CliffsTestPrep®

Regents Global History Geography Workbook

CliffsTestPrep®

Regents Global History and Geography Workbook

An American BookWorks Corporation Project

Contributing Authors

Adam Turek Herman
Bayside High School,
Bayside, NY

Andy Szeto
Bayside High School,
Bayside, NY

Melissa Stepanian
Bayside High School,
Bayside, NY

Wiley Publishing, Inc.

Publisher's Acknowledgments

Editorial

Acquisition Editor: Greg Tubach

Project Editor: Suzanne Snyder

Copy Editor: Elizabeth Kuball

Technical Editor: Marcus Stadelmann

Composition

Proofreader: Carole Arielle Mennelle

Wiley Publishing, Inc. Composition Services

CliffsTestPrep® Regents Global History and Geography Workbook

Published by:
Wiley Publishing, Inc.
111 River Street
Hoboken, NJ 07030-5774
www.wiley.com

Copyright © 2008 Wiley, Hoboken, NJ

Published by Wiley, Hoboken, NJ
Published simultaneously in Canada

Library of Congress Cataloging-in-Publication data is available from the publisher upon request.

ISBN 13: 978-0-4701-6781-6
ISBN 13: 978-0-4701-6781-5

Printed in the United States of America
10 9 8 7 6 5 4 3 2 1

Table of Contents

Sample Thematic Essay Questions

Introduction

About This Book

The New York State Global History and Geography Regents Examination is not an easy one, but we've tried to create a unique book for you that will help you prepare for this exam in a logical manner. Why is it unique? Instead of presenting pages and pages of review material, like most other test preparation books, this book focuses solely on the test questions themselves. It has long been accepted that the more you practice on the types of questions that will appear on the actual examination, the better you'll do on the final test. Therefore, what we've done in this book is present you with hundreds of questions and answers—all from previous Regents exams.

To present these questions in a logical manner, we've divided the book into sections based on the *topical divisions* that you'll find on the actual Global History and Geography Exam. Then we present all the multiple-choice questions and essay questions on a particular topic, in one chapter, so you can practice answering those questions as you go along. We've provided the answer explanations right after each question to help reinforce your knowledge. Read the question, answer it to the best of your ability, and then *immediately* check the answer to see if it's correct. We've tried to focus primarily on the correct answers here, although when a question might be somewhat confusing, we've also explained why the other answers are incorrect. In most instances that correct answers are factual, so if you get the correct answer, there is no need to explain why the other answers are incorrect.

The four major sections into which we've divided the book are

- World History
- Geography
- Economics
- Civics, Citizenship, and Government

However, within each topic, we've also included the subtopics that are normally covered on the exam. You'll find each answer coded by this subtopic. By using these subtopics, you can quickly determine where you need additional help. These topics include

- Ancient World
- Expanding Zones of Exchange
- Global Interactions (topics from 1200–1650)
- First Global Age
- Age of Revolution

- Crisis and Achievement (1900–1945)
- Twentieth Century Since 1945
- Global Connections/Interactions (modern issues)

As you go through the book, it's up to you to answer the question before you look at the answers. You're "on your honor" to test yourself. There's no grade at the end, of course, so if you look at the answers first, you're only cheating yourself. You will want to practice answering test questions and writing essay answers as much as possible.

A word about the essays in this book: Unlike many other books you've undoubtedly used for test preparation, we do not give you long, in-depth essays. Frankly, we don't believe that reading someone else's essay is much help to you. Instead we focus on the elements that comprise a good essay. Studies have shown that students often have trouble with the basic organization of an essay, which has led to poor writing skills. What we've given you are the basic elements of what should be in each essay. Each essay is accompanied by a general overview of how to organize your essay, what you should cover in it, and the basic elements of writing the essay. By studying these explanations, you'll learn how to approach the actual essay questions on your final Global History and Geography Exam.

Organization of the Test

The Global History and Geography Exam is a three-hour exam, and covers a wide range of the topics that you've studied throughout the year. The following types of questions comprise the three separate parts of this exam:

- Fifty multiple-choice questions
- A thematic essay question
- A document-based question

The document-based question consists of two parts—a series of short answer questions based on given documents, cartoons, illustrations, and so on, followed by an analytical essay.

The Multiple-Choice Format

Most of the standardized tests that you've taken throughout your educational career have probably contained multiple-choice questions. For some reason, these types of questions give a large percentage of test takers a difficult time. If you approach these questions carefully, they're easier than you think.

Let's analyze the concept of the multiple-choice question: Keep in mind that these questions are created to test your abilities to recognize the correct answer from four choices, at least on this specific exam. Other tests may have more or fewer choices.

Questions are comprised of several parts:

- The question stem (i.e., the question)
- The correct choice
- Distracters

As test-item writers create questions, they normally approach it as follows:

- One choice is absolutely correct.
- One or two choices are absolutely incorrect (distracters).
- One or two choices may be similar to the correct answer, but might contain some information that is not quite accurate or on target, or even might not answer the specific question (distracters).

How do you approach these questions? First, read the question and see whether you know the answer. If you know it automatically, then you can look at the choices and select the correct one. But keep in mind that the answers to the multiple-choice questions on the Global History and Geography Exam are based on specific material that you may have read or listened to. So it is important to keep this in mind as you go through the passages. Do not bring in any outside knowledge. Just focus on the question and the material on which it is based.

The easiest way to answer a multiple-choice question is to use the time-honored approach of *process of elimination*—especially if you don't know the answer right from the start.

You start by eliminating choices that do not seem logical, or those that you know immediately are incorrect. If you can start by eliminating one of those choices, you now have only three choices left. You've reduced your odds of selecting the correct answer from one out of four (25 percent) to one out of three (33⅓ percent), which is a lot better.

Can you eliminate another answer choice? Perhaps one doesn't sound quite right, or it doesn't seem to pertain to the passage you just read. If you can eliminate another choice, you've increased your odds to one out of two (50 percent).

Now, unless you know the correct answer, you can guess.

Pay attention to words like *always* and *never*—most things in the world are not *always* or *never*. Also, be careful if a question asks you to choose which of the choices is *not*. . . ! Watch the wording also on questions that state "All are correct *except*. . . "!

Scoring

The scoring on this test is based on your answers to the multiple-choice questions, the thematic essay, the document-based questions and the analytical document-based essay. Your score will be based on the average on the complete exam, including all of the different sections.

Because there are 50 multiple-choice questions, worth 55 percent of the total score, it pays to understand how to answer these types of questions. The preceding review, should give you a strong head-start, and, of course, understanding the material is key.

The thematic essay question counts for 15 percent of the exam. You will be given a specific concept (the theme) and then a task, which will ask you to discuss and describe situations and individuals that may relate to this theme. Fortunately, you will also be given hints on people or situations to use and to avoid. Make sure you read the guidelines that follow the question. Use these guidelines to check your work. These guidelines, which are usually the same from test to test are:

- Develop all aspects of the task.
- Support the theme with relevant facts, examples, and details.
- Use a logical and clear plan of organization, including an introduction and a conclusion that are beyond a restatement of the theme.

These are basic essay-writing skills. As you write, make sure you refer back to these pointers, because they will help you organize your essay.

The combined Part I (multiple-choice questions) and Part II (thematic essay) are worth a total of 70 percent of your score; the document-based essay question is worth 30 percent. The question consists of two sections, each worth 15 percent:

- Short answers in which you will be asked questions based on 6 to 8 documents and you are asked to provide a short response
- An essay question, which is based on the same topics as the short-answer documents

This section is designed to test your ability to read, understand, and interpret historical documents. You will be given the historical context of the questions that follow, and then your specific task. The task will ask you to respond to the short-answer questions using your knowledge of global history. Then, utilizing the information from your answers, write an essay. Again, as in the thematic essay section, you will be given guidelines to follow:

- Develop all aspects of the task.
- Incorporate information from at least five documents.
- Incorporate relevant outside information.
- Support the theme with relevant facts, examples, and details.
- Use a logical and clear plan of organization, including an introduction and a conclusion that are beyond a restatement of the theme.

Use these guidelines as you write and continually check back to make sure you're including all the information that is required by the question.

The Global History and Geography Exam is not difficult, as long as you read carefully and follow the instructions throughout. Practice answering the multiple-choice questions in the book to become familiar with the style and approach that you'll find on the actual exam. Also, take the time to work out an approach to the various essays that you'll find here. You don't need to write entire essays, but you should try to write an outline for each, highlighting the important factors that relate to the question or task given in the question. Then compare it to the material we provide. If you've omitted a lot of information in your outline, go back and reread the material. Double-check the question or task. Try to determine what you overlooked. Fortunately, the guidelines to Parts II and III are provided and you should continually check back to make sure you have included everything that's required.

Remember: The more you practice, the better you'll do on your actual exam!

But now it's time to start working. Good luck!

World History

Multiple Choice

Directions: For each of the following questions, select the choice that best answers the question or completes the statement.

---

1. Which belief is shared by Hindus and Buddhists?

(1) Everyone should have the same social status.
(2) People should pray five times a day.
(3) The soul can be reincarnated.
(4) Material wealth is a sign of the blessing of the gods.

Correct answer: (3) A belief that is shared by Hindus and Buddhists is that the soul can be reincarnated, or reborn in alternate forms. Hindus do not believe that everyone should have the same social status, as indicated in their acceptance of the caste system. Unlike the Hindus, Buddhists do not believe in the material wealth as a determinant of social status. Only Muslims are required to pray five times a day in the direction of Mecca. *(Ancient World)*

---

2. Some historians suggest that, as a result of the Mongol invasions of Russia, the Russian people were

(1) united with the Ottomans.
(2) converted to Christianity.
(3) freed from serfdom.
(4) cut off from most of Western Europe.

Correct answer: (4) Some historians suggest that as a result of the Mongol invasions of Russia, the Russian people were cut off from most of Western Europe. For more than two centuries, Russia was ruled by the Mongols. The Mongol rule cut off ties from Western Europe. As a result, the Russians could not benefit from the intellectual and technological movements during the Renaissance and the Enlightenment. There was no significant attempt to westernize Russia until the eighteenth century, when it was started by Peter the Great. Russians introduced Christianity prior to the Mongol invasion. However, the Russians never united with the Ottomans. *(Global Interactions)*

---

3. Many achievements of Islamic civilization reached European society by way of the

    (1) Crusades and eastern Mediterranean trading networks.

    (2) merchant guilds and the Industrial Revolution.

    (3) Middle Passage and the Columbian Exchange.

    (4) conquests of the Germanic tribes and trade along the Silk Road.

Correct answer: (1) Many achievements of Islamic civilization reached European society by way of the Crusades and eastern Mediterranean trading networks. Christians and Muslims were at war over the control of the Holy Land from the late 1000s to the late 1200s. The Crusaders were able to bring back new products and innovations from the Muslim world. This is an example of cultural diffusion. *(Expanding Zones of Exchange)*

---

4. At the time of the Protestant Reformation, the medieval church in Western Europe was criticized for

    (1) sponsoring explorations to the Middle East.

    (2) allowing the Bible to be printed and distributed to the people.

    (3) being too concerned with worldly power and riches.

    (4) refusing to sell indulgences to peasants.

Correct answer: (3) Prior to the Protestant Reformation, the medieval church in Western Europe was criticized for being too concerned with worldly power and riches. Church officials were condemned for the sale of church pardons and appointments to pay for lavish art projects. The church never sponsored explorations to the Middle East. Fearing that the authority of church officials would be undermined, the printing of the Bible was not allowed by the medieval Church. *(Global Interactions)*

Base your answer to question 5 on the quote below and on your knowledge of social studies.

    . . . If from now on the King starts by rising early and going to bed late, and if the ministers take oaths among themselves to cut out the evils of parties and merriment, be diligent in cultivating frugality and virtue, do not allow private considerations from taking root in their minds, and do not use artifice as a method of operation in government affairs, then the officials and common people will all cleanse and purify their minds and be in great accord with his will. . . .

    —Yi Hang-no, Korean Royal Adviser

---

5. Which Confucian principle is reflected in this statement?

    (1) The ruler must set an example for the people.

    (2) Respect for elders is the foundation of civilization.

    (3) Virtue increases with education.

    (4) Compassion and sympathy for others is important.

Correct answer: (1) The Confucian principle reflected in this statement is that the ruler must set an example for the people. A ruler must act in the interest of the people; or he will be replaced under the Mandate of Heaven. In his collection of works called *The Analects,* Chinese philosopher Confucius stressed the importance of education, respect for elders and compassion for others. However, these ideas were not conveyed in the passage. *(Ancient World)*

---

6. Which action would best complete this partial outline?

I. Byzantine heritage

  A. Blended Christian beliefs with Greek art and philosophy

  B. Extended Roman engineering achievements

  C. Preserved literature and science textbooks

  D. _____

  (1) Adapted the Roman principles of justice

  (2) Used a senate as the chief governing body

  (3) Led crusades to capture Rome from the Huns

  (4) Helped maintain Roman rule over Western Europe

Correct answer: (1) The phrase that would best complete this partial outline is that the Byzantine heritage adapted the Roman principles of justice. In addition to religion, arts, and science, the Byzantine Empire was responsible for preserving the legal writings of the ancient Romans. Spearheaded by Emperor Justinian long after the collapse of Rome, this compilation of legal reasoning and knowledge is known as the Justinian Code. *(Expanding Zones of Exchange)*

---

7. The expeditions of Hernán Cortés and Francisco Pizarro resulted in the

  (1) destruction of the Aztec and Inca empires.

  (2) capture of Brazil by Portugal.

  (3) colonization of North America by Portugal.

  (4) exploration of the Philippines and East Indies.

Correct answer: (1) The expeditions of Hernán Cortés and Francisco Pizarro resulted in the destruction of the Aztec and Inca empires. Aided by superior military technology, these Spanish explorers were able to conquer the Aztec and Inca empires in a short period of time. Cortés and Pizarro never reached the Philippines and the East Indies. Furthermore, their voyages never led to the colonization of North America by Portugal or the capture of Brazil. Brazil was captured by a Portuguese explorer named Pedro Cabral. *(The First Global Age)*

---

8. One result of the Opium War was that China

  (1) adopted democratic reforms.

  (2) gained control of Hong Kong.

  (3) regained control of Manchuria.

  (4) was divided into spheres of influence.

Correct answer: (4) One result of the Opium War was that China was divided into spheres of influence. Spheres of influence were sections of China that were under the control of foreign nations such as Britain, France, and Japan. These countries were given special trading rights. The Chinese and the British were at war over the trading of opium in 1840–1843 and 1856–1860. The military strength of China was no match to the British. Upon its defeat, the Chinese were forced to sign the Treaty of Nanking. The terms required the Chinese to pay substantially and give up control of Hong Kong. The Chinese did not adopt democratic reforms as a result of the Opium War, as China would continue to be governed by an emperor. In addition, China never regained control of Manchuria after the war. *(Age of Revolutions)*

Base your answer to Question 9 on the cartoon below and on your knowledge of social studies.

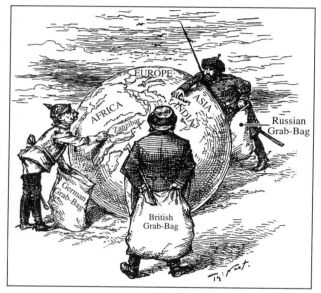

THE WORLD'S PLUNDERERS
"It's English, you know."

Source: Thomas Nast, *Harper's Weekly,* June 20, 1885 (adapted)

9. This Thomas Nast cartoon shows the

(1) competition between European nations for overseas territories after the Berlin Conference.
(2) aggressive action of the Triple Alliance before World War I.
(3) spread of communism throughout the world during the nineteenth century.
(4) concern of European nations for the welfare of developing nations at the end of the nineteenth century.

Correct answer: (1) This Thomas Nast cartoon shows the competition between European nations for overseas territories after the Berlin Conference. The cartoon indicates that Europeans were increasingly interested in Africa in the late nineteenth century. This is known as the "Scramble for Africa." The Europeans would further their imperialistic aims by exerting their powers on the Asian continent later. *(Age of Revolution)*

Base your answer to Question 10 on the bullet points below and on your knowledge of social studies.

- Japan resigns from the League of Nations, 1933
- Rome-Berlin-Tokyo Axis formed, 1936
- Japan invades China, 1937
- United States places embargo on scrap iron, steel, and oil exports to Japan, 1941

10. Which event occurred immediately after this series of developments?

    (1) Manchuria became a Japanese protectorate.
    (2) Pearl Harbor was attacked.
    (3) The Japanese fleet was destroyed.
    (4) The atomic bomb was dropped on Hiroshima.

Correct answer: (2) Pearl Harbor was attacked immediately after this series of developments. On December 7, 1941, Japan launched a naval attack on Pearl Harbor. More than 2,400 people were killed by the attack. As a result, President Franklin D. Roosevelt asked Congress to declare war on Japan. The atomic bomb was not dropped until 1945. *(Crises and Achievement [1900–1945])*

Base your answer to question 11 on the excerpt below and on your knowledge of social studies. This excerpt is taken from a poem written about World War I.

> If I should die, think only this of me:
> That there's some corner of a foreign field
> That is for ever England. There shall be
> In that rich earth a richer dust concealed;
> A dust whom England bore, shaped, made aware,
> Gave, once, her flowers to love, her ways to roam,
> A body of England's, breathing English air,
> Washed by the rivers, blest by suns of home. . . .
>
>   —Rupert Brooke, "The Soldier"

11. Which idea is expressed in this excerpt from Brooke's poem?

    (1) pacifism
    (2) neutrality
    (3) nationalism
    (4) anarchy

Correct answer: (3) The idea of nationalism is expressed in this excerpt from Brooke's poem. The poem, written by poet Rupert Brooke, inspired the English nation during World War I. It reminded the nation of the importance of patriotism. Brooke did not express the idea of neutrality, or a policy in which a country does not take sides in a conflict. A pacifist does not believe in wars to resolve conflicts. An anarchist does not believe in government. *(Crises and Achievement [1900–1945])*

---

12. A major result of the Nuremberg trials after World War II was that

    (1) Germany was divided into four zones of occupation.
    (2) the United Nations was formed to prevent future acts of genocide.
    (3) the North Atlantic Treaty Organization (NATO) was established to stop the spread of communism.
    (4) Nazi political and military leaders were held accountable for their actions.

Correct answer: (4) A major result of the Nuremberg trials after World War II was that Nazi political and military leaders were held accountable for their actions. The Nuremberg trials prosecuted those who participated in war crimes during World War II, notably the murder that took place in the concentration camps. The United Nations and NATO were created to promote international peace and stop the spread of communism. However, the Nuremberg trials were not directly related to the establishment of the United Nations and NATO. Germany was not divided into four zones of occupation as the result of the Nuremberg trials. *(Crises and Achievement [1900–1945])*

---

13. Which statement related to the recent history of Pakistan is not fact, but an opinion?

    (1) Pakistan gained its independence from Britain in 1947.
    (2) The majority of the people who live in Pakistan are Muslims.
    (3) Pakistan would be better off if it were still part of India.
    (4) Mohammed Ali Jinnah was a major leader in Pakistan's independence movement.

Correct answer: (3) The statement that Pakistan would be better off if it were still part of India is an opinion. There is no scientific way to prove whether Pakistan would be better off if it were still part of India, nor could that statement be supported by historical research. The other statements are facts. *(Twentieth Century Since 1945)*

Base your answer to Question 14 on the passage below and on your knowledge of social studies.

. . . I have walked that long road to freedom. I have tried not to falter; I have made missteps along the way. But I have discovered the secret that after climbing a great hill, one only finds that there are many more hills to climb. I have taken a moment here to rest, to steal a view of the glorious vista that surrounds me, to look back on the distance I have come. But I can rest only for a moment, for with freedom comes responsibilities, and I dare not linger, for my long walk is not yet ended.

—Nelson Mandela, *Long Walk to Freedom,* Little, Brown and Co., 1994

14. When Mandela referred to "climbing a great hill," he was referring to the struggle to

(1) end apartheid in South Africa.
(2) modernize South Africa's economy.
(3) end economic sanctions against South Africa.
(4) stop majority rule in South Africa.

Correct answer: (1) When Mandela referred to "climbing a great hill," he was referring to the struggle to end apartheid in South Africa. Mandela was imprisoned for nearly three decades for his protest of apartheid. Minority Europeans had been in control of South Africa until the end of apartheid in 1991, which gave black South Africans full political rights. Additionally, this brought an end to economic sanctions by the international community. Nelson Mandela does not mention the modernization of South Africa's economy in this passage. *(Twentieth Century Since 1945)*

15. Which belief is shared by an African person who practices animism and a Japanese person who practices Shinto?

(1) Only one God rules the universe.
(2) Periodic fasting is essential to spiritual purity.
(3) Spirits exist in both living and nonliving things.
(4) All suffering is caused by desire and selfishness.

Correct answer: (3) Spirits exist in both living and nonliving things is a belief shared by an African who practices animism and a Japanese who practices Shinto. Neither animism nor Shintoism is monotheistic (that is, neither believes in the existence of only one God). Unlike Muslims, both animists and Shintoists do not fast periodically. Buddhists believe that all suffering is caused by desire and selfishness. *(Ancient World)*

16. Which title would best complete this partial outline?

I. _____

   A. Formation of secret alliances
   B. Conflict over colonies in Africa
   C. Military buildup of European armies and navies
   D. Assassination of Archduke Ferdinand

(1) Scramble for Africa
(2) Causes of World War I
(3) Results of World War II
(4) Reasons for the United Nations

Correct answer: (2) The title that would best complete this partial outline is "Causes of World War I." As part of its own imperialistic goal, each European nation competed aggressively for colonies in Africa before World War I. This, in part, explains the massive military buildup. Triple Alliance and Triple Entente were the secret alliances formed before World War I. These secret alliances were instrumental for war when Archduke Ferdinand was assassinated by a Serbian nationalist, which sparked World War I. *(Global Connections/Interactions)*

Base your answer to Question 17 on the bullet points below and on your knowledge of social studies.

- Many of Africa's traditional musical instruments are made of gourds and shells.
- Ancient Egyptians wrote on papyrus, a reed found growing near the Nile River.
- A major feature of Japanese art is the relationship between humans and nature.

17. Which concept is illustrated in these statements?

   (1) role of education in the ancient world
   (2) development of traditional government
   (3) effect of artistic expression on religion
   (4) impact of geography on cultural development

Correct answer: (4) The impact of geography on cultural development is illustrated in these statements. Because of its abundance on the African continent, for example, locals have used gourds and shells to create musical instruments. The same reasoning applies to the use of papyrus by the ancient Egyptians. *(Ancient World)*

18. One way in which the Five Relationships of Confucianism, the Ten Commandments, and the Eightfold Path are similar is that they

   (1) promote polytheism.
   (2) establish gender equality.
   (3) provide codes of behavior.
   (4) describe secularism.

Correct answer: (3) One way in which the Five Relationships, the Ten Commandments, and the Eightfold Path are similar is that they provide codes of behavior. Chinese philosopher Confucius stated the importance of maintaining social and political order in his Five Relationships. The teachings of Confucius were recorded by his followers in *The Analects*. The Five Relationships, the Ten Commandments, and the Eightfold Path do not promote gender equality. With a strong focus on religion, the Ten Commandments and the Eightfold Path do not promote secularism. Additionally, the Ten Commandments do not promote polytheism, which is the belief in many gods. A religious belief in one god is called monotheism. *(Ancient World)*

19. The Phoenicians are often referred to as the "carriers of civilization" because they

    (1) introduced Islam and Christianity to Central Africa.

    (2) established colonies throughout northern Europe.

    (3) developed the first carts with wheels.

    (4) traded goods and spread ideas throughout the Mediterranean region.

Correct answer: (4) The Phoenicians are often referred to as the "carriers of civilization" because they traded goods and spread ideas throughout the Mediterranean region. The Phoenicians were the first civilization to develop a phonetic alphabet system. It was most likely developed for merchants to keep accurate records. The Phoenician alphabet would eventually evolve into the alphabet we use today. The Phoenicians did not introduce Islam and Christianity to Central Africa, nor did they establish colonies throughout northern Europe, or develop the first carts with wheels. *(Ancient World)*

20. The exchange of silks and spices and the spread of Buddhism along the Silk Road are examples of

    (1) cultural diffusion.

    (2) self-sufficiency.

    (3) ethnocentrism.

    (4) desertification.

Correct answer: (1) The exchange of silks and spices and the spread of Buddhism along the Silk Road are examples of cultural diffusion. The spreading of new ideas from one place to another is called cultural diffusion. The Silk Road was an active commercial trade route stretched from China to Rome and was established during the Han Dynasty. Chinese merchants made enormous profits by bringing products such as silks and spices to other parts of the world. *(Expanding Zones of Exchange)*

Base your answer to Question 21 on the passage below and on your knowledge of social studies.

1. In the name of Allah, Most
Gracious, Most Merciful.
2. Praise be to Allah,
The Cherisher and Sustainer of the Worlds;
3. Most Gracious, Most Merciful;
4. Master of the Day of Judgement.
5. Thee do we worship,
And Thine aid we seek.
6. Show us the straight way,
7. The way of those on whom
Thou hast bestowed Thy Grace,
Those whose (portion)
Is not wrath,
And who go not astray.

—'Abdullah Yūsuf 'Alí, ed., *The Meaning of The Holy Qur'ān,* Amana Publications, 1999

15

21. Which concept is best reflected in this passage?

   (1) baptism
   (2) karma
   (3) monotheism
   (4) animism

Correct answer: (3) The concept is best reflected in this passage is monotheism. The followers of Islam believe in monotheism, which is the belief in one god. The excerpt stresses the importance of showing obedience to Allah. In Christianity, baptism is a process that indicates one's rebirth by belief in Jesus' atonement and resurrection. Animism is a religion that stresses the existence of spirit in nature. The followers of Hinduism believe that the actions of a person's present life would have an impact on his next. *(Ancient World)*

22. Which accomplishments are associated with the Gupta Empire?

   (1) adoption of democracy and construction of the Pantheon
   (2) defeat of the Roman Empire and adoption of Christianity
   (3) establishment of Pax Mongolia and founding of a Chinese dynasty
   (4) writing of Sanskrit language classics and development of the decimal numeral system, including the concept of zero

Correct answer: (4) The accomplishments associated with the Gupta Empire are writing of Sanskrit language classics and development of a decimal numeral system, including the concept of zero. The Indians prospered during the Gupta Dynasty. Writers during this period produced lasting literary work in the Sanskrit language. The most famous writer of this time was Kalidasa. The development of decimal numeral system including the the concept of zero led to advances in mathematics, particularly in the field of algebra. *(Expanding Zones of Exchange)*

23. Kievan Rus' adopted the Eastern Orthodox religion, the Cyrillic alphabet, and different styles of art and architecture through contact with

   (1) traders from South Asia
   (2) conquering invaders from Mongolia
   (3) crusaders from Western Europe
   (4) missionaries from the Byzantine Empire

Correct answer: (4) Kievan Rus' adopted the Eastern Orthodox religion, the Cyrillic alphabet, and different styles of art and architecture through contact with missionaries from the Byzantine Empire. Kievan Rus' was able to adopt different ideas from the Byzantine Empire because of its geographic proximity. This is an example of cultural diffusion. *(Global Interactions)*

24. Which statement about the Golden Age of Islam is a fact rather than an opinion?

   (1) Islamic art was more abstract than Greek art.
   (2) Muslims were the best early mathematicians.
   (3) Islamic society preserved Greek and Roman culture.
   (4) Muslim artists had more talent than European artists.

Correct answer: (3) The statement about Islamic society preserving Greek and Roman culture is a fact. A consensus is necessary in order for a statement to be a fact. Other statements are opinions because no consensus can be made. The Golden Age of Islam marked the height of intellectual growth. Muslim scholars translated Greek and Roman works in major universities. The period also saw the advancement in mathematics, which includes the development of Arabic numbers. *(Expanding Zones of Exchange)*

25. Which two cultures most influenced the development of early Japan?

   (1) Greek and Roman
   (2) Chinese and Korean
   (3) Egyptian and Mesopotamian
   (4) Indian and Persian

Correct answer: (2) Chinese and Korean were two cultures that most influenced the development of early Japan. Their influence, combined with native traditions, created a unique culture for the Japanese. This is an example of cultural diffusion. The Chinese and Korean cultures provided a foundation for Japanese customs and traditions. For example, the Japanese borrowed their system of writing as well as Buddhism from China. *(Global Interactions)*

26. The foreign policy of many Russian rulers supported the country's desire for

   (1) access to inland cities.
   (2) more mineral resources.
   (3) extensive canal systems.
   (4) warm-water ports.

Correct answer: (4) The foreign policy of many Russian rulers supported the country's desire for warm-water ports. The access to warm-water ports was vital in maintaining its commercial interests. Since frozen ports were not accessible during the winter, Russia began to seek warm-water ports. Peter the Great, an absolute ruler, started quest. In addition to securing ports, Peter the Great saw the need to westernize the nation. The capital, St. Petersburg, was part of this effort. *(First Global Age)*

Base your answer to Question 27 on the map below and on your knowledge of social studies.

Spread of the Black Death

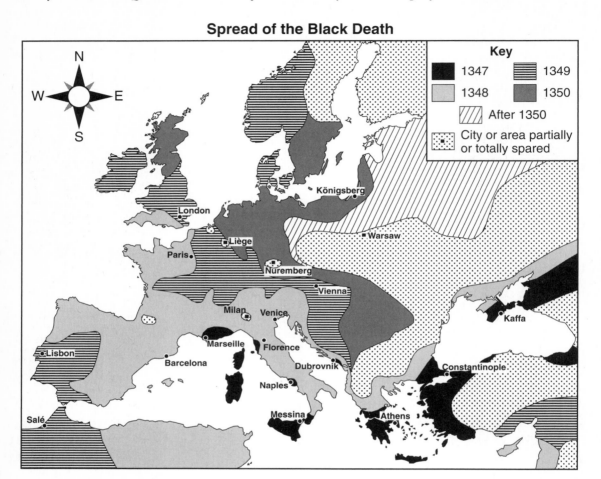

Source: Richard Bulliet et al., *The Earth and Its Peoples: A Global History,* Houghton Mifflin, 2001 (adapted)

27. Which area of Europe was *least* affected by the Black Death?

(1) southwestern Europe
(2) Mediterranean Coast
(3) Eastern Europe
(4) British Isles

Correct answer: (3) Eastern Europe was *least* affected by the Black Death. The plague was most devastating in densely populated cities. People living in Western Europe took the hardest hit during the plague.

Since few cities were located in Eastern Europe, the people were least affected by the Black Death. In addition, the cold climate slowed the spread of the plague in Eastern Europe. *(Expanding Zones of Exchange)*

Base your answer to Question 28 on the illustrations below and on your knowledge of social studies.

Aztec Civilization (A.D. 1200 to 1535)

Inca Civilization (A.D. 1200 to 1535)

Source: Sue A. Kirne, *World Studies: Global Issues and Assessments,* N & N Publishing, 1995 (adapted)

---

28. These illustrations suggest that early Latin American civilizations

    (1) were based on European societies.
    (2) used advanced technology to build complex structures.
    (3) incorporated early Roman architectural design.
    (4) were strongly influenced by Renaissance humanism.

Correct answer: (2) These illustrations suggest that early Latin American civilizations used advanced technology to build complex structures. According to the illustrations, the Aztecs made use of their engineering ingenuity by constructing sophisticated monuments such as the Grand Pyramids. In addition, the Incans built an extensive road system to overcome the geographical barriers posed by the Andes Mountain range. *(Age of Revolutions)*

---

29. Sir Isaac Newton, Galileo Galilei, and Johannes Kepler are all directly associated with the

    (1) Industrial Revolution.
    (2) Scientific Revolution.
    (3) English Revolution.
    (4) Agricultural Revolution.

Correct answer: (2) Sir Isaac Newton, Galileo Galilei, and Johannes Kepler are all directly associated with the Scientific Revolution. Famous for their contributions in science, these men used scientific methods to support their findings. However, the findings of these Renaissance scientists were often banned by authority, especially the Catholic Church. For example, Galilei was challenged by the Church for stating that the sun, not the Earth, was the center of the universe. *(Age of Revolutions)*

30. The Enlightenment and the American Revolution were both major influences on nineteenth-century uprisings in

    (1) Latin America.
    (2) the Middle East.
    (3) Vietnam.
    (4) Japan.

Correct answer: (1) The Enlightenment and the American Revolution were both major influences on nineteenth-century uprisings in Latin America. Both the Enlightenment and the American Revolution urged the people of Latin America to challenge Spanish authority, believing that people should possess the natural rights: life, liberty and property. The movement for Latin American independence from Spanish rule was most notably led by Simon Bolivar. *(Age of Revolutions)*

31. Before the French Revolution, the people of France were divided into three estates based mainly on their

    (1) education level.
    (2) geographic region.
    (3) social class.
    (4) religious beliefs.

Correct answer: (3) Before the French Revolution, the people of France were divided into three estates based mainly on their social class. The First Estate consisted of the religious officials such as bishops and cardinals. The Second Estate included the nobles and wealthy landholders. The Third Estate, which accounted for 97 percent of the French people, was comprised of the commoners. The three estates did not share political and economic powers, as most of the tax burden fell on the commoners. Because of this, the commoners would eventually revolt. *(Age of Revolutions)*

32. One similarity in the leadership of Jomo Kenyatta, José de San Martín, and Sun Yixian (Sun Yat-sen) is that they

    (1) supported nationalistic movements.
    (2) organized communist rebellions.
    (3) opposed trade with other nations.
    (4) established democratic rule in their countries.

Correct answer: (1) One similarity in the leadership of Jomo Kenyatta, José de San Martín, and Sun Yixian (Sun Yat-sen) is that they supported nationalistic movements. Jomo Kenyatta, a Kenyan nationalist, advocated and fought for independence from the British, which was achieved in 1963. Similar to Simon Bolivar, José de San Martín led a nationalist movement in Latin America in the nineteenth century, liberating Argentina. Sun Yixian was a nationalist leader who overthrew the Qing dynasty in China during the early twentieth century. *(Age of Revolutions)*

33. The Opium Wars in China and the expedition of Commodore Matthew Perry to Japan resulted in

    (1) the economic isolation of China and Japan.
    (2) an increase in Chinese influence in Asia.
    (3) the beginning of democratic governments in China and Japan.
    (4) an increase in Western trade and influence in Asia.

Correct answer: (4) The Opium Wars in China and the expedition of Commodore Matthew Perry to Japan resulted in an increase in Western trade and influence in Asia. China was a weak nation by the late eighteenth century. British merchants began to trade opium in China. Opium, a highly addictive drug, had a negative impact on the Chinese people. The British crushed the Chinese armies when its government attempted to ban opium, resulting in a series of conflicts known as the Opium Wars. The Treaty of Nanking granted trade access and territories to the British, including Canton and Hong Kong. Other nations would soon follow the British footsteps in establishing their own spheres of influences. Similarly, Commodore Matthew Perry arrived in Japan to seek new markets and trade ports. Amazed with the technological marvels of the Americans, the Japanese signed a trade agreement granting increased access. *(Age of Revolutions)*

34. What was a direct result of the Meiji Restoration in Japan?

    (1) Japan became a modern industrial nation.
    (2) The Tokugawa Shogunate seized control of the government.
    (3) Russia signed a mutual trade agreement.
    (4) Japan stayed politically isolated.

Correct answer: (1) As a direct result of the Meiji Restoration Japan became a modern industrial nation. Beginning in the late nineteenth century, the Meiji Restoration relaxed the long-standing isolation policies. This launched the commercial relationships between Japan and other western nations. Additionally, Japan borrowed ideas and innovations from the West. This is an example of cultural diffusion. Because of its willingness to modernize, Japan, became an industrial nation by the early twentieth century. *(Age of Revolutions)*

35. One reason for the outbreak of World War II was the

    (1) ineffectiveness of the League of Nations.
    (2) growing tension between the United States and the Soviet Union.
    (3) conflict between the Hapsburg and the Romanov families.
    (4) refusal of the German government to sign the Treaty of Versailles.

Correct answer: (1) One reason for the outbreak of World War II was the ineffectiveness of the League of Nations. The League of Nations was an international peacekeeping organization established after World War I. The primary goal of the organization was to encourage the international community to use diplomatic means to resolve conflicts by punishing aggression. Without the support of the United States, the Soviet Union and Germany, the League of Nations was weak. For example, the Treaty of Versailles, signed by the Germans, specified a ban on militarization by the Germans. However, the League could not stop Germany from rebuilding its military in the 1930s. Similarly, the League also did not prevent the invasion of Ethiopia by Italy in 1935. The growing tension between the United States and the Soviet Union did not occur until after World War II. The conflict between the Hapsburgs and the Romanovs did not lead to World War II. *(Crises and Achievement [1900–1945])*

---

36. Which United States foreign policy was used to maintain the independence of Greece and Turkey after World War II?

(1) containment
(2) neutrality
(3) nonalignment
(4) militarism

Correct answer: (1) Containment was used to maintain the independence of Greece and Turkey after World War II. The United States became increasingly concerned over the spread of communism in European countries after the war. Unlike the neutral stance after World War I, the United States became active in curtailing the communist influence in Southern and Western Europe. Containment was illustrated in the passing of the Truman Doctrine, through which the United States provided military and financial assistance to Turkey and Greece. The goal was to prevent Turkey and Greece to become a part of Soviet Union's satellite states. Some third-world countries chose to follow the policy of nonalignment by not choosing a side in the Cold War. *(Crises and Achievement [1900–1945])*

---

37. Which important principle was established as a result of the Nuremberg trials?

(1) Defeated nations have no rights in international courts of law.
(2) Individuals can be held accountable for "crimes against humanity."
(3) Soldiers must follow the orders of their superiors.
(4) Aggressor nations must pay war reparations for damages caused during wars.

Correct answer: (2) Individuals can be held accountable for "crimes against humanity." This important principal was established as a result of the Nuremberg trials. Many German officials and former leaders were either imprisoned or received death sentences for their actions during World War II. *(Crises and Achievement [1900–1945])*

---

38. The policy of strict racial separation and discrimination that was implemented in the Republic of South Africa is called

(1) collectivization.
(2) apartheid.
(3) intifada.
(4) communism.

Correct answer: (2) The policy of strict racial separation and discrimination that was implemented in the Republic of South Africa is called apartheid. The policy resulted in racial segregation in South African public places such as schools, beaches, and restaurants. White South Africans and blacks were required to ride on separate buses. The practice ended in 1990, and Nelson Mandela became the fist black African elected as president of South Africa. *(Twentieth Century Since 1945)*

---

39. The treatment of the Armenians by Ottoman Turks in the late nineteenth and early twentieth centuries and the treatment of Muslims by the Serbs of Yugoslavia in the 1990s are both examples of

   (1) coalition rule.
   (2) liberation theology.
   (3) universal suffrage.
   (4) human rights violations.

Correct answer: (4) The treatment of the Armenians by Ottoman Turks in the late nineteenth and early twentieth centuries and the treatment of Muslims by the Serbs of Yugoslavia in the 1990s are both examples of human rights violations. Armenians were persecuted by the Ottoman Turks through taxation and discrimination. This led to a nationalist movement in the early twentieth century. The suppression of the nationalist movement by the Ottoman Turks led to killings of many Armenians. To drive out all Muslims, the Serbs began to conduct ethnic cleansing in their territories in the late twentieth century. The movement was led by its president Slobodan Milosevic, who was prosecuted for war crimes in the early twenty-first century. *(First Global Age)*

---

40. The doctrines of the Roman Catholic, Eastern Orthodox, and Protestant churches are all based on the

   (1) concept of reincarnation.
   (2) principles of Christianity.
   (3) teachings of Muhammad.
   (4) leadership of the pope.

Correct answer: (2) The doctrines of the Roman Catholic, Eastern Orthodox, and Protestant churches are all based on the principles of Christianity. The three doctrines share similar Christian beliefs, including belief in Jesus and the Bible. However, only the Roman Catholic Church relies on the leadership of the pope. Events such as the Great Schism and Protestant Reformation led to divisions within the Christian faith. The concept of reincarnation, or the rebirth of a soul, comes from Hinduism; while the teachings of Muhammad constitute the foundation of the Muslim faith. *(Ancient World)*

---

41. Heavy military losses in World War I, food and fuel shortages, and opposition to the czar led to the

   (1) French Revolution
   (2) Russian Revolution
   (3) Chinese Revolution
   (4) Cuban Revolution

Correct answer: (2) Heavy military losses in World War I, food and fuel shortages, and opposition to the czar led to the Russian Revolution. Nicolas II did little to relieve the suffering of the people during

World War I. This led to widespread opposition. These conditions led to the rise of Lenin and Communism in Russia. To gain the support of the people, Lenin promised the Russian people "peace, land, and bread." *(Crises and Achievement [1900–1945])*

Base your answer to Question 42 on the bullet points below and on your knowledge of social studies.

- Scholars take civil service examinations for government positions.
- Students form Red Guard units to challenge counterrevolutionaries.
- Students demonstrate for democratic reforms in the capital and are killed by government troops.

42. These statements describe the changing role of students in which nation?

(1) Japan
(2) China
(3) Russia
(4) India

Correct answer: (2) These statements describe the changing role of students in China. The roles of students changed dramatically over the course of Chinese history. To become a government official, each student must pass civil service examinations. This practice, which is more than 1,000 years old, allowed emperors to choose candidates based on their merits. During the Cultural Revolution, students were taught communist beliefs and obedience to Mao Zedong. To ensure loyalty to the Communist Party, scholarly activities were not encouraged. In the late twentieth century, students protested in Tiananmen Square for democratic reforms in China. Troops were dispatched to suppress the student revolt. *(Ancient World)*

43. What is the main reason the Neolithic Revolution is considered a turning point in world history?

(1) Fire was used as a source of energy for the first time.
(2) Spoken language was used to improve communication.
(3) Domestication of animals and cultivation of crops led to settled communities.
(4) Stone tools and weapons were first developed.

Correct answer: (3) The Neolithic Revolution is considered a turning point in world history. The Neolithic (or Agricultural) Revolution led to the development of permanently settled communities. The domestication of animals and cultivation of crops freed humans from the need to constantly search for food. Thus, it allowed humans to pursue other economic and social activities. Fire, spoken language, and stone tools were not characteristics of the Neolithic Revolution. *(Ancient World)*

44. The Pillars of Emperor Asoka of the Mauryan Empire and the Code of Hammurabi of Babylon are most similar to the

(1) ziggurats of Sumeria.
(2) map projections of Mercator.
(3) Great Sphinx of the Egyptians.
(4) Twelve Tables of the Romans.

Correct answer: (4) The Pillars of Emperor Asoka of the Mauryan Empire and the Code of Hammurabi of Babylon are most similar to the Twelve Tables of the Romans. Asoka was emperor of the Mauryan Empire during the second century B.C.E. He erected stone pillars throughout his empire to publicize new laws and political philosophy. King Hammurabi of Babylon provided a set of law codes, which clearly listed a punishment for each specific crime. Similar to the law codes of Asoka and Hammurabi, the Romans collected their law codes in the Twelve Tables. *(Ancient World)*

---

45. One similarity between animism and Shinto is that people who follow these belief systems

(1) practice filial piety.
(2) worship spirits in nature.
(3) are monotheistic.
(4) are required to make pilgrimages.

Correct answer: (2) One similarity between animism and Shinto is that people who follow these belief systems worship spirits in nature. Both belief systems emphasized the importance of nature. For example, the followers of Shinto believed that natural disasters such as typhoons and tsunamis are controlled by spirits. Therefore, Shinto followers often say prayers to show deference to the spirits in the ocean. Neither belief system is monotheistic (believes in only one god). *(Ancient World)*

Base your answer to Question 46 on the bullet points below and on your knowledge of social studies.

- Buddhist temples are found in Japan.
- Most Indonesians study the Koran.
- Catholicism is the dominant religion in Latin America.

---

46. These statements illustrate a result of

(1) westernization.
(2) cultural diffusion.
(3) economic nationalism.
(4) fundamentalism.

Correct answer: (2) These statements illustrate a result of cultural diffusion. Cultural diffusion occurs when ideas are passed on from one region to another. Buddhism, for example, originated in India in the sixth century B.C.E. Missionaries were responsible for spreading the Buddhist doctrines to China, Korea, and Japan. The Japanese transformed the religion and created a new branch called Zen Buddhism. This was not an example of either westernization or fundamentalism. *(Ancient World)*

---

47. Which group introduced the Cyrillic alphabet, Orthodox Christianity, and domed architecture to Russian culture?

(1) Mongols
(2) Vikings
(3) Jews
(4) Byzantines

Correct answer: (4) The Byzantines introduced the Cyrillic alphabet, Orthodox Christianity, and domed architecture to Russian culture. To convert the Russian people to Christianity, the Byzantine emperor sent Greek missionaries to Russia. The introduction of the Cyrillic alphabet helped spread the Christian faith. The Byzantines also brought other ideas from their Golden Age to Russia, including music, art, and its domed architectural style. *(Expanding Zones of Exchange)*

---

48. One of the major achievements of Byzantine Emperor Justinian was that he

    (1) established a direct trade route with Ghana.
    (2) defended the empire against the spread of Islam.
    (3) brought Roman Catholicism to his empire.
    (4) preserved and transmitted Greek and Roman culture.

Correct answer: (4) One of the major achievements of Byzantine Emperor Justinian was that he preserved and transmitted Greek and Roman culture. For example, Justinian assembled a group of legal scholars to collect and revise the ancient Roman laws. The compilation became known as the Justinian Code. Other achievements from the Byzantine Empire included art, philosophy, and music. *(Expanding Zones of Exchange)*

---

49. Both European medieval knights and Japanese samurai warriors pledged oaths of

    (1) loyalty to their military leader.
    (2) devotion to their nation-state.
    (3) service to their church.
    (4) allegiance to their families.

Correct answer: (1) Both European medieval knights and Japanese samurai warriors pledged oaths of loyalty to their military leader. Medieval knights and Japanese samurai—warriors known for strict discipline, obedience, and honor—were both products of feudalistic societies. Lords from both feudal societies relied on them to ensure security for their people from foreign intruders. *(Expanding Zones of Exchange)*

---

50. What was a significant effect of Mansa Musa's pilgrimage to Mecca?

    (1) The African written language spread to southwest Asia.
    (2) Military leaders eventually controlled Mali.
    (3) Islamic learning and culture expanded in Mali.
    (4) The trading of gold for salt ended.

Correct answer: (3) Mansa Musa's pilgrimage to Mecca was significant because it led to the expansion of Islamic learning and culture in Mali. Mansa Musa was an emperor of Mali. He was responsible for the introduction of Islam to the empire. Timbuktu, the capital of Mali, was known for its institutions of higher learning. With the support of Mansa Musa, Timbuktu became a hub for the Islamic faith. *(Global Interactions)*

51. A direct impact that the printing press had on sixteenth-century Europe was that it encouraged the

(1) spread of ideas.
(2) beginnings of communism.
(3) establishment of democracy.
(4) development of industrialization.

Correct answer: (1) A direct impact that the printing press had on sixteenth-century Europe was that it encouraged the spread of ideas. A German printer named Johannes Gutenberg invented the printing press using the movable type in the mid-fifteenth century. The printing press led to declining costs in book production, which provided people with increased access to education and spread of learning. The first book in wide-circulation was the Gutenberg Bible. The printing press was an important catalyst behind the Renaissance and the Protestant Reformation. *(Expanding Zones of Exchange)*

52. Which technological advancement helped unify both the Roman and the Inca empires?

(1) astrolabe
(2) road system
(3) gunpowder
(4) wheeled carts

Correct answer: (2) The road system helped unify both the Roman and the Inca empires. In addition to commercial purposes, the extensive road system allowed the military to dispatch troops throughout the Roman Empire. Similarly, the Incans were able to overcome their geographic barriers by creating a system of roads. The astrolabe, gunpowder, and wheeled carts were not invented by the Romans or the Incans. *(Ancient World)*

53. Cervantes' literary classic *Don Quixote,* the rule of Isabella and Ferdinand, and the art of El Greco are associated with the

(1) Golden Age in Spain
(2) Hanseatic League in Germany
(3) Glorious Revolution in England
(4) Renaissance in Italy

Correct answer: (1) Cervantes' literary classic *Don Quixote,* the rule of Isabella and Ferdinand, and the art of El Greco are associated with the Golden Age in Spain. The marriage of Isabella and Ferdinand was a political move that brought two kingdoms together. Their leadership turned Spain into a powerful nation and a leader in American exploration. When exploration proved profitable, Spain used its resources in sponsoring artistic pursuits. The period saw the writings of Cervantes and artwork by El Greco. *(Global Interactions)*

Base your answer to Question 54 on the graphic organizer below and on your knowledge of social studies.

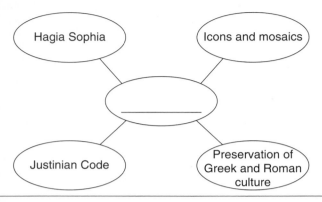

54. Which title best completes this graphic organizer?

    (1) Arab Accomplishments
    (2) Achievements of Meso-American Civilizations
    (3) Russian Law and Architecture
    (4) Byzantine Achievements

Correct answer: (4) The title that best completes this graphic organizer would be Byzantine achievements. The Hagia Sophia, icons, and mozaics represent Byzantine art and architecture, while the Justinian Code and preservation of Greek and Roman culture explain Byzantine law and culture. Since the Hagia Sophia is so closely related to Byzantine architecture, Arab Accomplishments, Meso-American Civilizations, and Russian Law would not apply. *(Ancient World)*

55. Which statement best describes a result of the encounter between Europeans and native populations of Latin America?

    (1) Native societies experienced rapid population growth.
    (2) European nations lost power and prestige in the New World.
    (3) Large numbers of natives migrated to Europe for a better life.
    (4) Plantations in the New World used enslaved Africans to replace native populations.

Correct answer: (4) The statement that best describes a result of the encounter between Europeans and native populations of Latin America was, "Plantations in the New World used enslaved Africans to replace native populations." Europe was home to some of the powerful nations during the Age of Exploration. The discovery of the New World created a need for enslaved labor. When Native Americans proved to be an inefficient labor source, European merchants began to bring African slaves to the New World in the sixteenth century. *(First Global Age)*

Base your answer to Question 56 on the statements below and on your knowledge of social studies.

. . . The Laws ought to be so framed, as to secure the Safety of every Citizen as much as possible. . . . The Equality of the Citizens consists in this; that they should all be subject to the same Laws. . . .

—*Documents of Catherine the Great,* W. F. Reddaway, ed., Cambridge University Press (adapted)

56. These ideas of Catherine the Great of Russia originated during the

(1) Age of Exploration.
(2) Age of Enlightenment.
(3) Protestant Reformation.
(4) French Revolution.

Correct answer: (2) These ideas of Catherine the Great of Russia originated during the Age of Enlightenment. Also known as the Age of Reason, the Enlightenment was the intellectual movement in the eighteenth century in which logic and reasons triumphed over traditional values. A product of the Enlightenment, Catherine the Great created fair laws to ensure the safety of the people. She also believed in equality before the law, regardless of a person's social status. *(First Global Age)*

57. The Bolshevik Party in 1917 gained the support of the peasant class because it promised them

(1) "Peace, Land, and Bread"
(2) "Liberty, Equality, Fraternity"
(3) abolition of the secret police
(4) democratic reforms in all levels of government

Correct answer: (1) The Bolshevik Party in 1917 gained the support of the peasant class because they promised them "Peace, Land, and Bread." Vladmir Lenin applied Marxist ideas to war-torn Russia. The Bolsheviks did not propose democratic reforms or use the French Revolution–era slogan "Liberty, Equality, Fraternity" in 1917. *(Age of Revolution)*

58. Which area, once controlled by Britain, suffered mass starvation in the 1840s, and became an independent Catholic nation in 1922?

(1) Scotland
(2) India
(3) Ghana
(4) Ireland

Correct answer: (4) Ireland, once controlled by Britain, suffered mass starvation in the 1840s, and became an independent Catholic nation in 1922. Ireland suffered from a widespread potato famine in the 1840s. More than 1 million people died from what became known as the Great Hunger. The famine was exacerbated by the indifference of the British government. This strengthened Ireland's resolve to become an independent nation. Scotland, India, and Ghana were never affected by the potato famine. *(Crises and Achievement)*

---

59. Which name would best complete this partial outline?

I. African Nationalists of the Twentieth Century

   A.   Leopold Senghor

   B.   Jomo Kenyatta

   C.   Julius Nyerere

   D.   _____

   (1) Atatürk [Mustafa Kemal]

   (2) Ho Chi Minh

   (3) José de San Martín

   (4) Kwame Nkrumah

Correct answer: (4) Kwame Nkrumah would best complete this partial outline. An African nationalist, Nkrumah argued that the people must achieve self-determination, or have the freedom to make decisions about its political affairs. To this end, Kwame Nkrumah led the Gold Coast (present-day Ghana) to independence in 1957. The other leaders were not twentieth-century African nationalists. *(Twentieth Century Since 1945)*

---

60. Since 1948, a major reason for the conflict between Arabs and Israelis is that each side

   (1) wants the huge oil reserves that lie under the disputed land.

   (2) believes that the United States favors the other side in the conflict.

   (3) claims sovereignty over the same land.

   (4) seeks to control trade on the eastern end of the Mediterranean Sea.

Correct answer: (3) Since 1948, a major reason for the conflict between Arabs and Israelis is that each side claims sovereignty over the same land. The British were committed to set up a permanent Jewish state in Palestine under the Balfour Declaration. With the backing of the newly formed United Nations, the promise became reality at the end of World War II. Since then, Arabs and Israelis have been involved in numerous conflicts over the same land. Recent efforts to end the half-century-old conflict have been ineffective. *(Twentieth Century Since 1945)*

61. In the 1980s, Mikhail Gorbachev's attempts to change the Soviet Union resulted in

    (1) an increase in tensions between India and the Soviet Union.
    (2) a strengthening of the Communist Party.
    (3) a shift from producing consumer goods to producing heavy machinery.
    (4) a series of economic and political reforms.

Correct answer: (4) In the 1980s, Mikhail Gorbachev's attempts to change the Soviet Union resulted in a series of economic and political reforms. Gorbachev believed in introducing new economic and political ideas to reform Russia. The policy of glasnost, or openness, led to the end of censoring of news media by the Russian government. His new economic policies, perestroika, called for limited capitalistic ideas in Russia. *(Twentieth Century Since 1945)*

Base your answer to Question 62 on the cartoon below and on your knowledge of social studies.

Source: Ziraldo Alves Pinto, Ziraldo/Rio de Janeiro, Brazil, Cartoonists and Writers Syndicate.

62. What is the main idea of this Brazilian cartoon?

    (1) Relations between Latin America and the United States are mutually beneficial.
    (2) The United States wants to cut off political and economic relations with Latin America.
    (3) Latin American nations are self-sufficient and need not rely on the United States.
    (4) The United States wants to control its relationships with Latin America.

Correct answer: (4) The main idea of this Brazilian cartoon is that the United States wants to control its relationships with Latin America. The United States dictated terms of trade in Latin America for much of the twentieth century. Because of this, the relations between Latin America and the United States are not mutually beneficial. In the 21st century, Brazil had been trying, with moderate success, to find other economic partners to free itself from American domination. *(Twentieth Century Since 1945)*

Base your answer to Question 63 on the headlines below and on your knowledge of social studies.

"Tensions Increase over Kashmir"

"Hindus and Muslims Clash in Calcutta Riots"

"Threat of Nuclear Conflict Worries World"

---

63. These headlines refer to events in which region?

(1) Latin America
(2) sub-Saharan Africa
(3) subcontinent of India
(4) East Asia

Correct answer: (3) The headlines refer to events in the subcontinent of India. As an overwhelming majority, Hindus often clashed with minority groups such as the Sikhs and the Muslims in India. Lack of unity makes maintaining a democratic government more difficult for Indians. In addition, nations such as India and Pakistan compete in a nuclear arms race to protect their nations. However, nations in the world community recognized its dangers and attempted to stop the proliferation of military weapons. As recently as the early twenty-first century, the world community urged these nations to stop further nuclear testing and development. *(Twentieth Century Since 1945)*

---

64. One way in which the Tang Dynasty, the Gupta Empire, and the European Renaissance are similar is that they all included periods of

(1) religious unity.
(2) democratic reforms.
(3) economic isolation.
(4) cultural achievements.

Correct answer: (4) One way in which the Tang Dynasty, the Gupta Empire, and the European Renaissance are similar is that they all included periods of cultural achievements. For example, European Renaissance saw the rebirth of Greek and Roman cultures. The artists and intellectuals in this period challenged traditional values and authority. Similarly, the Tang Dynasty and the Gupta Empire marked the golden age of their own arts and literary achievements. *(Ancient World)*

---

65. The Armenian Massacre, the "killing fields" of the Khmer Rouge, and Saddam Hussein's attacks against the Kurds are examples of

(1) apartheid.
(2) enslavement.
(3) human rights violations.
(4) forced collectivization.

Correct answer: (3) The Armenian Massacre, the "killing fields" of the Khmer Rouge, and Saddam Hussein's attacks against the Kurds are examples of human rights violations. Armenians were oppressed by the Ottoman Turks through heavy taxation and discrimination. This led to a nationalist movement in the early twentieth century. The suppression of the nationalist movement by the Ottoman Turks led to the extermination of many Armenians. Similarly, Saddam Hussein and Pol Pot launched attacks on selected groups of people as part of their ethnic cleansing campaign in the late twentieth century. *(Crises and Achievement [1900–1945])*

---

66. In Western Europe, the Middle Ages began after the collapse of which empire?

(1) Mughal
(2) Roman
(3) Ottoman
(4) Byzantine

Correct answer: (2) In Western Europe, the Middle Ages began after the collapse of the Roman Empire. The collapse of the Roman Empire led Europe into a period called the Dark Ages, which was characterized by political turmoil, a decline in learning, and the absence of centralized governments. To ensure its security, medieval people turned to feudalism and manorialism. The political and economic instabilities also gave rise to the Roman Catholic Church. *(Expanding Zones of Exchange)*

Base your answers to questions 67 and 68 on the chart below and on your knowledge of social studies.

Executions During the Reign of Terror

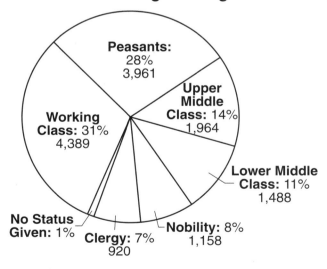

Peasants: 28% 3,961
Upper Middle Class: 14% 1,964
Working Class: 31% 4,389
Lower Middle Class: 11% 1,488
No Status Given: 1%
Clergy: 7% 920
Nobility: 8% 1,158

Source: Dennis Sherman et al., eds., World Civilizations: Sources, Images, and Interpretations, McGraw-Hill (adapted)

67. During which revolution did these executions occur?

(1) French
(2) Russian
(3) Chinese
(4) Cuban

Correct answer: (1) These executions occurred during the French Revolution. The storming of the Bastille marked the end of absolute monarchy in France. With the outcry of "Liberty, Equality, and Fraternity," France transformed itself into a republic. To ensure the success of the republic and foreign intrusions, Maximilien Robespierre began his Reign of Terror. Thousands were beheaded. *(Age of Revolutions)*

68. Which statement is best supported by information found in the chart on the previous page?

(1) Clergy were spared from the Reign of Terror.
(2) The Reign of Terror affected all classes equally.
(3) The Reign of Terror crossed social and economic boundaries.
(4) Peasants were the most frequent victims of the Reign of Terror.

Correct answer: (3) The statement best supported by information found in the chart is that the Reign of Terror crossed social and economic boundaries. The chart indicated that people from different walks of lives were executed. *(Age of Revolutions)*

Base your answer to Question 69 on the headlines below and on your knowledge of social studies.

"Germany, Austria-Hungary, and Italy Form Triple Alliance"

"Serbian Nationalism Grows in Balkans"

"Archduke Franz Ferdinand Assassinated in Bosnia"

69. The events in these headlines contributed most directly to the

(1) beginning of World War I
(2) outbreak of the Cold War
(3) development of communist rule in Europe
(4) strengthening of European monarchies

Correct answer: (1) The events in these headlines contributed most directly to the beginning of World War I. Triple Alliance and Triple Entente were the secret alliances formed before World War I as part of massive military buildups. Each nation was obliged to aid another nation in the alliance when necessary. These secret alliances were instrumental for war when Archduke Ferdinand was assassinated by a Serbian nationalist. *(Crises and Achievement [1900–1945])*

70. According to Buddhist principles, believers can end personal suffering by

   (1) doing good deeds.
   (2) eliminating selfish desires.
   (3) making pilgrimages to Mecca.
   (4) relying on divine help.

Correct answer: (2) According to Buddhist principles, believers can end personal suffering by eliminating selfish desires. Siddhartha Gautama, the founder of Buddhism, expressed his beliefs through *The Four Noble Truths. The Four Noble Truths* emphasized that everything in life is about suffering. Suffering can cease, however, if people do not give in to their selfish desires. Making pilgrimages to Mecca is not a requirement of the followers of Buddhism; it is a component of the Islamic religion. Doing good deeds and relying on divine help are characteristics of Christianity. *(Ancient World)*

71. Christianity, Islam, and Judaism are similar in that they all ask their followers to

   (1) believe in reincarnation.
   (2) strive for nirvana.
   (3) follow a code of behavior.
   (4) practice polytheism.

Correct answer: (3) Christianity, Islam, and Judaism are similar in that they all ask their followers to follow a code of behavior. Each of these major religions is monotheistic and provides a code of conduct such as the Koran and the Bible. In general, these codes are observed by followers to achieve a greater good. Hinduism includes a belief in reincarnation, while Buddhism encourages people to strive for nirvana. *(Ancient World)*

72. Shintoism and animism share a belief in the importance of

   (1) reincarnation.
   (2) spirits in nature.
   (3) the Bible.
   (4) missionaries.

Correct answer: (2) Shintoism and animism share a belief in the importance of spirits in nature. Spirits exist in both living and nonliving things is a belief shared by an African who practices Animism and a Japanese who practices Shinto. Reincarnation is a belief of Hinduism, while the value of the Bible and missionaries were features of Christianity. *(Ancient World)*

73. After the western Roman Empire fell to Germanic invaders in the fifth century C.E., the eastern part of the empire eventually became known as the

   (1) Byzantine Empire.
   (2) Carthaginian Empire.
   (3) Islamic Empire.
   (4) Persian Empire.

Correct answer: (1) After the western Roman Empire fell to Germanic invaders in the fifth century C.E., the eastern part of the empire eventually became known as the Byzantine Empire. Under the leadership of Emperor Constantine, the Byzantine Empire continued to rise in power. The Byzantines were instrumental in preserving the Greco-Roman cultures. The Carthaginian Empire was based in North Africa, while the spread of Islam and the Persian Empire gained power in the Middle East. *(Ancient World)*

---

74. The Age of Pericles in Athens, the Gupta Empire in India, and the Tang Dynasty in China all experienced a Golden Age with

    (1) advancements in the principles of democratic governments.

    (2) outstanding contributions in the arts and sciences.

    (3) the end of foreign domination.

    (4) the farthest expansion of their borders.

Correct answer: (2) The Age of Pericles in Athens, the Gupta Empire in India, and the Tang Dynasty in China all experienced a Golden Age with outstanding contributions in the arts and sciences. The Age of Pericles was generally considered the golden age of Athens. His achievements included his efforts to make Athenian democracy stronger and his leadership in social advancements. Similarly, the Gupta Empire saw advancements such as art, literature, science, and mathematics. The Tang Dynasty in China featured advancements in terms of science and technology, such as movable type and prosperity from trade along the Silk Road. *(Ancient World)*

---

75. The travels of Marco Polo resulted in the

    (1) introduction of gunpowder to China.

    (2) decline of Mongol rule in China.

    (3) expansion of trade between China and Europe.

    (4) use of Confucian teachings in Europe.

Correct answer: (3) The travels of Marco Polo resulted in the expansion of trade between China and Europe. The travels of Marco Polo jumpstarted a trading relationship between the Chinese and the Europeans. Gunpowder was invented by the Tang Dynasty in the 800s. The decline of the Mongol Empire took place by the end of the Yuan Dynasty in the late 1300s to 1400s after Marco Polo's journey to China in 1275. Confucian teachings did not provide a major impact in Europe. *(Global Interactions)*

Base your answer to Question 76 on the statements below and on your knowledge of social studies.

- In less than 50 years, it was the largest unified land empire in history.
- In 1279, it was the first foreign group to gain complete control of China.
- It made the caravan routes across Asia safe for trade and travel.
- When attempting to conquer Japan in 1274 and 1281, its fleets were destroyed by storms.

76. Which empire is most closely associated with these statements?

(1) Persian
(2) Gupta
(3) Ottoman
(4) Mongol

Correct answer: (4) The empire most closely associated with these statements is the Mongol Empire. The Mongols were led by rulers such as Genghis Khan and Kublai Khan. During the Yuan Dynasty, the Mongols took over territories spanning from China to Persia. Trading routes such as the Silk Road were developed to increase trade between China and the Middle East. *(Global Interactions)*

77. The wealth and power of Mali's ruler, Mansa Musa, were significant because they contributed to the

(1) start of the Crusades.
(2) spread of Islam.
(3) growth of European imperialism.
(4) rise of Arab nationalism.

Correct answer: (2) The wealth and power of Mali's ruler, Mansa Musa, were significant because they contributed to the spread of Islam. Mansa Musa was a devout Muslim, who made a hajj, or journey, to Mecca from 1324 to 1325. Upon returning, Mansa Musa built mosques and universities in Timbuktu. Because of this, Timbuktu became a center of learning in the Mali Empire. Mansa Musa's reign did not interfere with the Crusades, which had been fought from about 1093 to 1291, or the rise of European imperialism during the late 1800s. Additionally, Mansa Musa did not influence Arab nationalism. *(Global Interactions)*

78. An important effect of the Protestant Reformation in Europe was that it strengthened the

(1) power of monarchies.
(2) power of the pope.
(3) belief in polytheism.
(4) unity of Europe.

Correct answer: (1) An important effect of the Protestant Reformation in Europe was that it strengthened the power of monarchies. Martin Luther wrote in his Ninety-Five Theses against the sale of indulgences. This led to widespread fear of many monarchs, speculating whether they might also be able to break away from the Roman Catholic Church. In response to the pope's refusal to divorce his wife, for example, Henry VIII of England broke away from the Roman Catholic Church. Henry VIII then established the Anglican Church, or the Church of England. *(Global Interactions)*

37

79. The need to possess warm-water ports greatly influenced the foreign policy of which nation?

   (1) England
   (2) Russia
   (3) France
   (4) Egypt

Correct answer: (2) The need to possess warm-water ports greatly influenced the foreign policy of Russia. Peter the Great of Russia sought to gain ports on the Baltic Sea. A massive army was assembled to accomplish this goal. However, Catherine the Great would successfully acquire Black Sea ports in 1795. On the other hand, England and France were more concerned with imperialism than securing warm-water ports. *(First Global Age)*

80. The astrolabe and improvements in cartography helped Europeans to

   (1) launch the Crusades.
   (2) defeat the Mongols.
   (3) expel the Moors.
   (4) explore the Western Hemisphere.

Correct answer: (4) The astrolabe and improvements in cartography helped Europeans to explore the Western Hemisphere. These innovations provided the necessary catalyst for Europeans to explore around the world and expand power. The Crusades were fought over religious conflict between the Christians and the Muslims. Additionally, these inventions did not contribute to the defeat of the Mongols or the expulsion of the Moors. *(First Global Age)*

Base your answer to Question 81 on the chart below and on your knowledge of social studies.

Population of Four British Cities: 1801–1891				
Year	*Birmingham*	*Leeds*	*Liverpool*	*Manchester*
1801	74,000	53,000	80,000	90,000
1861	296,000	207,000	444,000	339,000
1891	523,000	429,000	704,000	645,000

81. Which event caused this population shift in Great Britain?

   (1) the bubonic plague
   (2) emigration to the Americas
   (3) the Industrial Revolution
   (4) rebellions in Ireland

Correct answer: (3) The Industrial Revolution caused a population shift in Great Britain. The need for laborers during the Industrial Revolution led to population increase in the cities. The bubonic plague, emigration (migration) to the Americas, and rebellions in Ireland caused the population of England to decrease, rather than increase as is shown in the chart. *(Age of Revolutions)*

Base your answer to Question 82 on the passage below and on your knowledge of social studies.

. . . But after a long period of commercial intercourse [trade], there appear among the crowd of barbarians both good persons and bad, unevenly. Consequently there are those who smuggle opium to seduce the Chinese people and so cause the spread of the poison to all provinces. Such persons who only care to profit themselves, and disregard their harm to others, are not tolerated by the laws of heaven and are unanimously hated by human beings. His Majesty the Emperor, upon hearing of this, is in a towering rage. He has especially sent me, his commissioner, to come to Kwangtung [Guangdong Province], and together with the governor-general and governor jointly to investigate and settle this matter. . . .

—"Letter of Advice to Queen Victoria" from Lin Zexu (Lin Tse-Hsü), Chinese Commissioner of Canton, 1839

---

82. This letter to Queen Victoria relates most directly to the outbreak of the

   (1) Chinese Civil War.
   (2) Sino-Japanese War.
   (3) Communist Revolution.
   (4) Opium Wars.

Correct answer: (4) This letter to Queen Victoria relates most directly to the outbreak of the Opium Wars. This letter is written from the Chinese Commissioner of Canton during the height of the Age of Imperialism. Opium, a highly addictive drug, provided negative influences on the Chinese society. Because the letter is written to the British about opium, it did not address the conflict between the Chinese and the Japanese. Additionally, the letter was written in 1839, not during the Communist Revolution in the late twentieth century. *(Age of Revolutions)*

---

83. The theory of Social Darwinism was sometimes used to justify

   (1) the establishment of communist governments in Asia.
   (2) Latin American revolutions in the early nineteenth century.
   (3) the independence movement in India.
   (4) European imperialism in the late nineteenth century.

Correct answer: (4) The theory of Social Darwinism was sometimes used to justify European imperialism in the late nineteenth century. Social Darwinism supports the theory of survival of the fittest. The theory proposed that only strong nations will survive. To this end, strong European nations used Social Darwinism to justify the colonization of weaker nations. Social Darwinism does not support communism, the Latin American revolutions, or the independence movement in India. *(Age of Revolutions)*

84. Japan's increased foreign trade during the Meiji Restoration was closely related to its

   (1) need to maintain a traditional society.

   (2) desire for a modern industrialized society.

   (3) colonization by Western nations.

   (4) encouragement of foreign investment.

Correct answer: (2) Japan's increased foreign trade during the Meiji Restoration was closely related to its desire for a modern industrialized society. During the Age of Imperialism, Japan felt the pressure to westernize in order to compete with other nations. This move was necessary in order to prevent Japan from being the victim of European imperialism. During the Meiji Restoration, the Japanese were involved in foreign trade and wanted to industrialize. At this point, Japan looked to break away from its traditional society. *(Age of Revolutions)*

85. Which event occurred first and led to the other three?

   (1) rise of fascism in Europe

   (2) Bolshevik Revolution

   (3) World War I

   (4) signing of the Treaty of Versailles

Correct answer: (3) World War I occurred first leading to the other three events. World War I broke out in 1914. The Bolshevik Revolution occurred in 1917 in Russia. When World War I ended in 1919, the Treaty of Versailles was signed. Fascism began to rise in Europe in 1922 with Benito Mussolini and Adolf Hitler (1933). *(Crises and Achievement [1900–1945])*

86. The early twentieth-century Zionist movement calling for the establishment of a Jewish homeland was an example of

   (1) imperialism.

   (2) nationalism.

   (3) capitalism.

   (4) isolationism.

Correct answer: (2) The early twentieth-century Zionist movement calling for the establishment of a Jewish homeland was an example of nationalism. Nationalism is defined as pride or love for one's country. During the Zionist movement, Jews sought to establish their permanent homeland. Imperialism is defined as the control of a stronger country taking over a weaker country for social, political, economic, religious, and militaristic reasons. Capitalism is an economic system where the market controls the economy. Under isolationism, a nation chooses to stay out of the politics of foreign nations. *(Crises and Achievement [1900–1945])*

Base your answer to Question 87 on the passage below and on your knowledge of social studies.

. . . Passive resistance is a method of securing rights by personal suffering, it is the reverse of resistance by arms. When I refuse to do a thing that is repugnant [objectionable] to my conscience, I use soul-force. For instance, the Government of the day has passed a law which is applicable to me. I do not like it. If by using violence I force the Government to repeal the law, I am employing what may be termed body force. If I do not obey the law and accept the penalty for its breach, I use soul-force. It involves sacrifice of self. . . .

—M. K. Gandhi, Hind Swaraj or *Indian Home Rule,* Navajivan Publishing (1938)

87. This statement reflects the belief that individuals

(1) have no control over events.
(2) can influence events by following moral guidelines.
(3) must use violence to influence events.
(4) can influence events by using military force.

Correct answer: (2) This statement reflects the belief that individuals can influence events by following moral guidelines. Under passive resistance, Gandhi believed that people may achieve their goals without resorting to violence. The people suffer for the sake of their own thoughts and desires. *(Age of Revolutions)*

88. Between the late 1800s and the end of World War II, Japan implemented a policy of imperialism mainly because Japan

(1) admired the economic power of China.
(2) lacked coal, iron, and other important resources.
(3) wanted to unify the governments of East Asia.
(4) feared the expansion of Nazi Germany in the Pacific.

Correct answer: (2) Between the late 1800s and the end of World War II, Japan implemented a policy of imperialism mainly because Japan lacked coal, iron, and other important resources. In order to produce more goods, countries need raw materials. During the Age of Imperialism, strong nations sought to imperialize in order to gain access to natural resources and new markets for their manufactured goods. Coal and iron were needed to support the industrial sector. *(Crises and Achievement [1900–1945])*

89. The partition of India and the division of Yugoslavia were similar in that both were divided

(1) as a result of the Berlin Conference.
(2) because of religious or ethnic differences.
(3) to form communist and noncommunist states.
(4) to conform to United Nations guidelines.

Correct answer: (2) The partition of India and the division of Yugoslavia were similar in that both were divided because of religious or ethnic differences. In India, conflict existed between its Hindu majority and Pakistan's Muslim majority. Kashmir, between Pakistan and India, has been a source of recent conflict. In Yugoslavia, many religions and ethnicities existed together, such as Orthodox Christian Serbs, Roman Catholic Croats, and Muslim Albanians. This led to a constant struggle ending in separation from

Yugoslavia and independence for Croatia, Slovenia, Bosnia and Herzegovina, and Macedonia. The Berlin Conference of 1884 and 1885 divided Africa during the Age of Imperialism, which did not affect India or Yugoslavia. In addition, these divisions did not involve the formation of communist and noncommunist states or the United Nations. *(Age of Revolutions)*

---

90. One similarity in the histories of Germany and Vietnam is that both nations

    (1) were once divided but have since been reunited.

    (2) remained nonaligned during the Cold War period.

    (3) have chosen a democratic form of government in recent years.

    (4) were once colonized by other European nations.

Correct answer: (1) One similarity in the histories of Germany and Vietnam is that both nations were once divided but have since been reunited. During the Cold War, Germany and Vietnam divided among noncommunist and communist states. Afterward, both were reunited. While Germany became a nation under capitalism, Vietnam became entirely communist. This question does not involve imperialism or colonization. *(Age of Revolutions)*

---

91. Control of the Bosporus and Dardanelles straits was a strategic objective in both World War I and World War II because these straits

    (1) link Africa to Europe.

    (2) allow waterway passage into Germany.

    (3) separate Italy from the Balkan peninsula.

    (4) provide access from the Black Sea to the Mediterranean Sea.

Correct answer: (4) Control of the Bosporus and Dardanelles straits was a strategic objective in both World War I and World War II, because these straits provide access from the Black Sea to the Mediterranean Sea. The Bosporus and Dardanelles do not link Africa to Europe, allow for a water passage into Germany, or separate Italy from the Balkan peninsula. *(Crises and Achievement [1900–1945])*

---

92. Which historical development showed the desire of a group to gain independence from a colonial power?

    (1) rise of the Nazi Party in Germany

    (2) Solidarity movement in Poland

    (3) Tiananmen Square uprising in China

    (4) Sepoy Mutiny in India

Correct answer: (4) The Sepoy Mutiny in India showed the desire of a group to gain independence from a colonial power, Great Britain. Indians revolted during the Sepoy Mutiny because of their refusal to fight with guns covered in beef or pork fat. The Hindus and the Muslims rebelled against the British in the hopes of gaining independence. In Poland, the trade union revolted against communism-they revolted against both, the USSR and their own communist government for political change. In China, students revolted against the government of Deng Xiaoping at Tiananmen Square. *(Age of Revolutions)*

93. Which statement describes a similarity between the French Revolution and the Bolshevik Revolution in Russia?

(1) The leaders in power before the revolutions favored changing the political system in their country.
(2) Both revolutions were the result of government denial of basic human rights and stressful economic conditions.
(3) Most of the revolutionary support was provided by radicals from other countries.
(4) The new democracies created by the revolutions gave people greater representation in their governments.

Correct answer: (2) A similarity between the French Revolution and the Bolshevik Revolution in Russia was that both revolutions were the result of government denial of basic human rights and stressful economic conditions. The Third Estate in France sought for natural rights under the governance of King Louis XVI. In Russia, the Bolsheviks rose against Czar Nicholas II claiming that their rights and livelihood were being ignored. Both Czar Nicholas II and King Louis XVI did not allow for political changes. In both cases, the people revolted against the government, creating some change. *(Age of Revolutions)*

Base your answer to Question 94 on the bullet points below and on your knowledge of social studies.

- Block printing, gunpowder, and the abacus were developed.
- Porcelain making and black-ink painting on silk paper were perfected.
- The compass was discovered and used to improve the determination of direction when sailing.

94. These advances are associated with the

(1) Tang and Song dynasties of China.
(2) Gupta Empire in India.
(3) Ghana and Mali civilizations of Africa.
(4) Byzantine Empire in the Middle East.

Correct answer: (1) These advances are associated with the Tang and Song dynasties of China. During the Gupta Empire, advancements were made in India in terms of art, literature, science, and mathematics. The Ghana and Mali civilizations focused on gold and salt. The Byzantine Empire featured icons, mosaics, and political advancements such as Justinian's Code. *(Expanding Zones and Exchange)*

Base your answer to Question 95 on the headlines below and on your knowledge of social studies.

"Archaeologists Revise Historical Interpretations After New Discovery"

"New Research Sheds Light on Causes of World War I"

"Computer Technology Helps Reconstruct Ancient Languages"

95. These headlines indicate that the understanding of historical facts

    (1) remains the same over time.

    (2) is passed down from one generation to another.

    (3) reflects a variety of personal opinions.

    (4) is shaped by the available evidence.

Correct answer: (4) These headlines indicate that the understanding of historical facts is shaped by the available evidence. Historians and archaeologists are two examples of researchers whose work help to improve our understanding of the past. New advancement of technology is also valuable in this cause. *(Ancient World)*

96. Which belief is most closely associated with the teachings of Siddhartha Gautama (Buddha)?

    (1) People are born into a specific caste.

    (2) Believers must follow the Ten Commandments.

    (3) Followers must fast during Ramadan.

    (4) People can overcome their desires by following the Eight-Fold Path.

Correct answer: (4) According to Buddhist principles, believers can end personal suffering by eliminating selfish desires. Siddhartha Gautama, the founder of Buddhism, expressed some of his beliefs through the Eight-Fold Path, which called on its followers to lead an ethical life. Suffering can cease, however, if people do not give in to their selfish desires. *(Ancient World)*

97. What was the immediate cause of World War I in Europe?

    (1) start of the civil war in Russia

    (2) sinking of the British liner, *Lusitania*

    (3) assassination of the heir to the throne of the Austro-Hungarian Empire

    (4) attack on Poland by the German army

Correct answer: (3) The immediate cause of World War I in Europe was the assassination of the heir to the throne of the Austro-Hungarian Empire. The start of civil war in Russia and the sinking of the British liner *Lusitania* both occurred once the war had started, while the attack on Poland by the German army was the start of World War II. With all the various causes of World War I, the one defining immediate cause of the war was the assassination of the archduke, heir to the throne of the Austro-Hungarian Empire. *(Crisis & Achievement (1900–1945)*

98. The Armenian massacre, the Holocaust, and the Rape of Nanking are examples of

(1) appeasement policies.
(2) resistance movements.
(3) Russification efforts.
(4) human rights violations.

Correct answer: (4) The Armenian massacre, the Holocaust, and the Rape of Nanking are examples of human rights violations. The many examples of rape, torture, and killings in all of these instances make them human rights violations. None of the above are appeasement policies, resistance movements, or Russification efforts. *(Crisis & Achievement (1900–1945)*

Base your answer to Question 99 on the actions below and on your knowledge of social studies.

- Showing respect for parents
- Maintaining family honor
- Honoring all elders

99. Which term is most closely related to these three actions?

(1) nirvana
(2) animism
(3) filial piety
(4) hadj (hajj)

Correct answer: (3) Filial piety is most closely related to these three actions. These Confucian principles called for respect for parents, maintaining family honor, and honoring all elders. The family was a model of the society. The followers of these principles believed that these actions would maintain social order and harmony. *(Ancient World)*

100. The travels of Marco Polo and of Ibn Battuta were similar, in that these travels

(1) led to nationalistic movements.
(2) helped to spread the ideas of religious leaders.
(3) stimulated the expansion of trade.
(4) supported democratic forms of government.

Correct answer: (3) The travels of Marco Polo and of Ibn Battuta were similar, in that these travels stimulated the expansion of trade. The travels of Marco Polo resulted in the expansion of trade between China and Europe. They jump-started a trading relationship between the Chinese and the Europeans. The travels of Ibn Battuta gave other regions a detailed description of the city of Timbuktu, a center of learning and trade in the West African kingdom of Mali. *(Global Interactions)*

---

101. In the early 1500s, Martin Luther's Ninety-five Theses, Henry VIII's Act of Supremacy, and John Calvin's *Institutes of the Christian Religion* contributed to

   (1) a decline in the power of the Catholic Church.
   (2) an increased sense of nationalism in Tudor England.
   (3) the growing power of the feudal nobility in Europe.
   (4) a major conflict among Eastern Orthodox Christians.

Correct answer: (1) In the early 1500s, Martin Luther's Ninety-five Theses, Henry VIII's Act of Supremacy, and John Calvin's *Institutes of the Christian Religion* contributed to a decline in the power of the Catholic Church. Martin Luther wrote in his Ninety-five Theses against the sale of indulgences. In response to the pope's refusal to allow him to divorce his wife, Henry VIII of England broke away from the Roman Catholic Church. Henry VIII then established the Anglican Church, or the Church of England. An important effect of the Protestant Reformation in Europe was that it strengthened the power of monarchs. *(Global Interactions)*

Base your answer to Question 102 on the information below and on your knowledge of social studies.

Edict of 1635 Ordering the Closing of Japan

- Japanese ships are strictly forbidden to leave for foreign countries.

- No Japanese is permitted to go abroad. If there is anyone who attempts to do so secretly, he must be executed. The ship so involved must be impounded and its owner arrested, and the matter must be reported to the higher authority.

- If any Japanese returns from overseas after residing there, he must be put to death. . . .

- Any informer revealing the whereabouts of the followers of padres (Christians) must be rewarded accordingly. If anyone reveals the whereabouts of a high ranking padre, he must be given one hundred pieces of silver. For those of lower ranks, depending on the deed, the reward must be set accordingly. . . .

   —David John Lu, *Sources of Japanese History,* McGraw-Hill, 1974

---

102. These rules reflect the Japanese policy of

   (1) totalitarianism.
   (2) appeasement.
   (3) interdependence.
   (4) isolationism.

Correct answer: (4) These rules reflect the Japanese policy of isolationism. To maintain their political power, Tokugawa shoguns kept the Japanese from exchanging of ideas or having contact with westerners. The document suggests that violators would face death. Despite its reluctance to become interdependent, Japan prospered during this period. The document does not provide any information about interdependence, totalitarianism, or appeasement. *(Global Interactions)*

103. The heliocentric model, the development of inductive reasoning, and the work of Descartes are all associated with which revolution?

    (1) Neolithic
    (2) Agricultural
    (3) Green
    (4) Scientific

Correct answer: (4) The heliocentric model, the development of inductive reasoning, and the work of Descartes are all associated with the Scientific Revolution. Sir Isaac Newton, Galileo Galilei, and Johannes Kepler were Renaissance scientists associated with the Scientific Revolution. Known for their contributions in science, these men used logic and evidence to support their claims. However, the findings were often challenged by the traditional authority, especially the Roman Catholic Church. For example, Galilei's claim that the sun, not the earth, was the center of the universe, was challenged vehemently by the church officials. *(Age of Revolutions)*

104. Which idea became a central belief of the Enlightenment?

    (1) The use of reason would lead to human progress.
    (2) Mathematics could be used to solve all human problems.
    (3) The ancient Romans had the best form of government.
    (4) People should give up their natural rights to their rulers.

Correct answer: (1) The idea that became a central belief of the Enlightenment was that the use of reason would lead to human progress. Enlightenment philosophers such as John Locke and Jean Jacques Rousseau sought to inform people of the value of their natural rights and the benefits of democracy. *(Age of Revolutions)*

Base your answer to Question 105 on the statements below and on your knowledge of social studies.

Statement A: We worked in a place that was noisy and dangerous. We did the same work over and over again. Many workers, often children, lost fingers, limbs, and even their lives.

Statement B: Government should not interfere in business. To do so would disrupt the balance of supply and demand.

Statement C: Government has a duty to interfere in order to best provide its people with a happy and safe life.

Statement D: Advances in agricultural techniques and practices resulted in an increased supply of food and raw materials, causing a movement of the farmers from the countryside to the city.

105. All of these statements describe events or viewpoints that relate to the

    (1) Protestant Reformation.
    (2) Commercial Revolution.
    (3) Industrial Revolution.
    (4) Berlin Conference.

Correct answer: (3) All of these statements describe events or viewpoints that relate to the Industrial Revolution. The Industrial Revolution caused a population increase in the cities of Great Britain. The need for laborers during the Industrial Revolution led to population increase in the cities. While some people advocated for laissez-faire capitalism, others were concerned with the safety of the workers. *(Age of Revolutions)*

Base your answer to Question 106 on the poem excerpt below and on your knowledge of social studies.

The White Man's Burden

Take up the White Man's burden—
Send forth the best ye breed—
Go, bind your sons to exile
To serve your captives' need;
To wait, in heavy harness,
On fluttered folk and wild—
Your new-caught sullen peoples,
Half devil and half child. . . .

—Rudyard Kipling, 1899

---

106. This stanza from Kipling's poem is most closely associated with the belief that it was the duty of Western colonial powers to

(1) learn from the people they conquered.
(2) teach their colonies how to produce manufactured goods.
(3) civilize the people they controlled.
(4) welcome less developed countries as equals.

Correct answer: (3) This stanza from Kipling's poem is most closely associated with the belief that it was the duty of Western colonial powers to civilize the people they controlled. The theory of Social Darwinism, implied in the poem, was sometimes used to justify European imperialism in the late nineteenth century. Social Darwinism supports the theory of survival of the fittest. The theory proposed that only strong nations will survive. To this end, strong European nations used Social Darwinism to justify the colonization of weaker nations. *(Age of Revolutions)*

---

107. Between 1845 and 1860, which factor caused a large decline in Ireland's population?

(1) famine
(2) civil war
(3) plague
(4) war against Spain

Correct answer: (1) Between 1845 and 1860, famine caused a large decline in Ireland's population. Once controlled by Britain, Ireland suffered a mass starvation in the 1840s from a widespread potato famine. More than 1 million people died from what became known as the Great Hunger. The famine was exacerbated by the indifference of the ruling powers of Great Britain, which strengthened Ireland's resolve to become an independent nation. *(Age of Revolutions)*

108. The ability of the Ottoman Empire to expand its borders depended on

    (1) military assistance from western Europe.
    (2) extensive trade with the Americas.
    (3) alliances formed during World War I.
    (4) strategic location between Europe and Asia.

Correct answer: (4) The ability of the Ottoman Empire to expand its borders depended on strategic location between Europe and Asia. The Ottoman Empire was located at the crossroads of trade between Europe and Asia. Trade routes such as the silk route and the spice route crossed through the Ottoman Empire, giving control and money to the Ottoman caliphs. The Ottoman Empire did not receive military help from Western Europe or have extensive trade with the Americas. While the Ottoman Empire formed alliances at World War I, the empire expanded its borders well before then. *(First Global Age)*

109. One action that many governments took during World War I was to

    (1) encourage political dissent and freedom of the press.
    (2) regulate their economic systems to increase production.
    (3) prevent women from seeking employment in factories.
    (4) raise tariffs to encourage trade.

Correct answer: (2) One action that many governments took during World War I was to regulate their economic systems to increase production. Because men qualified for military services were deployed for war, women were needed to work in the factories. Warring nations required supplies and goods, so posing tariffs or other forms of taxes would be detrimental to the war effort. Political dissent and negative press were generally discouraged during the war. *(Crises and Achievement [1900–1945])*

110. Which event is most closely associated with the start of World War II in Europe?

    (1) invasion of Poland by Nazi forces
    (2) signing of the Munich Agreement
    (3) building of the Berlin Wall
    (4) assassination of Archduke Franz Ferdinand

Correct answer: (1) The invasion of Poland by Nazi forces is most closely associated with the start of World War II in Europe. Failing to respond after a series of aggressions by the Germans, nations such as France and Britain eventually declared war on Germany in 1939. The signing of the Munich Agreement was an example of appeasing, or giving in to, the Germans. This agreement allowed the Germans to seize the Sudetenland. The building of the Berlin Wall happened after World War II. The assassination of Archduke Franz Ferdinand was the immediate cause of World War I. *(Crises and Achievement [1900–1945])*

111. Although Cuba has lost support from many nations, one reason Fidel Castro has remained in power is that he has

  (1) established free trade with the United States.
  (2) opposed communism.
  (3) prohibited the practice of Catholicism.
  (4) raised the standard of living for many Cubans.

Correct answer: (4) Although Cuba has lost support from many nations, one reason Fidel Castro has remained in power is that he has raised the standard of living for many Cubans. Castro overthrew an oppressive government under Fulgencio Batista in 1959 and established a communist dictatorship. The United States strongly opposed Cuba's connection with the USSR. Its economy suffered greatly because of American sanctions. *(Twentieth Century Since 1945)*

Base your answer to Question 112 on the statement below and on your knowledge of social studies.

. . . The Parties agree that an armed attack against one or more of them in Europe or North America shall be considered an attack against them all and consequently they agree that, if such an armed attack occurs, each of them, in exercise of the right of individual or collective self-defense . . . will assist the Party or Parties so attacked by taking forthwith, individually and in concert with the other Parties, such action as it deems necessary, including the use of armed force, to restore and maintain the security of the . . . area. . . .

112. Which organization includes this statement in its charter?

  (1) Warsaw Pact
  (2) United Nations
  (3) Organization of American States
  (4) North Atlantic Treaty Organization

Correct answer: (4) The North Atlantic Treaty Organization includes this statement in its charter. Established after the World War II (1949), this peacekeeping organization illustrated the importance of collective security. Noncommunist countries began to form alliances in the period known as the Cold War. The USSR formed its own alliance called the Warsaw Pact. *(Twentieth Century Since 1945)*

113. A similarity between Peter the Great of Russia and Deng Xiaoping of the People's Republic of China was that each

  (1) resisted economic and social reforms in his country.
  (2) rejected the culture of his country in favor of a foreign culture.
  (3) promoted economic and technological modernization of his country.
  (4) experienced foreign invasions of his country that almost succeeded.

Correct answer: (3) A similarity between Peter the Great of Russia and Deng Xiaoping of the People's Republic of China was that each promoted economic and technological modernization of his country. The need to possess warm-water ports greatly influenced the foreign policy of Russia. Peter the Great of Russia sought to gain ports on the Baltic Sea, hoping the ports would lead to more trade and cultural diffusion with foreign countries; however, Catherine the Great successfully acquired Black Sea ports in 1795. Similarly, Deng Xiaoping attempted to increase China's industrial output through the Four Modernizations. *(Twentieth Century Since 1945)*

114. In the late twentieth century, what was a problem common to the Balkans, Rwanda, and Indonesia?

(1) disposal of nuclear waste
(2) ethnic or religious conflicts
(3) drought and famine
(4) overcrowding of urban centers

Correct answer: (2) Ethnic or religious conflicts was a problem common to the Balkans, Rwanda, and Indonesia in the late Twentieth century. For example, the Balkans was one such area where different religions and ethnic groups existed. Several geographic features in the Balkans, including location, have helped lead to the cultural diversity of the region. After a period of violence, Yugoslavia was divided among different ethnic groups into countries such as Croatia and Slovenia. *(Twentieth Century Since 1945)*

115. In the years following the Meiji Restoration in Japan and the unification of Germany in the nineteenth century, both nations experienced

(1) an increase in military production and strengthened military forces.
(2) a reduction in tensions with neighboring nations.
(3) a restructuring of government that included popularly elected monarchs.
(4) a decrease in the reliance on industrialization and trade.

Correct answer: (1) In the years following the Meiji Restoration in Japan and the unification of Germany in the nineteenth century, both nations experienced an increase in military production and strengthened military forces. During the Age of Imperialism, Japan felt the pressure to westernize in order to compete with other nations. This move was necessary in order to prevent Japan from being the victims of European imperialism. During the Meiji Restoration, the Japanese were involved in foreign trade and wanted to industrialize. At this point, Japan looked to break away from its traditional society. Similarly, Germany tried to free itself from the French dominance. *(Age of Revolutions)*

116. One way in which Alexander II, Catherine the Great, and Boris Yeltsin played similar roles in Russian history was that they

(1) led communist revolutions.
(2) encouraged reforms.
(3) were subjects of Stalinist purges.
(4) supported territorial expansion.

Correct answer: (2) One way in which Alexander II, Catherine the Great, and Boris Yeltsin played similar roles in Russian history was that they encouraged reforms. For example, the collapse of the USSR marked the end of communism in other European states in recent years. Boris Yeltsin struggled to convert Russia from a communist state to a democracy. His reforms called for increased capitalistic elements in the Russian economy. Similarly, Catherine the Great was instrumental in reforming Russia. Her achievements included securing warm-water ports in the Black Sea. *(First Global Age)*

Base your answer to Question 9 on the bullet points below and on your knowledge of social studies.

- Berlin airlift
- Cuban missile crisis
- Nuclear arms race

---

117. These events were part of an era known as the

 (1) Age of Imperialism.
 (2) Scientific Revolution.
 (3) Enlightenment.
 (4) Cold War.

Correct answer: (4) These events were part of an era known as the Cold War. During the Cold War, the United States and the Soviet Union were at odds over political philosophies. Many nations were aligned with either the noncommunist United States or the communist Soviet Union. Although these two countries were never at war during this period, nations such as Germany and Cuba became hot spots over the spread of communism. The two countries also felt the need to increase military spending to better protect their political and economic interests. *(Crises and Achievement [1900–1945])*

---

118. Which civilization first developed a civil service system, invented gunpowder, and manufactured porcelain?

 (1) Aztec
 (2) Chinese
 (3) Japanese
 (4) Roman

Correct answer: (2) The Chinese civilization first developed a civil service system, invented gunpowder, and manufactured porcelain. Many early advances in civilization, such as the ones listed in this question, tie back to ancient China. Aztec, Japanese, and Roman civilizations made advancements, but development of gunpowder is considered a Chinese invention. *(Ancient World)*

---

119. Which two belief systems teach that there are spirits in nature?

 (1) Shinto and Animism
 (2) Hinduism and Confucianism
 (3) Judaism and Christianity
 (4) Islam and Buddhism

Correct answer: (1) The two belief systems that teach that there are spirits in nature are Shinto and Animism. These two religions look to items in nature, such as plants and animals, and see the spirits of the gods residing in them. Judaism, Christianity, and Islam are all monotheistic religions and see no basis for spirits in nature. Confucianism is more of a philosophy instead of a belief system, and it has no writings on spirits. The only answer that works, therefore, is Shinto and Animism. *(Expanding Zones of Exchange)*

---

120. A major contribution of the Golden Age of Islam was the

   (1) development of mercantilism.
   (2) creation of the first polytheistic religion.
   (3) spread of democratic ideals.
   (4) advancement of mathematics and science.

Correct answer: (4) A major contribution of the Golden Age of Islam was the advancement of mathematics and science. New concepts in medicine, science, and math, such as algebra, were being formed in this age. The Golden Age of Islam did not lead to the development of mercantilism or the spread of democratic ideals. Because Islam was a monotheistic religion, it certainly did not create the first polytheistic religion. *(Expanding Zones of Exchange)*

---

121. Which civilization best completes the heading of the partial outline below?

   I. I. _____

   A. Spread of Islam
   B. Gold and salt trade
   C. Growth of Timbuktu
   D. Pilgrimage of Mansa Musa

   (1) Benin
   (2) Kush
   (3) Mali
   (4) Egyptian

Correct answer: (3) The civilization that best completes the heading of the partial outline would be Mali. The Mali civilization of Africa was responsible for the spread of Islam, the gold and salt trade, the growth of Timbuktu, and the pilgrimage of Mansa Musa. *(Methodology of Global History/Geography)*

---

122. Historians value the writings of Marco Polo and Ibn Battuta because they

   (1) serve as primary sources about trade and culture.
   (2) provide the basis for European holy books.
   (3) include advice on how to be a democratic ruler.
   (4) present unbiased views of life in Africa and Asia.

Correct answer: (1) Historians value the writings of Marco Polo and Ibn Battuta because they serve as primary sources about trade and culture. These writings provide direct information on the time periods, giving us insights on the time period. These writings do not provide the basis for European holy books, include advice on how to be a democratic ruler, or present an unbiased view of life in Africa and Asia. *(First Global Age)*

---

123. Which factor contributed to the beginning of the Renaissance in Italian cities?

   (1) occupation by foreign powers
   (2) interaction with Latin America
   (3) surplus of porcelain from Japan
   (4) access to important trade routes

Correct answer: (4) The access to important trade routes contributed to the beginning of the Renaissance in Italian cities. The crusades opened up new trade doors to Europeans, bringing in spices and other luxuries. No occupation by foreign powers preceded the Renaissance, nor was there an interaction with Latin America or a surplus from Japan. The new trade routes were the major beginning of the Italian Renaissance, which then spread throughout Europe. *(First Global Age)*

Base your answer to Question 124 on the bullet points below and on your knowledge of social studies.

- 1340s—Mongols, merchants, and other travelers carried disease along trade routes west of China.
- 1346—The plague reached the Black Sea ports of Caffa and Tana.
- 1347—Italian merchants fled plague-infected Black Sea ports.
- 1348—The plague became an epidemic in most of Western Europe.

---

124. Which conclusion can be made based on these statements?

   (1) The plague primarily affected China.
   (2) The interaction of people spread the plague.
   (3) Port cities were relatively untouched by the plague.
   (4) The plague started in Western Europe.

Correct answer: (2) Based on these statements, you can make the conclusion that the interaction of people spread the plague. The timeline given shows how the plague spread through trade and traders, infecting crops of people in all different coastal cities. The statements do not point toward China or only to Western Europe. Given the cities mentioned, port cities were heavily affected by the plague, leaving human contact spreading the plague as the viable answer. *(Methodology of Global History/Geography)*

Base your answer to Question 125 on the quotation below and on your knowledge of social studies.

"To him who wishes to follow me, I offer hardships, hunger, thirst, and all the perils of war."

   —Garibaldi's Memoirs

125. This quotation from Garibaldi is most closely associated with Italian

(1) exploration.
(2) nationalism.
(3) imperialism.
(4) neutrality.

Correct answer: (2) The quotation from Garibaldi is most closely associated with Italian nationalism. Garibaldi was a major leader in unifying Italy, and in his memoirs, he discusses his nationalistic goals. There is no example of exploration, imperialism, or neutrality in this quote. Instead, Garibaldi talks about Italians joining him in a nationalistic movement in his quest for unifying Italy, a nationalistic movement. *(Age of Revolution)*

Base your answer to Question 126 on the quotation below and on your knowledge of social studies.

. . . I am willing to admit my pride in this accomplishment for Japan. The facts are these: It was not until the sixth year of Kaei (1853) that a steamship was seen for the first time; it was only in the second year of Ansei (1855) that we began to study navigation from the Dutch in Nagasaki; by 1860, the science was sufficiently understood to enable us to sail a ship across the Pacific. This means that about seven years after the first sight of a steamship, after only about five years of practice, the Japanese people made a trans-Pacific crossing without help from foreign experts. I think we can without undue pride boast before the world of this courage and skill. As I have shown, the Japanese officers were to receive no aid from Captain Brooke throughout the voyage. Even in taking observations, our officers and the Americans made them independently of each other. Sometimes they compared their results, but we were never in the least dependent on the Americans. . . .

—Eiichi Kiyooka, trans., *The Autobiography of Fukuzawa Yukichi,* The Hokuseido Press, 1934

126. Which set of events is most closely associated with the nation described in this passage?

(1) end of the Opium War → creation of European spheres of influence
(2) end of the Tokugawa Shogunate → beginning of the Meiji Restoration
(3) fall of the Manchus → rise of Sun Yixian (Sun Yat-sen)
(4) imperialism in China → start of World War II

Correct answer: (2) The set of events that is most closely associated with the nation described in this passage would be the end of the Tokugawa Shogunate → beginning of the Meiji Restoration. The passage repeatedly refers to Japan. The Opium War and Manchu Dynasty are both Chinese events, and have nothing to do with Japan. Imperialism in China leading to the start of World War II is a Japanese cause and effect, but it deals with a time period after the passage. *(Age of Revolution)*

127. When some European leaders agreed to Hitler's demands concerning Czechoslovakia in 1938, they were supporting a policy of

(1) détente.
(2) balance of power.
(3) collective security.
(4) appeasement.

Correct answer: (4) When some European leaders agreed to Hitler's demands concerning Czechoslovakia in 1938, they were supporting a policy of appeasement. Appeasement is the policy where governments give into hostile demands in order to avoid a war. This is the definition of what European leaders did when they ceded sections of Czechoslovakia to Hitler in 1938 without firing a shot in protest. Détente, balance of power, and collective security do not apply to this situation, because it was a simple case of surrender for "peace in our time." *(Crisis & Achievement (1900–1945)*

---

128. One reason Germany's invasion of Poland in 1939 was successful is that Poland

    (1) lacked natural barriers.
    (2) was located along the North Sea.
    (3) lacked natural resources.
    (4) was close to the Balkans.

Correct answer: (1) One reason that Germany's invasion of Poland in 1939 was successful is that Poland lacked natural barriers. Poland was a geographically flat nation, and the Germans were able to roll right in. The location of Poland along the North Sea, the lack of natural resources, and proximity to the Balkans had nothing to do with the ease of the Polish occupation. The fact that Germany could drive tanks right through the country in days was why the invasion was so successful. *(Crisis & Achievement (1900–1945)*

---

129. What was one reason that India was divided into two nations in 1947?

    (1) Indian leaders disagreed about India's role in the United Nations.
    (2) Great Britain feared a unified India would be a military threat.
    (3) The Soviet Union insisted that India should have a communist government.
    (4) Differences between the Hindus and the Muslims created religious conflict.

Correct answer: (4) One reason that India was divided into two nations in 1947 was that the difference between Hindus and the Muslims created a religious conflict. The Hindu majority of India was not generally cooperative with the Muslim practices, nor were the Muslims tolerant of Hindu beliefs. The creation of two states led to a peaceful settlement. The division did not occur because of disagreement about India in the United Nations, a threat to British security, or Soviet influence. *(Twentieth Century Since 1945)*

---

130. Which event illustrates the policy of containment?

    (1) Nuremberg trials (1945–1946)
    (2) Hungarian revolt (1956)
    (3) launching of Sputnik (1957)
    (4) naval blockade of Cuba (1962)

Correct answer: (4) The event that illustrates the policy of containment would be the naval blockade of Cuba. In order to stop the USSR from controlling land in the Western Hemisphere, the United States blockaded Cuba, stopping the Soviet Union from sending in more military supplies. The Nuremberg trials show justice after World War II, while the Hungarian revolt and Sputnik both illustrate major Cold War events. *(Twentieth Century Since 1945)*

131. One similarity between the Korean War and the Vietnam War is that both wars were

(1) resolved through the diplomatic efforts of the United Nations.
(2) fought as a result of differing political ideologies during the Cold War.
(3) fought without foreign influence or assistance.
(4) caused by religious conflicts.

Correct answer: (2) One similarity between the Korean War and the Vietnam War is that both wars were fought as a result of differing political ideologies during the Cold War. The Cold War raged between the United States and the Soviet Union, with capitalism fighting communism. These wars were not both resolved by the United Nations, and neither of them was fought without foreign influence or caused by religious conflicts. *(Twentieth Century Since 1945)*

Base your answer to Question 132 on the photograph below and on your knowledge of social studies.

The Berlin Wall

Source: http://imagesrvr.epnet.com/embimages/imh/archivephoto/full/g1952059.jpg

132. This 1989 photograph symbolizes the

(1) end of the Cold War.
(2) importance of the Berlin airlift.
(3) creation of a divided Germany.
(4) fear of Nazism among Germans.

Correct answer: (1) The 1989 photograph symbolizes the end of the Cold War. This man, tearing into the Berlin Wall, is tearing down the separation between East and West Berlin. This image is not showing the importance of the Berlin airlift, creation of a divided Germany, or the fear of Nazism among Germans. Instead, this is showing how the Berlin Wall fell, as Europe began to reunite and the Cold War was ending. *(Twentieth Century Since 1945)*

133. Which sequence of events is listed in the correct chronological order?

(1) Crusades → French Revolution → Renaissance
(2) French Revolution → Crusades → Renaissance
(3) Crusades → Renaissance → French Revolution
(4) Renaissance → Crusades → French Revolution

Correct answer: (3) The sequence of events listed in the proper chronological order is Crusades → Renaissance → French Revolution. The Crusades opened up new markets and ideas, leading into the Renaissance. The Renaissance was an explosion of culture and philosophy in Europe, giving way to thinkers like John Locke. It was the ideas of John Locke that inspired the French Revolution, confirming this as the correct order. *(First Global Age)*

Base your answer to Question 134 on the graph below and on your knowledge of social studies.

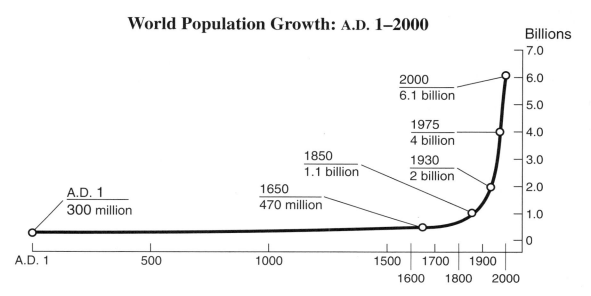

World Population Growth: A.D. 1–2000

Source: Population Reference Bureau and de Blij and Murphy, *Human Geography: Culture, Society, and Space,* John Wiley & Sons, 1999 (adapted)

134. Which statement can be supported by the information in the graph?

(1) The population of the world remained the same from 1 C.E. to 1650 C.E.

(2) Most of the world's population growth took place during the period from 1000 C.E. to 1500 C.E.

(3) The population growth rate decreased during the period from 1650 C.E. to 1800 C.E.

(4) The world's population tripled between 1930 C.E. and 2000 C.E.

Correct answer: (4) The statement that can be supported using the information on the graph is that the world's population tripled between 1930 C.E. and 2000 C.E. The sharp increase in population is evident at the end of the map. The population did not remain the same from 1 C.E. to 1650 C.E., nor did the growth take place between 1000 C.E. to 1500 C.E., nor did the growth rate decrease during the period of 1650 C.E. to 1800 C.E. The only statement that is supported by the graph is that the world's population tripled between 1930 C.E. and 2000 C.E. *(Methodology of Global History/Geography)*

135. Which period of history had the greatest influence on the Enlightenment ideas of natural law and reason?

(1) Pax Romana
(2) Middle Ages
(3) Age of Exploration
(4) Scientific Revolution

Correct answer: (4) The Scientific Revolution had the greatest influence on the Enlightenment ideas of natural law and reason. The ideas of the Scientific Revolution, specifically looking at man and the role of man, led Enlightenment thinkers to re-evaluate man and man's capacity. Pax Romana, the Middle Ages, and the Age of Exploration had little if any influence on the Enlightenment ideas of natural law and reason. *(Age of Revolution)*

136. During the twentieth century, global attention was drawn to the Armenians of the Ottoman Empire, the Tutsis of Rwanda, and the Muslims of Kosovo because these groups were all victims of

(1) nuclear power accidents.
(2) human rights violations.
(3) environmental disasters.
(4) the AIDS epidemic.

Correct answer: (2) During the twentieth century, global attention was drawn toward the Armenians of the Ottoman Empire, the Tutsis of Rwanda, and the Muslims of Kosovo, because these groups were all victims of human rights violations. Innocent people in each example were being beaten, tortured, and killed because of their ethnicity. This is the very definition of human rights violations. These groups were not victims of nuclear power accidents, environmental disasters, or the AIDS epidemic. Their only crime was being different, and they were brutalized because of it. *(Twentieth Century Since 1945)*

137. Olympic games, the poems of Homer, and Hellenistic culture are associated with which ancient civilization?

(1) Egyptian
(2) Greek
(3) Roman
(4) Phoenician

Correct answer: (2) Olympic games, the poems of Homer, and Hellenistic culture are associated with the ancient Greek civilization. There are no fancy tricks or pneumonic devices to help with this question. Any question that asks about the origins of the Olympic games will always tie back to ancient Greece. Homer was a Greek poet, and Hellenistic culture sees its base in ancient Greece with Alexander. *(Ancient World)*

---

138. Which heading best completes the partial outline below?

    I. _____

      A. Development of medical encyclopedias

      B. Development of algebra and astronomical tables

      C. Production of cotton textiles and wooden carpets

      D. Production of literature, calligraphy, and geometric art

    (1) Achievements of Feudal Societies
    (2) Inventions during the Neolithic Revolution
    (3) Issues of the Protestant Reformation
    (4) Contributions of the Islamic Civilization

Correct answer: (4) The partial outline would best be headed by the title Contributions of the Islamic Civilization. The development of algebra, specifically, is an Islamic development and certainly not an invention of the Neolithic Revolution. Feudal societies were not well known for their medical encyclopedias, and the Protestant Reformation did not have anything to do with development or productions of goods. *(Ancient World)*

---

139. Which fact relating to early Japan was a result of the other three?

    (1) Japan experienced earthquakes and volcanic eruptions.
    (2) The Japanese developed a nature-based belief called Shinto.
    (3) Tsunamis and typhoons sometimes destroyed coastal Japanese villages.
    (4) Mountains are found throughout the islands of Japan.

Correct answer: (2) The Japanese nature-based belief called Shinto is the fact that relates to the other three. The Japanese people needed a reason to explain the natural disasters that affected Japan: earthquakes, volcanoes, typhoons, and tsunamis, as well as the mountains found throughout the islands of Japan. Therefore, the nature-based belief system called Shinto formed. *(Ancient World)*

Base your answer to Question 140 on the picture below and on your knowledge of social studies.

140. This statue is most closely associated with which religion?

    (1) Buddhism
    (2) Islam
    (3) Jainism
    (4) Christianity

Correct answer: (1) The statue most closely associates with Buddhism. Based on the position in which the statue is sitting, as well as the clothing and apparel (for example, the dot on forehead), the answer would not be Islam, Christianity, or Jainism, leaving Buddhism as the correct answer. *(Ancient World)*

141. Which action could be considered an effect of the Protestant Reformation?

    (1) posting of the Ninety-five Theses
    (2) decline in the power of the Roman Catholic Church
    (3) sale of indulgences
    (4) end of religious warfare

Correct answer: (2) The decline in the power of the Roman Catholic Church could be considered an effect of the Protestant Reformation. The sale of indulgences and the posting of the Ninety-five Theses are both causes of the Reformation, leading to Luther forming a branch of Christianity. Religious warfare exists today, so the Protestant Reformation clearly did not end it. *(Age of Revolution)*

Base your answer to Question 142 on the passage below and on your knowledge of social studies.

In 1469, Isabella of Castile married Ferdinand of Aragon. This marriage between the rulers of two powerful kingdoms opened the way for a unified state. Using their combined forces, the two monarchs made a final push against the Muslim stronghold of Granada. In 1492, Granada fell. . . .

—Elisabeth Ellis and Anthony Esler, *World History: Connections to Today,* Prentice Hall, 1997

142. What is being described in this passage?

    (1) a crusade to the Holy Land
    (2) the reasons for the voyages of Columbus
    (3) the Spanish Reconquista
    (4) the start of the Italian Renaissance

Correct answer: (3) The Spanish Reconquista is being described in this passage. Isabella and Ferdinand were both Spanish rulers in the late fifteenth century; they would not be starting a crusade to the Holy Land or starting the Italian Renaissance. Although the timing is correct for the reasons for the voyages of Columbus, the passage discusses pushing the Moors out of Granada, which was the Reconquista. *(First Global Age)*

143. One way in which the Scientific Revolution and the Enlightenment were similar is that they:

    (1) encouraged the spread of new ideas.
    (2) strengthened traditional institutions.
    (3) led to the Protestant Reformation.
    (4) rejected Renaissance individualism.

Correct answer: (1) One way in which the Scientific Revolution and the Enlightenment were similar is that they encouraged the spread of new ideas. The Protestant Reformation occurred before the Enlightenment or the Scientific Revolution, and neither of these strengthened traditional institutions. Quite the opposite, the Scientific Revolution and the Enlightenment caused difficulty for existing institutions by accepting Renaissance individualism and encouraging the spread of new ideas. *(Age of Revolution)*

144. In the late 1800s, one response of workers in England to unsafe working conditions was to

    (1) take control of the government.
    (2) return to farming.
    (3) set minimum wages.
    (4) form labor unions.

Correct answer: (4) In the late 1800s, one response of workers in England to unsafe working conditions was to form labor unions. Workers could not return to farming, because larger farms had bought up their farms, and there was no work to be had in the fields. The labor unions worked to set minimum wages and take control of the government, so the formation of labor unions was the way in which English workers responded to unsafe conditions. *(Age of Revolution)*

---

145. During World War I, which group of people were victims of genocide?

(1) Arabs in Egypt
(2) Palestinians in Syria
(3) Algerians in France
(4) Armenians in the Ottoman Empire

Correct answer: (4) During World War I, the Armenians in the Ottoman Empire were victims of genocide. Genocide is when you destroy a complete race of people. The Armenians, who were forced to march through the Syrian desert, separated from their families, and otherwise persecuted by the Ottoman Turks, were clearly victims during this time period. *(Crisis & Achievement (1900–1945)*

---

146. The Treaty of Versailles punished Germany for its role in World War I by

(1) forcing Germany to accept blame for the war and to pay reparations.
(2) dividing Germany into four occupied zones.
(3) supporting economic sanctions by the United Nations.
(4) taking away German territory in the Balkans and Spain.

Correct answer: (1) The Treaty of Versailles punished Germany for its role in World War I by forcing Germany to accept blame for the war and to pay reparations. The division of Germany, and the United Nations are both results of World War II. The payment of reparations is a World War I punishment, and not one repeated in World War II. *(Crisis & Achievement (1900–1945)*

---

147. The main reason Japan invaded Southeast Asia during World War II was to

(1) recruit more men for its army.
(2) acquire supplies of oil and rubber.
(3) satisfy the Japanese people's need for spices.
(4) prevent the United States from entering the war.

Correct answer: (2) The main reason Japan invaded Southeast Asia during World War II was to acquire supplies of oil and rubber. The islands that make up the Japanese mainland are lacking in natural resources, a fact that Japan compensated for with an aggressive imperialist policy of invasion and conquering. This is why, during World War II, the Japanese felt they needed to go into Southeast Asia to acquire supplies, keeping them dominant in Asia. *(Crisis & Achievement (1900–1945)*

148. The political climate of the Cold War caused the world's two superpowers to

    (1) cooperate in halting the spread of communism.
    (2) colonize Africa and Asia.
    (3) compete economically and militarily.
    (4) protect human rights.

Correct answer: (3) The political climate of the Cold War caused the world's two superpowers to compete economically and militarily. Because the Soviet Union was communist and the United States was democratic, and because each side wanted to contain the other side, they competed for dominance in the world. The two fundamental competitions took place over the economic security and the military might of both sides, rather than colonization or protection of human rights. *(Twentieth Century Since 1945)*

149. The political ideas of Ho Chi Minh, Fidel Castro, and Saloth Sar [- (Pol Pot)] were strongly influenced by the writings of

    (1) Confucius.
    (2) Mohandas Gandhi.
    (3) Desmond Tutu.
    (4) Karl Marx.

Correct answer: (4) The political ideas of Ho Chi Minh, Fidel Castro, and Pol Pot were strongly influenced by the writings of Karl Marx. The leaders in this question each wanted a communist nation, controlled by the people as opposed to the wealthy elite. The writings they applied to the formation of these nations came from Karl Marx, whose vision for a world controlled not by the wealthy elite, but by the workers, appealed to these revolutionary leaders. *(Twentieth Century Since 1945)*

150. In India, urbanization affected society by

    (1) reinforcing Hindu beliefs.
    (2) encouraging native arts and crafts.
    (3) weakening the traditional caste system.
    (4) increasing the number of farmers.

Correct answer: (3) In India, urbanization affected society by weakening the traditional caste system. With people moving out of the villages into the cities, there was less emphasis on your heritage and what caste your parents were in. Rather, the focus went to your individual talents. *(Twentieth Century Since 1945)*

151. The late twentieth-century conflicts in Rwanda, Yugoslavia, and India were similar in that each was caused by the

    (1) deforestation conducted by multinational companies.
    (2) collapse of communism.
    (3) intervention of United Nations peacekeeping forces.
    (4) rivalries between ethnic groups.

Correct answer: (4) The late twentieth-century conflicts in Rwanda, Yugoslavia, and India were similar in that each was caused by the rivalries between ethnic groups. These ethnic groups had historic conflicts brewing, and they came to a head at the end of the twentieth century. Intervention by the United Nations and deforestation do not apply, and the collapse of communism is an indirect cause of some, but not all, of the conflicts. *(Twentieth Century Since 1945)*

---

152. During which period did the domestication of animals and growing of crops first occur?

    (1) Iron Age
    (2) Old Stone Age
    (3) Neolithic Revolution
    (4) Scientific Revolution

Correct answer: (3) The domestication of animals and the growing of crops first occurred during the period of the Neolithic Revolution. The Neolithic Revolution represents the first movements toward villages and civilizations, moving humans away from a more nomadic lifestyle. The Iron Age, Stone Age, and Scientific Revolution, while all examples of periods, have nothing to do with animals or crops, so the Neolithic Revolution becomes the only possible correct choice. *(Ancient World)*

---

153. The religious terms *Four Noble Truths, Eightfold Path,* and *nirvana* are most closely associated with

    (1) Judaism.
    (2) Islam.
    (3) Shintoism.
    (4) Buddhism.

Correct answer: (4) The religious terms *Four Noble Truths, Eightfold Path,* and *nirvana* are most closely associated with Buddhism. The concept of nirvana, or a level of existence in a perfect environment, is a Buddhist concept. Judaism, Islam, and Shintoism have no references to nirvana, Four Noble Truths, or the Eightfold Path. *(Ancient World)*

---

154. The Golden Age of Muslim culture was best known for its

    (1) attempts to colonize North America.
    (2) frequent conflicts between Christians and Jews.
    (3) advances in mathematics, science, and medicine.
    (4) policies to reduce trade between the Middle East and China.

Correct answer: (3) The Golden Age of Muslim culture was best known for its advances in mathematics, science, and medicine. New concepts in medicine, science, and math, such as algebra, were being formed in this age. The Golden Age of Islam did not lead to attempts to colonize North America or policies to reduce trade between the Middle East and China, nor did it lead to frequent conflicts between Christians and Jews. *(Ancient World)*

155. What was one influence of Mongol rule on the history of Russia?

    (1) Contact with kingdoms in western Europe greatly increased.
    (2) The Chinese writing system was introduced and adopted.
    (3) Most Russians converted from Orthodox Christianity to Islam.
    (4) Russian leaders adopted the idea of strong, centralized control of the empire.

Correct answer: (4) The Mongol rule influenced the history of Russia by Russian leaders adopting the idea of strong, centralized control of the empire. In the wake of Mongol conquest over Russia, cultural influences took over, and the concept of a strong centralized government came to Russia. Russians did not increase contact with Western Europe, adopt the Chinese writing system, or convert to Islam. *(First Global Age)*

Base your answer to Question 157 on the statements below and on your knowledge of social studies.

- Timbuktu is known as a great center of learning and trade.
- Walls of Great Zimbabwe reveal a powerful and rich society.
- Complex culture produces brass sculptures in Benin.

156. What generalization can be made on the basis of these statements?

    (1) Religious beliefs were the most important element in many African societies.
    (2) Some African societies achieved a high level of economic and cultural development.
    (3) North African societies were more advanced than South African societies.
    (4) Most African societies were hundreds of years behind Asian societies in using technology.

Correct answer: (2) Based on these statements, you can generalize that some African societies achieved a high level of economic and cultural development. Between the learning in Timbuktu, the architecture in Great Zimbabwe, and the culture in Benin, African societies were rich and cultural. The examples given do not tie into religion, showing North African versus South African superiority, or the technological advancements of Africa. *(First Global Age)*

157. Which statement best expresses the Western perspective regarding Rudyard Kipling's "white man's burden"?

    (1) Europeans should preserve traditional cultures in Africa and Asia.
    (2) Europeans must protect existing African and Asian economies.
    (3) Europeans suffered great hardships in exploring new trade routes to Asia.
    (4) Europeans had a duty to introduce the benefits of their civilization to non-European peoples.

Correct answer: (4) The statement that Europeans had a duty to introduce the benefits of their civilization to non-European peoples best expresses the Western perspective regarding the "white man's burden." According to Kipling, Africans were uncivilized, and it was the responsibility of Europeans to "save" them. Kipling had no intention of preserving traditions in Africa or Asia, protecting their economies, or dealing with the hardships in exploring new trade routes. *(Age of Revolution)*

158. The movement started by journalist Theodor Herzl to promote an independent Jewish state in Palestine is referred to as

    (1) the Reconquista.
    (2) the Diaspora.
    (3) Utopianism.
    (4) Zionism.

Correct answer: (4) The movement started by journalist Theodore Herzl to promote an independent Jewish state in Palestine is referred to as Zionism. Theodore Herzl is a name that is always tied to Zionism and Nationalism. The Reconquista and Utopianism have nothing to do with the Jewish state of Palestine, and the Diaspora refers to the dispersed ethnic population of the Jewish people. Thus, the only answer left would be Zionism. *(Age of Revolution)*

159. During the Indian independence movement, many Muslims in India demanded a separate state of Pakistan to

    (1) remain under British control.
    (2) prevent future invasions from Afghanistan and China.
    (3) address concerns about their status as a religious minority.
    (4) protect the sacred rivers, the Indus and the Ganges.

Correct answer: (3) During the Indian independence movement, many Muslims in India demanded a separate state of Pakistan to address concerns about their status as a religious minority. The Muslims did not want to be controlled by a majority Hindu government or ruled by people they felt would not treat them equally. They certainly did not demand a separate state to remain under British control or to prevent future invasions from Afghanistan and China. The Pakistanis did not demand a separate state to protect their sacred rivers either. *(Twentieth Century Since 1945)*

Base your answer to Question 160 on the stamp below and on your knowledge of social studies.

68

160. This commemorative stamp was issued 50 years after the Marshall Plan. George Marshall was honored because he had

(1) insisted that Germany and the other Axis Powers pay for starting World War II.
(2) proposed economic aid from the United States to rebuild the economies of European Nations.
(3) formed the European Union so that Western Europe could rebuild its own economy.
(4) encouraged Western European nations to accept aid from the Soviet Union.

Correct answer: (2) The commemorative stamp shown honors George Marshall because he proposed economic aid from the United States to rebuild the economies of European nations. The Marshall Plan was designed to help all nations rebuild their economies, and worked out quite well, to Marshall's credit. The Marshall Plan did not insist that the Axis Powers pay for starting World War II, nor did it form the European Union so that Western Europe could rebuild it's own economy. Marshall certainly did not encourage Western European nations to accept aid from the Soviet Union; rather, he wanted to preserve democracy. *(Twentieth Century Since 1945)*

161. One way in which Lech Walesa, Mikhail Gorbachev, and Nelson Mandela are similar is that each

(1) led the people of his nation toward a more democratic government.
(2) fought for power for the black majority over the white minority.
(3) worked to end communism in his country.
(4) refused to participate in the United Nations.

Correct answer: (1) One way in which Lech Walesa, Mikhail Gorbachev, and Nelson Mandela are similar is that each led the people of his nation toward a more democratic government. Each of the nationalists above were responsible for bringing their nations into democratic governments in the late twentieth-century. Only Nelson Mandela fought for power for the black majority, and only Walesa and Gorbachev worked to end communism. None of the nations refused to participate in the United Nations. *(Twentieth Century Since 1945)*

Base your answer to Question 162 on the bullet points below and on your knowledge of social studies.

- Creation of NATO (North Atlantic Treaty Organization) and the Warsaw Pact
- Construction of the Berlin Wall
- Cuban missile crisis

162. These events are most closely associated with

(1) World War I.
(2) World War II.
(3) the Cold War.
(4) the Persian Gulf War.

Correct answer: (3) The events listed are most closely associated with the Cold War. The creation of NATO and the Warsaw Pact, the building of the Berlin Wall, and the Cuban missile crisis are all examples of escalating tensions and military buildups. These events occurred after both World War I and World War II, and well before the Persian Gulf War. *(Twentieth Century Since 1945)*

Base your answer to Question 163 on the bullet points below and on your knowledge of social studies.

- Chernobyl experiences nuclear disaster.
- Chlorofluorocarbons (CFC) deplete the ozone layer.
- Rivers and seas are polluted throughout the world.

163. Which conclusion can best be drawn from these statements?

   (1) Modern technology can have serious negative effects.
   (2) Today's environment renews itself.
   (3) Only developing nations have environmental problems.
   (4) Most environmental problems originate in Europe.

Correct answer: (1) The best conclusion that can be drawn from the statements is that modern technology can have serious negative effects. Each one of the statements has led to the damage of the environment, and shown the negative side effects of industrialization. The statements do not show the environment renewing itself, nor do they show that only developing nations or European nations have environmental problems. The Chernobyl nuclear disaster, for instance, occurred in the Soviet Union, a fully developed nation. *(Global Connections/Interactions)*

164. One similarity between the Reign of Terror during the French Revolution and the Cultural Revolution in China was that both

   (1) limited the power of absolute leaders.
   (2) illustrated the power of public opinion in forming national policy.
   (3) established social stability and economic growth.
   (4) used violent methods to eliminate their opponents.

Correct answer: (4) One similarity between the Reign of Terror during the French Revolution and the Cultural Revolution in China was that both used violent methods to eliminate their opponents. Both the Reign of Terror and the Cultural Revolution were violent, bloody, purges of anyone who may stand against the revolutionary leaders. Neither of them limited the power of absolute leaders, illustrated the power of public opinion in forming national policy, or established social stability and economic growth. Rather, both of these events brutally and violently eliminated the opponents to the revolutionary leaders and created a harsh rule in France and China. *(Global Connections/Interactions)*

165. Revival of trade in Western Europe, decline of feudalism, revival of interest in learning, and cultural interaction with the Middle East are associated with the

   (1) impact of the Crusades.
   (2) effects of the barter system.
   (3) growth of the Maya Empire.
   (4) rise of Charlemagne.

Correct answer: (1) Revival of trade in Western Europe, decline of feudalism, revival of interest in learning, and the cultural interaction with the Middle East are associated with the impact of the Crusades. The Crusades, by sending young men to the Middle East, changed Europe significantly, leading to all the changes seen above. The barter system, the growth of the Maya Empire, and the rise of Charlemagne, while each significant, did not have the widespread impact that the Crusades had, as seen with the examples given. *(First Global Age)*

Base your answer to Question 166 on the map below and on your knowledge of social studies.

Spread of the Black Death

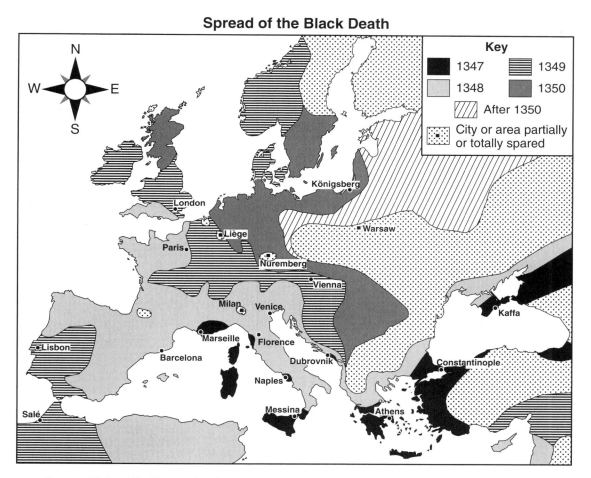

Source: Richard Bulliet et al., *The Earth and Its Peoples: A Global History,* Houghton Mifflin, 2001 (adapted)

166. The map shows that the Black Death

    (1) began in England and Ireland and then spread eastward.

    (2) spread slowly over several decades.

    (3) affected most areas of Western Europe.

    (4) was most severe in Italy.

Correct answer: (3) The map shows the Black Death affected most areas of Western Europe. All the major regions in Western Europe are affected, with the course of the Black Death passing through many of the main cities of Europe. The map does not show the Black Death beginning in England and Ireland, seeing how there are earlier dates in Sicily for instance. The map also does not show a slow spread, because all the dates are within a decade. Finally, the map does not show how severe death was, so you cannot say it was most severe in Italy. *(Global Interactions)*

167. What was a long-term impact of Marco Polo's trips to China?

    (1) The Silk Roads replaced the all-water route to Asia.

    (2) The Chinese forced the Europeans to trade only in Peking.

    (3) China was isolated from other countries.

    (4) Trade increased between China and Europe.

Correct answer: (4) The long-term impact of Marco Polo's trips to China was that trade increased between China and Europe. By Marco Polo traveling to China, he opened new pathways of trade and created mutual markets for goods. The Silk Road did not replace the all-water route to Asia, nor did the Chinese force the Europeans to trade only in Peking. Certainly China was not isolated, since Marco Polo's visit was specifically to open the trade routes. *(Global Interactions)*

168. In Western Europe, Martin Luther's Ninety-five Theses and Henry VIII's Act of Supremacy led to

    (1) an end to Christian unity.

    (2) a strengthening of economic unity.

    (3) better relations between peasants and merchants.

    (4) fewer violent outbreaks between ethnic groups.

Correct answer: (1) In Western Europe, Martin Luther's Ninety-five Theses and Henry VIII's Act of Supremacy led to an end to Christian unity. These two actions began the Protestant Reformation, which led to people practicing Christianity in different ways, with different practices to follow. These actions did not lead to a strengthening of economic unity, nor did it lead to better relations between peasants and merchants or fewer violent outbreaks between ethnic groups. Quite the opposite, these events caused violence, large rifts in Europe, and strained relationships in places. *(Age of Revolution)*

Base your answer to Question 169 on the bullet points below and on your knowledge of social studies.

    ■ Leonardo da Vinci used movement and perspective in his work.

    ■ Machiavelli's *The Prince* advised rulers on how to gain and maintain power.

    ■ Humanist scholars examined worldly subjects and classical culture.

169. Which period is associated with these statements?

   (1) French Revolution
   (2) Renaissance
   (3) Early Middle Ages
   (4) Enlightenment

Correct answer: (2) The period associated with these statements is the Renaissance. Leonardo da Vinci is the Renaissance man, so any questions about his time period will always come back to the Renaissance. The French Revolution, Early Middle Ages, and Enlightenment are all periods in history, but as soon as Leonardo da Vinci comes up, the answer will come back to the Renaissance. *(Age of Revolution)*

170. The Aztec use of the calendar and the Maya writing system both illustrate that pre-Columbian cultures in the Americas

   (1) traded extensively with Africa.
   (2) flourished prior to European contact.
   (3) declined because of invasion and disease.
   (4) converted others to Islam.

Correct answer: (2) The Aztec use of the calendar and the Maya writing system both illustrates that pre-Columbian cultures in America flourished prior to European contact. Both of these examples show the culture that existed in the Americas before European contact, and that Europeans came to an evolved and complex civilization, not a group of savages. *(First Global Age)*

171. What was a major cause of the French Revolution?

   (1) inequalities in the tax structure
   (2) economic success of mercantilism
   (3) failure of the Congress of Vienna
   (4) Continental System in Europe

Correct answer: (1) A major cause of the French Revolution was the inequalities in the tax structure. The Third Estate was bearing a heavy tax burden and was home to the poorest of people to begin with. The other choices—the economic success of mercantilism, the failure of Congress of Vienna, and the Concert of Europe—are not causes of the French Revolution. *(Age of Revolution)*

172. The British government took control of the Suez Canal and Singapore during the nineteenth century in order to

   (1) sell petroleum to these territories.
   (2) gain more converts to Christianity.
   (3) ensure safe passage on strategic waterways.
   (4) transport laborers directly to the Americas.

Correct answer: (3) The British government took control of the Suez Canal and Singapore during the nineteenth century in order to ensure safe passage on strategic waterways. The Suez Canal and Singapore were both vital to trade, so the British took them to keep them safe. There was no effort to sell petroleum to these territories, gain more converts to Christianity, or use them to transport laborers to the Americas. *(Age of Revolution)*

---

173. The Sepoy Rebellion was to India as the Boxer Rebellion was to

(1) Russia.
(2) China.
(3) Japan.
(4) Italy.

Correct answer: (2) The Sepoy Rebellion was to India as the Boxer Rebellion was to China. The Boxer Rebellion, coming at the end of the Qing Dynasty, was a rebellion against the British controlling China, while the Sepoy Rebellion was a rebellion against the British controlling India. Russia, Japan, and Italy had no such rebellions to compare. *(Age of Revolution)*

---

174. One reason for Japan's rapid industrialization during the Meiji Restoration was that Japan had

(1) rejected Western ideas.
(2) used its access to the sea for fishing.
(3) relied on traditional isolationist policies.
(4) reformed its political and economic systems.

Correct answer: (4) One reason for Japan's rapid industrialization during the Meiji Restoration was that Japan had reformed its political and economic system. During the Meiji Restoration, Japanese leaders adopted Western cultures reforming their own systems to better compete with the Western world. They certainly did not reject Western ideas, or use its access to the sea for fishing, and most definitely did not rely on isolationist policies. Quite the opposite, the Meiji Restoration brought Japan into the modern world. *(Age of Revolution)*

---

175. Many historians believe that the harsh terms found in the Treaty of Versailles helped lead to

(1) Italy's unification.
(2) Turkey's modernization.
(3) revolutions in Russia.
(4) World War II.

Correct answer: (4) Many historians believe that the harsh terms found in the Treaty of Versailles helped lead to World War II. Germany being bankrupted and humiliated led to all sorts of negative feelings, feelings that Hitler came in and exploited. The Treaty of Versailles occurred after Italy's unification and revolutions in Russia, and the terms had little to do with Turkey's modernization. *(Crisis & Achievement (1900–1945)*

Geography

Multiple Choice

Directions: For each of the following questions, select the choice that best answers the question or completes the statement.

---

1. Which geographic feature had the greatest influence on the development of ancient civilizations?

   (1) dense forests
   (2) mountain passes
   (3) smooth coastlines
   (4) river valleys

Correct answer: (4) River valleys had the greatest influence on the development of ancient civilizations. River valleys, such as the Nile River, the Yellow River, and the Tigris and Euphrates rivers, were important for the development of agriculture, trade, and transportation. Dense forests, mountain passes, and smooth coastlines were usually considered barriers to the development of ancient civilizations. For example, smooth coastlines in Africa prevented the development of trade with other regions. *(Ancient World)*

---

2. What is one characteristic of a society that practices subsistence agriculture?

   (1) growth of surplus crops for export
   (2) production of crops mainly for its own use
   (3) establishment of large, state-owned farms
   (4) dependence on the use of slave labor for the production of crops

Correct answer: (2) One characteristic of a society that practices subsistence agriculture is the production of crops for its own use. A farmer who uses this agricultural practice usually yields just enough crops for the family with no surplus. Unlike the large state-owned farms, a subsistence farm is usually small in scale and does not depend on the use of slave labor. *(Ancient World)*

---

3. In India, Bangladesh, and much of Southeast Asia, agricultural productivity is most affected by the

   (1) seasonal monsoons.
   (2) unnavigable rivers.
   (3) numerous deserts.
   (4) cold climate.

Correct answer: (1) In India, Bangladesh, and much of Southeast Asia, agricultural productivity is most affected by the seasonal monsoons. Arriving usually in June, the wet monsoons bring rainfall and extreme heat to the region. If the wet monsoons produce too much rain, rivers such as the Indus and Ganges will overflow and destroy crops on the farms. Deserts in Southeast Asia have not affected the productivity of farmers. *(Ancient World)*

---

4. Which statement about the geography of Africa is most accurate?

(1) Much of the land in Africa is below sea level.
(2) The variety of geographic barriers has served to promote cultural diversity.
(3) Africa has an irregular coastline with many natural harbors.
(4) Much of the land in Africa is tundra and forest.

Correct answer: (2) The most accurate statement about the geography of Africa is that the variety of geographic barriers has served to promote cultural diversity. The Sahara Desert in North Africa, for example, served as a barrier for its people from migrating or traveling to sub-Saharan Africa. Africa does not have many natural harbors for commercial purposes. Much of the land in Africa is not below sea level. A tundra climate is not found in Africa, as much of the region is generally warm. *(Global Interaction)*

---

5. Which statement best describes an impact of geography on the history of the Korean peninsula?

(1) Large deserts have led to isolation.
(2) Location has led to invasion and occupation by other nations.
(3) Lack of rivers has limited food production.
(4) Lack of natural resources has prevented development of manufacturing.

Correct answer: (2) The statement that best describes an impact of geography on the history of the Korean peninsula is that location has led to invasion and occupation by other nations. Korea's proximity to China and Japan had been detrimental to its sovereignty and independence. Both countries have invaded and conquered Korea several times. Since the Korean peninsula produced an extensive coastline, food production is not limited. Despite lacking natural resources, South Korea is still able to develop a strong and competitive manufacturing economy. *(Global Interactions)*

Base your answer to Question 6 on the bullet points below and on your knowledge of social studies.

- Oceans are an important source of food in Japan.
- Terrace farming is used in many parts of China.
- Irrigation systems are widely used in India.

---

6. Which conclusion can best be drawn from these statements?

(1) Many civilizations use irrigation to improve crop production.
(2) People adapt to meet the challenges of their geography.
(3) Fish provide adequate protein for the Japanese.
(4) Most nations are dependent on the same food source.

Correct answer: (2) The conclusion that can best be drawn from these statements is that people adapt to meet the challenges of their geography. Although limited in other natural resources, Japan relies on fish as an important source of food. Terrace farming allows farmers in China to plant crops on unleveled lands. Similarly, irrigation systems allow Indian farmers to use rainwater efficiently to water their crops. People in different parts of the world have created ways to combat geographic constraints. *(Ancient World)*

---

7. Which social scientists are best known for studying the physical artifacts of a culture?

   (1) geographers
   (2) archaeologists
   (3) economists
   (4) sociologists

Correct answer: (2) Archaeologists are social scientists best known for studying the physical artifacts of a culture. By excavating artifacts, archaeologists are able to make inferences about the early civilizations. Geographers study the relationship between the people and their surroundings. Economists attempt to answer questions about the factors of production. Sociologists focus on the development of human society, including social behavior and institutions. *(Methodology of Global History/Geography)*

---

8. Which statement most accurately describes how geography affected the growth of the ancient civilizations of Egypt and Mesopotamia?

   (1) River valleys provided rich soil to grow plentiful crops.
   (2) Large deserts provided many mineral deposits.
   (3) Access to the Atlantic Ocean provided trade routes.
   (4) Large savanna areas provided protection from invaders.

Correct answer: (1) The statement that most accurately describes how geography affected the growth of the ancient civilizations of Egypt and Mesopotamia is that river valleys provided rich soil to grow plentiful crops. The proximity of river valleys such as the Nile and the Tigris and Euphrates provided people in both regions easy access to water for farming. The deserts, which lack mineral deposits, were barriers to invaders. However, the deserts made cultural development in both regions more difficult. Neither region had access to the Atlantic Ocean. *(Ancient World)*

Base your answer to Question 9 on the cartoon below and on your knowledge of social studies.

Source: Arcadio Esquivel, *La Nación,* Cartoonists & Writers Syndicate

9. This 2001 cartoon implies that nations in Central America are

(1) defeating enemies and overcoming all obstacles.
(2) requesting assistance in the battle against drought.
(3) facing several serious problems at the same time.
(4) waiting patiently until the economic crisis is over.

Correct answer: (3) This 2001 cartoon implies that nations in Central America are facing several serious problems at the same time. During the late twentieth century, Central American countries were plagued with natural disasters and economic issues. Countries such as Honduras and El Salvador were devastated by severe flooding, causing great property losses and destruction of crops. *(Twentieth Century Since 1945)*

10. Most of the world's known oil reserves are located near which geographic area?

(1) Persian Gulf
(2) North Sea
(3) Ural Mountains
(4) Gulf of Mexico

Correct answer: (1) Most of the world's known oil reserves are located near the Persian Gulf. Countries in the region include Iran, Iraq, Saudi Arabia, and Kuwait. Industrialized nations such as Great Britain and the United States rely heavily on oil production from the region. Because of this, the political and economic developments in the region are closely monitored by the world community. *(Twentieth Century Since 1945)*

11. Which geographic factor in Russia played a role in Napoleon's defeat in 1812 and Hitler's defeat at Stalingrad in 1943?

    (1) Siberian tundra
    (2) Caspian Sea
    (3) arid land
    (4) harsh climate

Correct answer: (4) Harsh climate in Russia played a role in Napoleon's defeat in 1812 and Hitler's defeat at Stalingrad in 1943. Both Napoleon and Hitler were defeated by the harsh winter during their war campaigns. Soldiers in both campaigns were unable to cope with the sub-zero temperature and lack of food sources and supplies in Russia. *(Age of Revolution)*

Base your answer to Question 12 on the bullet points below and on your knowledge of social studies.

- Height above sea level
- Distance from the equator
- Amount of rainfall
- Average daily temperature

12. Which aspect of geography is most influenced by the above factors?

    (1) natural boundaries
    (2) climate
    (3) topography
    (4) mineral resources

Correct answer: (2) Climate is most influenced by these factors. For example, the distance of a place from the equator influenced the climate. Because of its distance away from the equator, Greenland remained consistently cold. Similarly, the height above sea level of a region determines the average daily temperature. *(Ancient World)*

Base your answer to Question 13 on the bullet points below and on your knowledge of social studies.

- Large areas in the north and south received less than ten inches of rainfall annually.
- The presence of waterfalls and rapids slowed river travel.
- Highlands and steep cliffs limited exploration.

13. In which region did these geographic factors have an impact on European exploration and colonization?

    (1) South America
    (2) Southeast Asia
    (3) subcontinent of India
    (4) Africa

Correct answer: (4) In Africa, these geographic factors had an impact on European exploration and colonization. In the north, for example, the Sahara desert receive less than ten inches of rainfall annually. The lack of rainfall and intense heat makes it difficult for vegetation to grow in the region. The presence of waterfalls and rapids slowed river travel, which people relied on for commercial purposes in some regions. Highlands, steep cliffs, and other geographic barriers limited European exploration in the interior section of Africa. *(Ancient World)*

---

14. A similarity between Bantu migrations in Africa and migrations of the ancient Aryans into South Asia is that both moved

    (1) across the Atlantic Ocean.
    (2) from rural lands to urban areas.
    (3) in search of additional food sources.
    (4) for religious freedom.

Correct answer: (3) A similarity between Bantu migrations in Africa and migrations of the ancient Aryans into South Asia is that both moved in search of additional food sources. Both the Bantu people and the Aryans migrated to other areas to overcome their geographic barriers. For example, the Aryans chose to migrate to different parts of Asia to search for water sources and land for their domesticated animals. *(Expanding Zones of Exchange)*

---

15. Which factor led to the development of civilizations in ancient Mesopotamia?

    (1) political harmony
    (2) favorable geography
    (3) religious differences
    (4) universal education

Correct answer: (2) Favorable geography led to the development of civilizations in ancient Mesopotamia. The development of agriculture ensured a steady food source and population growth. Agriculture in Mesopotamia largely benefited from fertile soil and a water source. The Tigris and Euphrates rivers in Mesopotamia offered farmers with an excellent irrigation system. In addition, the rivers provided people with opportunities to trade and share new ideas. This is an example of cultural diffusion. *(Ancient World)*

---

16. The topography and climate of Russia have caused Russia to

    (1) depend on rice as its main source of food.
    (2) seek access to warm-water ports.
    (3) adopt policies of neutrality and isolation.
    (4) acquire mineral-rich colonies on other continents.

Correct answer: (2) The topography and climate of Russia have caused Russia to seek access to warm-water ports. Harsh winters led to the freezing of existing Russian seaports. This resulted in the stoppage of trade and transportation of vital resources. To address this problem, Russia began to seek access to warm-water ports through conquests near the Black Sea. In the late eighteenth century, Catherine the Great led a successful military campaign to accomplish this goal. *(Expanding Zones of Exchange)*

---

17. How did topography and climate affect the history of Africa?

   (1) The slave trade declined in western Africa.
   (2) Islam spread into southern Africa.
   (3) European colonization of central Africa was delayed.
   (4) Trade increased between southern and northern Africa.

Correct answer: (3) Topography and climate delayed the European colonization of central Africa. The African continent consists of various mountain ranges along its northern, western, and eastern sections. Such natural barriers made it difficult for Europeans to settle in Africa in pursuit of their imperialistic goals. *(Methodology of Global History/Geography)*

---

18. Italy, Korea, Spain, and India are similar in that each is considered

   (1) an archipelago
   (2) a peninsula
   (3) a landlocked nation
   (4) an island nation

Correct answer: (2) Italy, Korea, Spain, and India are similar in that each is considered a peninsula. A peninsula is a piece of land that is connected to a mainland but extends into a body of water. An archipelago is a series of islands, while a landlocked nation is completely surrounded by other countries. *(Methodology of Global History/Geography)*

---

19. Which geographic feature was common to the development of civilizations in ancient Egypt, China, India, and Mesopotamia?

   (1) river valleys
   (2) deserts
   (3) rain forests
   (4) mountains

Correct answer: (1) Civilizations in ancient Egypt, China, India, and Mesopotamia all developed around river valleys. River valleys were critical in the development of civilizations because they provided fertile soil and water. Deserts, rain forests, and mountains were examples of natural barriers for the development of civilizations. *(Ancient World)*

20. How did the Inca adapt to their physical environment?

    (1) They built large fishing fleets to feed their populations.
    (2) They built footbridges that connected their roads across the Andes.
    (3) They established extensive trade agreements with Europe.
    (4) They raised cattle and horses on the pampas.

Correct answer: (2) The Inca adapted to their physical environment by building footbridges that connected their roads across the Andes. Through various military campaigns, the Incan territory spread from the Andes Mountains and to the west coast of South America. The chief source of Incan economic activity was agriculture, not fishing or trading with the Europeans. Additionally, the Incas did not raise cattle or horses. *(First Global Age)*

21. The global problems of pollution, acid rain, and the breakdown of the ozone layer indicate a need for

    (1) greater international cooperation.
    (2) increased urbanization.
    (3) a balance of trade between nations.
    (4) an increase in space exploration.

Correct answer: (1) The global problems of pollution, acid rain, and the breakdown of the ozone layer indicate a need for greater international cooperation. Nations must come together to find solutions to these global problems. Many heads of state have gathered at various summits to discuss these issues. Urbanization would only increase these problems. Trade and space exploration would not help to alleviate these global issues. *(Global Connections/Interactions)*

22. Several geographic features in the Balkans, including location, have helped lead to the

    (1) peaceful development of the region.
    (2) development of democracy in the region.
    (3) cultural diversity of the region.
    (4) growing wealth of the region.

Correct answer: (3) Several geographic features in the Balkans, including location, have helped lead to the cultural diversity of the region. Yugoslavia was one such area where different religions and ethnicities existed. This is an example of cultural diversity. Recently, Yugoslavia was divided and different independent nations were created. Geography does not contribute to the Balkans' peace, democracy, or wealth. *(Twentieth Century Since 1945)*

23. Before the use of the Silk Road, how did geography affect early China?

(1) The mountains and deserts in western and southwestern China slowed the exchange of ideas.
(2) The northwestern region provided many fertile areas suitable for farming.
(3) The three major river systems provided barriers against invasion.
(4) The lack of deep-water ports on the eastern coast prevented China from developing trade with other nations.

Correct answer: (1) Before the use of the Silk Road, the mountains and deserts in western and southwestern China slowed the exchange of ideas. The Silk Road was an active trade route spanning from China to Rome during the Han Dynasty. The exchange of goods and ideas along the Silk Road is an example of cultural diffusion. Profitable goods such as spices and silk were traded along the Silk Road. *(Expanding Zones of Exchange)*

24. Which heading best completes this partial outline?

I. _____

    A. Natural boundaries of desert, mountains, and the sea

    B. Yearly flooding to enrich farmlands

    C. Old and Middle Kingdoms

    D. Production of papyrus plant

(1) Egypt—Gift of the Nile
(2) Mesopotamia—Land Between the Rivers
(3) China's Sorrow—Huang He River
(4) Harappa—City on the Indus

Correct answer: (1) "Egypt—Gift of the Nile" best completes this partial outline. Egypt is surrounded by desert, mountains, and the sea. Each geographic feature presents challenges for the people. For example, Egyptians relied on the Nile River to provide irrigation for their crops. However, flooding on the Nile could produce devastating damages for Egyptians. Additionally, learning was evident by their production of papyrus plant. *(Ancient World)*

25. Deforestation, acid rain, and the greenhouse effect are major world problems that indicate a need for

(1) cooperation between nations to reduce pollution and environmental destruction.
(2) the development of mass transit systems in developing nations.
(3) an increase in the worldwide production of oil.
(4) a reduction in crop production in some areas of the world.

Correct answer: (1) Deforestation, acid rain, and the greenhouse effect are major world problems that indicate a need for cooperation between nations to reduce pollution and environmental destruction. Urbanization and industrialization have been blamed for exacerbating these problems. Nations must come together to find solutions to these global problems. Many heads of state have gathered at various summits to discuss these issues. *(Global Connections/Interactions)*

---

26. The main purpose of a timeline is to show the

   (1) causes and effects of wars.
   (2) location of important places.
   (3) benefits of modern civilizations.
   (4) chronological relationship between events.

Correct answer: (4) The main purpose of a timeline is to show the chronological relationship between events. Many major world events happen within the same time in history, and it is easier to see the relationship by writing it down on paper in a timeline. Charts and maps would be used for other purposes, such as looking at causes and effects of wars, location of important places, and the benefit of modern civilizations. *(Methodology of Global History/Geography)*

Base your answer to Question 27 on the statement below and on your knowledge of social studies.

> Throughout history, people have lived on savannas, in deserts, in mountains, along river valleys, along coastlines, and on islands.

---

27. This statement demonstrates that people

   (1) adapt their surroundings.
   (2) develop a common language.
   (3) organize similar forms of government.
   (4) prefer to live in isolated areas.

Correct answer: (1) The statement demonstrates that people adapt to their surroundings. The statement looks at where people have lived throughout human history—anywhere from river valleys to deserts, from mountains to the plains. Humans adapt to this by consistently finding ways to live in their environment and create civilizations. The statement has nothing to do with a common language, form of government, or the type of land that people cultivate and create civilizations in. *(Methodology of Global History/Geography)*

28. How did the introduction of agriculture affect early peoples?

    (1) Societies became nomadic.
    (2) Food production declined.
    (3) Civilizations developed.
    (4) Birthrates decreased rapidly.

Correct answer: (3) The introduction of agriculture affected early peoples by the development of civilizations. With human beings able to produce a regular source of food, the need for a hunting-gathering society diminished, and tribes began to settle in a permanent location. Societies went from being nomadic into being based in cities, food production increased, and birthrates increased rapidly, leading to a time period called the Neolithic Revolution. *(Ancient World)*

29. Constantinople's location on the Bosporus Strait was one reason that the Byzantine Empire was able to

    (1) conquer the Russian city of Moscow.
    (2) spread Judaism throughout Western Europe.
    (3) control key trade routes between Europe and Asia.
    (4) unite the Eastern Orthodox and Roman Catholic churches.

Correct answer: (3) Constantinople's location on the Bosporus Strait enabled the Byzantine Empire to control key trade routes between Europe and Asia. The control over the strait meant that ships passing through the major ports from Europe to Asia, or vice versa, had to pass through Byzantine-controlled waters, giving the Byzantine Empire the edge over trade. This port did not give an edge to conquering Moscow, spreading Judaism, or uniting the Christian churches. *(Expanding Zones of Exchange)*

30. Which factors protected Russia from control by Napoleon's army?

    (1) religious and cultural similarities
    (2) industrialization and modernization
    (3) geographic size and location
    (4) political and economic instability

Correct answer: (3) The factors that protected Russia from control of Napoleon's army were the geographic size and location. Due to the large amount of land that Napoleon needed to conquer, as well as the freezing cold weather the French had to deal with, conquering Russia proved to be impossible for the French army. There were no religious and cultural similarities, industrialization and modernization, or political and economic instability to protect Russia. Only the large size of the country and cold weather protected the country from Napoleon's army. *(Age of Revolution)*

31. Which heading best completes the partial outline below?

I. _____

   A. Personal letter

   B. Autobiography

   C. Diary

   D. Driver's license

   (1) Primary Sources
   (2) Secondary Sources
   (3) Official Records
   (4) Published Records

Correct answer: (1) The partial outline would best be headed by the title Primary Sources. Primary sources are original documents, such as a diary, a personal letter, or an autobiography. An analysis, such as a history book, would be a secondary source. The examples given are not necessarily official records or published records; so primary sources still are the best heading. *(Methodology of Global History/Geography)*

32. Which geographic factor had the greatest influence on the early history of South Asia and China?

   (1) river valleys
   (2) island locations
   (3) vast coastlines
   (4) tropical rain forests

Correct answer: (1) The geographic factor that had the greatest influence on the early history of South Asia and China would be the river valleys. For any kind of early civilization to develop, including in South Asia (Indus Valley) or in China, the people needed fertile land to grow crops. River valleys are prime crop-growing areas, because they have fertile soil and manageable climates. A common theme that exists with all early histories, from Mesopotamia, Egypt, South Asia, and China, is that they settled in or near a river valley. *(Ancient World)*

33. One effect of rugged, mountainous geography on the civilization of ancient Greece was the development of

   (1) absolute monarchies.
   (2) separate, independent city-states.
   (3) extensive trade with the Persians.
   (4) belief in one God.

Correct answer: (2) One effect of rugged, mountainous geography on the civilization of ancient Greece was the formation of separate, independent city-states. The divisions between fertile lands meant that civilizations would form separately, and govern themselves individually, as a city-state, as opposed to easily unifying under an absolute monarchy, for example. Greece was also traditionally at odds with the Persians and had a well-established polytheistic culture. *(Ancient World)*

---

34. The archaeological evidence found at the Mesoamerican sites of Tenochtitlan and Machu Picchu suggests that these societies

  (1) consisted of hunters and gatherers.
  (2) were highly developed and organized cultures.
  (3) practiced a monotheistic religion.
  (4) followed a democratic system.

Correct answer: (2) The archeological evidence found at the Mesoamerican sites of Tenochtitlan and Machu Pichu suggests that these societies were highly developed and organized cultures. Evidence of a king, worship of many gods, and cities show us that the civilization was not democratic, monotheistic, or even hunter and gatherers, but rather suggests, as the answer says, highly developed and organized cultures. *(First Global Age)*

---

35. When Koreans call their land "a shrimp among whales," they are referring to

  (1) the mountains that cover much of the Korean peninsula.
  (2) the environmental damage caused by overfishing in the Pacific.
  (3) their traditional respect for the sea.
  (4) their location between powerful neighbors: Russia, China, and Japan.

Correct answer: (4) When Koreans call their land "a shrimp among whales," they are referring to their location between powerful neighbors: Russia, China, and Japan. Korea has a long history of being conquered by its neighbors, and it is the shrimp among these whales, consistently being gobbled up. The mountains that cover the Korean peninsula have nothing to do with Koreans calling their land a shrimp among whales, nor does the environmental damage or the respect for the sea. *(Age of Revolution)*

---

36. Which heading best completes the partial outline below?

  I. _____

  A. Maurya
  B. Gupta
  C. Delhi Sultanate
  D. Kushana

  (1) Empires of India
  (2) Latin American Civilizations
  (3) Empires of the Fertile Crescent
  (4) Dynasties of China

Correct answer: (1) The heading Empires of India best completes the partial outline. Maurya and Gupta were both Indian empires, and not civilizations of Latin America, empires of the Fertile Crescent, or dynasties of China. A good way to remember is that Gupta will always equal India. *(Methodology of Global History/Geography)*

---

37. The Panama Canal and Suez Canal are similar in that both

    (1) shortened shipping routes between major bodies of water.
    (2) were built by the British to expand their empire.
    (3) replaced the Silk Road as the world's main trade route.
    (4) directly connected the Atlantic and Pacific oceans.

Correct answer: (1) The Panama Canal and the Suez Canal are similar in that both shortened shipping routes between major bodies of water. The British did not build the Panama Canal, and neither canal replaced the Silk Road as the world's main trade route. Since the Suez canal did not directly connect the Atlantic and Pacific oceans, the only correct answer is that they both shortened shipping routes. *(Global Interactions)*

---

38. Which action taken by both Hitler and Napoleon is considered by historians to be a strategic military error?

    (1) invading Russia with limited supply lines
    (2) introducing combined ground and naval assaults
    (3) invading Great Britain by land
    (4) using conquered peoples as slave laborers

Correct answer: (1) Hitler and Napoleon invading Russia with limited supply lines is considered by historians to be a strategic error. Both Hitler and Napoleon's armies were severely depleted as a result, and it caused a turning point in both wars. Neither side invaded Great Britain by land. Only Napoleon introduced combined ground and naval assaults, and only Hitler used conquered people as slave laborers, so the only correct answer is invading Russia with limited supply lines. *(Global Interactions)*

Base your answer to Question 39 on the statements below and on your knowledge of social studies.

- The fertile soil of river valleys allowed early civilizations to develop and flourish.
- In the 1500s and 1600s, control of the Strait of Malacca determined who traded in the Spice Islands.
- Because Japan is an island that is mostly mountainous, people live in densely populated areas along the coast.

---

39. Which conclusion is best supported by these statements?

    (1) Major urban centers are found only along rivers.
    (2) The geography of a nation or region influences its development.
    (3) Without mountains and rivers, people cannot develop a culture.
    (4) The spread of new ideas is discouraged by trade and conquest.

Correct answer: (2) These statements best support the conclusion that the geography of a nation or a region influences its development. The statements discuss fertile soil of river valleys, control over waterways leading to control of trade, and the population patterns of Japan; all point toward the importance of geography. Major urban centers would only apply to the third statement, while the other two choices do not apply to any choice. Therefore, the answer is that geography of a nation or region influences its development. *(Methodology of Global History/Geography)*

---

40. Which statement about cultural diffusion in Asia is most accurate?

(1) Byzantine traders brought the Justinian Code to China.
(2) Roman legions introduced Christianity to India.
(3) Indian monks brought Islam to the Middle East.
(4) Chinese ideas and practices spread into Korea and Japan.

Correct answer: (4) The most accurate statement about cultural diffusion in Asia would be that Chinese ideas and practices spread into Korea and Japan. Many Chinese ideals and traditions spread throughout Asia, diffusing into Japanese and Korean cultures, and creating a new culture. Because Islam began in the Middle East, it would be impossible for Indian monks to bring Islam to the Middle East. Neither Roman legions in India nor Byzantine traders in China would be considered as accurate as Chinese ideas in Japan and Korea, making it the *best* answer. *(Ancient World)*

---

41. Which geographic feature made it difficult to unify South America?

(1) Andes Mountains
(2) Straits of Magellan
(3) Gulf of Mexico
(4) Argentinean pampas

Correct answer: (1) The Andes Mountains made it difficult to unify South America. A large, difficult-to-cross mountain range dividing the major parts of the continent created a major block in any effort to unify South America. The Straits of Magellan and Argentinean pampas were both easily overcome, and the Gulf of Mexico was not a South American geographic feature, so it did not come into play. *(Age of Revolution)*

---

42. Which factor is most responsible for the international importance of the Middle East?

(1) innovative political and social reforms
(2) superior weapons technology
(3) vital natural resources in a strategic location
(4) advanced scientific and industrial development

Correct answer: (3) The factor that is most responsible for the international importance of the Middle East is the vital natural resources in a strategic location. The Middle East has gained international importance because of its vast oil supply, a factor that continues to impact global affairs today. International importance of the Middle East did not happen because of innovative political and social reforms, weapons technology, or advanced scientific and industrial development. *(Twentieth Century Since 1945)*

---

43. Which heading best completes the partial outline below?

I. _____

- A. Seafood makes up a large part of the Filipino diet.
- B. Africans built hydroelectric plants along the Zambezi River.
- C. The majority of Russians live west of the Ural Mountains.
- D. The most densely populated area of India is the Ganges River Valley.

- **(1)** Rivers Are Barriers to Interdependence
- **(2)** Economic Issues Influence National Goals
- **(3)** Geography Affects Human Behavior
- **(4)** Governments Control the Actions of Citizens

Correct answer: (3) The heading that best completes the partial outline is Geography Affects Human Behavior. Each of the facts in the outline centers around geography, from the Ural Mountains to the Ganges River Valley, and each geographic feature somehow affects the way humans live. Not each fact is based off a river, nor is it based off of economic issues or government controls. The only heading that encompasses all facts is Geography Affects Human Behavior. *(Methodology of Global History/Geography)*

Base your answer to Question 44 on the quotation below and on your knowledge of social studies.

. . . The circumference of the city of Constantinople is eighteen miles; one-half of the city being bounded by the continent, the other by the sea, two arms of which meet here; the one a branch or outlet of the Russian, the other of the Spanish sea. Great stir and bustle prevails [dominates] at Constantinople in consequence of the conflux [meeting] of many merchants, who resort thither [come there], both by land and by sea, from all parts of the world for purposes of trade, including merchants from Babylon and from Mesopotamia, from Media and Persia, from Egypt and Palestine, as well as from Russia, Hungary, Patzinakia, Budia, Lombardy and Spain. In this respect the city is equalled only by Bagdad, the metropolis of the Mahometans. . . .

> —Rabbi Benjamin of Tudela, Manuel Komroff, ed., *Contemporaries of Marco Polo, Boni & Liveright*

---

44. This author would most likely agree with the idea that the

- **(1)** size of Constantinople limited trade.
- **(2)** cities of Western Europe were more impressive than Constantinople.
- **(3)** location of Constantinople contributed to its prosperity.
- **(4)** government of Constantinople failed to provide order.

Correct answer: (3) The author would most likely agree with the idea that the location of Constantinople contributed to its prosperity. The document discusses the central location of Constantinople and how many different regions were able to trade in Constantinople, creating a central hub of global commerce. The author would certainly not agree with the idea that the size of Constantinople limited trade, since the opposite happened. The author would disagree that the cities of Western Europe were more impressive or that the government of Constantinople failed to provide order, since the document points toward the greatness of Constantinople. *(Ancient World)*

45. One reason the Japanese followed a policy of expansionism before World War II was to gain

 (1) warm-water ports.
 (2) control of Tibet.
 (3) additional natural resources.
 (4) control of the Suez Canal.

Correct answer: (3) One reason the Japanese followed a policy of expansionism before World War II was to gain additional natural resources. Japanese resources are limited at best, so Japanese expansion was the best way for Japan to gain access to resources such as oil and, thereby, to modernize and compete as a world leader. Warm-water ports was a concern of the Soviet Union, while control of Tibet has been a Chinese concern and control over the Suez Canal was a British concern. *(Crisis & Achievement [1900–1945])*

46. How do some Latin American governments justify the destruction of the rain forests?

 (1) Cattle raising, farming, and mining in the rain forest will help the economy.
 (2) Manufacturers no longer use the latex produced by the trees of the rain forest.
 (3) People who live in the rain forest are moving to the cities.
 (4) Drug trafficking will decrease when the protection of the rain forests is gone.

Correct answer: (1) Some Latin American governments justify the destruction of the rain forest by stating that cattle raising, farming, and mining in the rain forest will help the economy. Stating that manufacturers no longer use latex would justify preserving the rain forest. *(Global Connections/Interactions)*

47. Which empire became powerful partly because of its location near the Mediterranean Sea?

 (1) German
 (2) Maya
 (3) Ming
 (4) Ottoman

Correct answer: (4) The empire that became powerful partly because of its location near the Mediterranean Sea was the Ottoman Empire. Basic geography tells us that the German, Ming, and Maya empires in no way bordered the Mediterranean Sea, so the only option left is the Ottoman Empire. *(Geography and Global Interactions)*

Base your answer to Question 48 on the map below and on your knowledge of social studies.

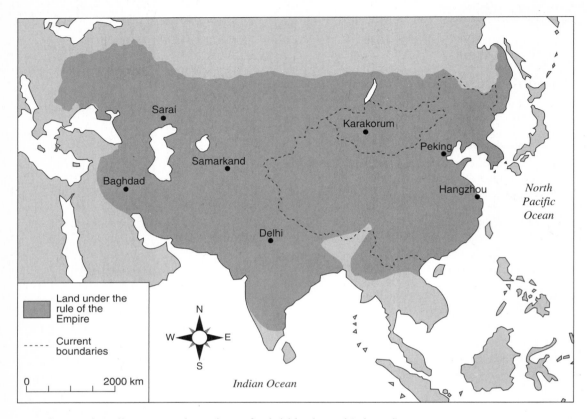

Source: http://www.artsmia.org/arts-of-asia/china/maps/ (adapted)

48. Which empire is the focus of this map?

    (1) Mongol
    (2) Songhai
    (3) Roman
    (4) Persian

Correct answer: (1) The Mongol Empire is the focus of the map. By having East Asia and a movement into West Asia and the Middle East, we know that this would not be a Roman or Persian map. Furthermore, the Songhai Empire never spread this far, leaving Mongolian Empire as the only possible focus of this map. *(Methodology of Global History/Geography)*

Economics

Multiple Choice

Directions: For each of the following questions, select the choice that best answers the question or completes the statement.

---

1. In Europe during the 1920s and 1930s, severe inflation, high unemployment, and fear of communism all contributed to the

   (1) overthrow of monarchies in Italy and Germany.
   (2) rise of Fascist governments in Italy, Germany, and Spain.
   (3) formation of the Common Market in Italy and Spain.
   (4) growth of democratic institutions.

Correct Answer: (2) In Europe during the 1920s and 1930s, severe inflation, high unemployment, and fear of communism all contributed to the rise of Fascist governments in Italy, Germany, and Spain. These desperate economic conditions gave rise to Mussolini in Italy, Hitler in Germany, and Franco in Spain. Opposed to democratic rule, these fascist leaders gained support by promising to improve the economic conditions of the people. The Common Market was not created during the 1920s and 1930s and monarchies were not overthrown in Italy and Germany in the 1920s and 1930s. (*Crisis and Achievement [1900–1945]*)

---

2. The continued importance of the Middle East to the global economy is based on its

   (1) research facilities.
   (2) exports of manufactured goods.
   (3) semi-arid climate.
   (4) quantity of oil reserves.

Correct Answer: (4) The continued importance of the Middle East to the global economy is based on its quantity of oil reserves. The Middle East is responsible for a significant portion of the world's oil output. Critical in the global economy, many industrialized nations depend on oil for its survival. As a result, the Middle East is constantly a potential conflict zone. A semiarid climate, exports of manufactured goods, and research facilities are not major factors that allow the Middle East to remain influential in the global economy. (*Twentieth Century Since 1945*)

3. Which headline would most likely have appeared in a pamphlet during the Industrial Revolution?

(1) "Michelangelo Completes Sistine Chapel"
(2) "Karl Marx Attacks Capitalism"
(3) "Martin Luther Speaks Out Against Sale of Indulgences"
(4) "John Locke Calls for the People to Choose the King"

Correct Answer: (2) The headline that would most likely have appeared in a pamphlet during the Industrial Revolution is "Karl Marx Attacks Capitalism." The ill effects of Industrial Revolution in Europe gave rise to workers' unrest. Siding with the workers, Karl Marx published the *Communist Manifesto* in 1848. His work argued that the workers must struggle against the factory owners to form a classless society. Michelangelo was an artist from the Renaissance; while John Locke was an Enlightenment philosopher. Martin Luther stood up against the Catholic Church during the Protestant Reformation. *(Age of Revolution)*

4. Which economic activity was the basis for most of the wealth and power of the West African empires of Ghana and Mali?

(1) hunting and gathering
(2) farming and cattle ranching
(3) trading in salt and gold
(4) working in bronze and brass

Correct Answer: (3) Trading in salt and gold was the basis for most of the wealth and power of the West African empires of Ghana and Mali. The empires of Ghana and Mali traded their gold for salt with nearby merchants. Because of its wealth, cities were developed along the trade routes. The most famous city was Timbuktu, a center of commerce, learning, and Islamic faith. Ghana and Mali were advanced empires, whose primary economic activities were not hunting and farming. *(Global Interactions)*

5. The *encomienda* system in Latin America was a direct result of the

(1) Crusades.
(2) Age of Exploration.
(3) Reformation.
(4) Age of Reason.

Correct Answer: (2) The encomienda system in Latin America was a direct result of the Age of Exploration. From 1400 to 1600, strong European nations were competing for trade routes and raw materials. Explorers were often commissioned to accomplish this goal. The success of explorers' voyages often led to enormous profits for the sponsoring nation. Created by Spain, the encomienda system provided the necessary labor from the natives. *(Age of Revolution)*

6. Which statement best describes a mixed economy?

(1) The government determines the production and distribution of goods and services.
(2) The products that consumers demand determine what goods are produced.
(3) Some industries are owned by the state, and others are privately owned.
(4) People produce the same goods, but in different amounts, every year.

Correct Answer: (3) The best statement that describes a mixed economy is that some industries are owned by the state, and others are privately owned. In a communist nation, the government determines the production and distribution of goods and services. On the other hand, the products that consumers demand determine what goods are produced in a capitalistic society. A mixed economy consists of characteristics from both the capitalistic and communist economies. Western countries such as Great Britain and Canada have mixed economies. *(Age of Revolution)*

7. Which leader based his rule on the ideas of Karl Marx and Friedrich Engels?

(1) Neville Chamberlain
(2) Vladimir Lenin
(3) Adolf Hitler
(4) Jiang Jieshi (Chiang Kai-shek)

Correct Answer: (2) Vladimir Lenin based his rule on the ideas of Karl Marx and Friedrich Engels. Karl Marx and Friedrich Engels were the authors of the *Communist Manifesto*. Vladimir Lenin applied Marxist ideas to war-torn Russia. To gain support, Lenin and the Bolsheviks promised the impoverished people "peace, land, and bread." Neville Chamberlain was a prime minister of England prior to World War II. His policy of appeasement encouraged German aggression on other European nations. Opposed to Communism, Adolf Hitler was a Nazi dictator responsible for the killing of millions of Jews during the Holocaust. Jiang Jieshi became the leader of China after the death of Sun Yixian. He fought unsuccessfully with the Communists during the Chinese Civil War and lost. *(Age of Revolution)*

Base your answer to Question 8 on the headlines in the bullet points below and on your knowledge of social studies.

- "India Strives for Grain Self-Sufficiency by 1970"
- "New Wheat Variety Grows in Arid Climate"
- "Chemical Fertilizer Use Rises 10% in 1960"
- "Sri Lanka's Rice Production Increases 25% in Three Years"

8. These newspaper headlines from the 1960s and 1970s describe some of the results of the

(1) Sepoy Mutiny.
(2) Kashmir crisis.
(3) Green Revolution.
(4) Computer Revolution.

Correct Answer: (3) These newspaper headlines from the 1960s and 1970s describe some of the results of the Green Revolution. The improvement in agricultural technology allowed farmers around the world to improve efficiency and increase production. In addition, the Green Revolution produced seeds and crops of better quality. Production increase means fewer famines and food shortages around the world. *(Global Connections/Interactions)*

---

9. Which factor contributed to the success of the Hanseatic League, the Kingdom of Songhai, and the British East India Company?

(1) location in the Middle East
(2) imperialism in Europe
(3) development of trade with other regions
(4) growth of the Ottoman Empire

Correct Answer: (3) The development of trade with other regions was a factor in contributing to the success of the Hanseatic League, the Kingdom of Songhai, and the British East India Company. The control of important trade routes and markets created great profits for these groups. For example, the British East India Company began to trade spices in the seventeenth century in India. The expansion of the spice trade led to great profits in the eighteenth century. *(Global Interactions)*

Base your answers to questions 10 and 11 on the quotation below and on your knowledge of social studies.

. . . The daily tasks of the women are to milk the cattle in the morning and evening, and to fetch water as required. By using their donkeys it is possible for them to bring back enough water to last two or three days. When the settlement moves, on average about once every five weeks, each woman is responsible for moving her hut and rebuilding it.

All the necessary movables, including hides, wooden containers and important struts in the framework of the hut, can normally be carried by two donkeys. Older women rely on their daughters, their younger co-wives, and their sons' wives for help in all these tasks. . . .

—Paul Spencer, *The Samburu,* University of California Press, 1965

---

10. Which type of economy would most likely be found in this society?

(1) command
(2) traditional
(3) free market
(4) manorial

Correct Answer: (2) A traditional economy would most likely to be found in this society. The Samburus were nomads, as they moved from one settlement to another. Because of this, their belongings had to be movable and lightweight. As hunter-gatherers, the Samburus were self-sufficient. *(Ancient World)*

11. Based on this passage, the Samburu people would be classified as

(1) commercial farmers.
(2) urban dwellers.
(3) nomads.
(4) serfs.

Correct Answer: (3) Based on this passage, the Samburu people would be classified as nomads. Moving from one settlement to another, the Samburus were considered nomads. Unlike commercial farmers, these people depended on hunting and gathering for survival. This was typical for societies during the Paleolithic Age. The development of agriculture during the Neolithic Age would lead to permanent settlement and domestication of animals. *(Ancient World)*

12. Which activity would be most characteristic of people in a traditional society?

(1) serving in government assemblies
(2) working in an industrialized city
(3) having the same occupation as their parents
(4) establishing a mercantile system of trade

Correct Answer: (3) Having the same occupation as their parents would be most characteristic of people in a traditional society. People in a traditional society worked in rural areas rather than industrialized cities. The society lacked a system of government and trade. Most people learned their occupational skills such as hunting and gathering from their parents. *(Ancient World)*

Base your answers to questions 13 and 14 on the speakers' statements below and on your knowledge of social studies.

Speaker A: Government should not interfere in relations between workers and business owners.

Speaker B: The workers will rise up and overthrow the privileged class.

Speaker C: Private property will cease to exist. The people will own the means of production.

Speaker D: A favorable balance of trade should be maintained by the use of tariffs.

13. Which two speakers represent Karl Marx's ideas of communism?

(1) A and B
(2) B and C
(3) B and D
(4) C and D

Correct Answer: (2) Speakers B and C represent Karl Marx's ideas of communism. Co-author of the *Communist Manifesto,* Karl Marx argued that poverty would lead to workers' *(proletariat)* revolting against the privileged class *(bourgeoisie).* The new society would eliminate the class system, with the people controlling the means of production. *(Age of Revolution)*

14. Which speaker is referring to laissez-faire capitalism?

   (1) A
   (2) B
   (3) C
   (4) D

Correct Answer: (1) Speaker A is referring to laissez-faire capitalism. According to laissez-faire capitalism, government should not interfere with the dealings and decisions made by business owners. Adam Smith, the author of *Wealth of Nations,* argued that government intervention in business would only curtail the growth of a nation's economy. Speakers B and C represent Karl Marx's ideas of communism. *(Age of Revolution)*

15. Which statement (below) describes one major aspect of a command economy?

   (1) Supply and demand determine what will be produced.
   (2) Most economic decisions are made by the government.
   (3) The means of production are controlled by labor unions.
   (4) The economy is mainly agricultural.

Correct Answer: (2) The statement that describes one major aspect of a command economy is, "Most economic decisions are made by the government." In a command economy, the government plays a significant role in determining all important factors of production. In a capitalistic society, supply and demand determine what to produce. The means of production are controlled by labor unions are jointly controlled by private business and the government. This is called a mixed economy. Agriculture is a major aspect in a traditional economy. *(Age of Revolution)*

Base your answer to Question 16 on the questions below and on your knowledge of social studies.

- What to produce?
- How to produce?
- For whom to produce?

16. Which social scientist studies how these questions would be answered for a specific society?

   (1) a sociologist
   (2) an economist
   (3) an anthropologist
   (4) a geographer

Correct Answer: (2) An economist studies what items are produced, how to produce them, and for whom they are produced. The social science of economics focuses on the production of goods and their purposes. Sociologists study societies while anthropologists study the development of man. Geographers are responsible for studying the interaction of people, environment, and resources. *(Ancient World)*

Base your answer to Question 17 on the statement below and on your knowledge of social studies.

The purpose of colonies is to ship raw materials to the colonial power and buy finished goods from the colonial power.

---

17. This statement reflects the basic idea of which economic system?

(1) socialism
(2) communism
(3) mercantilism
(4) capitalism

Correct Answer: (3) This statement reflects the basic idea of mercantilism. Under mercantilism, the purpose of colonies is to benefit the mother country. Colonies supply the mother country with raw materials and new markets for finished products. Under socialism, everyone in the system owns all property and controls the businesses. Under communism, the people control all means of production. *(First Global Age)*

---

18. Laissez-faire capitalism, as attributed to Adam Smith, called for

(1) heavy taxation of manufacturers.
(2) strict government control of the economy.
(3) minimal government involvement in the economy.
(4) government investments in major industries.

Correct Answer: (3) Laissez-faire capitalism, as attributed to Adam Smith, called for minimal government involvement in the economy. Adam Smith's economic theory of laissez-faire called for the hands-off approach of the economy by the government. Under laissez-faire capitalism, the government believed in minimal interference in addressing economic concerns. *(Age of Revolution)*

---

19. The reason that the Organization of Petroleum Exporting Countries (OPEC) greatly influences the world today is that it

(1) commands the loyalty of the worldwide Islamic community.
(2) develops and exports important technology.
(3) controls access to trade routes between the East and West.
(4) manages the oil supply that affects the global economy.

Correct Answer: (4) The reason that the Organization of Petroleum Exporting Countries (OPEC) greatly influences the world today is that it manages the oil supply that affects the global economy. The function of OPEC is to set prices of the world's oil by controlling oil production. OPEC does not involve Islam, technology, or trade routes. *(Twentieth Century Since 1945)*

20. What is a major reason for the differences in economic prosperity in various areas of the world today?

    (1) an unequal distribution of resources
    (2) the success of nationalist movements
    (3) religious unity between nations
    (4) membership in the United Nations

Correct Answer: (1) A major reason for the differences in economic prosperity in various areas of the world today is an unequal distribution of resources. Prosperity and wealth were determined by the accessibility of natural resources. The more resources a country has, the more prosperous it becomes. Economic differences do not involve nationalism, religion, or the United Nations. *(Global Connections / Interactions)*

21. One similarity between Stalin's five-year plans and Mao Zedong's Great Leap Forward was that both programs attempted to

    (1) increase industrial production.
    (2) privatize the ownership of land.
    (3) correct environmental pollution.
    (4) strengthen international trade.

Correct Answer: (1) One similarity between Stalin's five-year plans and Mao Zedong's Great Leap Forward was that both programs attempted to increase industrial production. The communist governments under the control of both Stalin and Mao wanted to the control industries for greater production. They did not want to privatize or give the land away and have the people control it. These plans did not involve the environment or trade. *(Age of Revolution)*

22. The growth of maritime and overland trading routes led to

    (1) decreased interest in inventions and technology.
    (2) the limited migration of peoples.
    (3) increased cultural diffusion.
    (4) the development of subsistence agriculture.

Correct Answer: (3) The growth of maritime and overland trading routes led to increased cultural diffusion. The maritime exploration of Zheng He was an example of cultural diffusion. Zheng He, a Chinese explorer during the Ming Dynasty, went on voyages to promote trade. As a result, different regions of the world came into contact with Chinese goods and ideas through tributes and exchanges. *(Ancient World)*

Base your answer to Question 23 on the passage below and on your knowledge of social studies.

. . . And we cannot reckon how great the damage is, since the mentioned merchants are taking every day our natives, sons of the land and the sons of our noblemen and vassals and our relatives, because the thieves and men of bad conscience grab them wishing to have the things and wares of this Kingdom which they are ambitious of; they grab them and get them to be sold; and so great, Sir, is the corruption and licentiousness [lack of restraint] that our country is being completely depopulated, and Your Highness should not agree with this nor accept it as in your service. . . .

—Nzinga Mbemba (King Affonso), Letters to the King of Portugal, 1526

23. Which event in African history is described in this passage?

(1) exploration of the African interior
(2) discovery of gold mines in Nigeria
(3) Belgium's takeover of the Congo
(4) Atlantic slave trade

Correct Answer: (4) The Atlantic slave trade is described in this passage. The European discovery of the New World led to a need for slave labor to work on the plantations. European traders began to bring slaves to the New World from Africa. The letter discusses King Affonso's disapproval and protest over the enslavement of his people. *(Global Interactions)*

24. The feudal systems in both medieval Europe and early Japan were characterized by

(1) a decentralized political system.
(2) religious diversity.
(3) an increased emphasis on education.
(4) the development of a wealthy middle class.

Correct Answer: (1) The feudal systems in both medieval Europe and early Japan were characterized by a decentralized political system. The collapse of the Roman Empire led to political and social chaos in Europe. In a feudal society, people relied on the local lords for protection. The knights were commissioned by the lords to provide military services. The feudal society of Japan was characterized by a similar political system. The warriors in this society were called the samurais. *(Expanding Zones of Exchange)*

25. During the Commercial Revolution, where did trading centers most often develop?

(1) in the mountains
(2) near grasslands
(3) along waterways
(4) on the tundra

Correct Answer: (3) During the Commercial Revolution, trading centers most often develop along waterways. During the thirteenth and fourteenth centuries, the rivers in the major city-states such as Venice became an important commercial link to the profitable Asian trade. Some Italian merchants benefited from enormous profits and became patrons of the arts. Their financial contribution was an important catalyst in the artistic and intellectual rebirth during the Renaissance. *(Global Interactions)*

26. What is a key principle of a market economy?

  (1) The means of production are controlled by the state.
  (2) Supply and demand determine production and price.
  (3) Employment opportunities are determined by social class.
  (4) Businesses are owned by the people collectively.

Correct Answer: (2) In a market economy, supply and demand determine production and price. Businesses and the means of production were determined by the economic cycles, not the government. People in the market economy have the power to pursue employment opportunities of their choice. *(Age of Revolution)*

27. Which two major ideas are contained in the writings of Karl Marx?

  (1) survival of the fittest and natural selection
  (2) class struggle and revolutionary change
  (3) separation of powers and checks and balances
  (4) monotheism and religious tolerance

Correct Answer: (2) Two of the major ideas contained in the writings of Karl Marx are class struggle and revolutionary change. The author of the *Communist Manifesto,* Marx argued that poverty and poor working conditions would lead workers to revolt over the privileged class. The new society would be classless, with the people controlling the means of production. Marx did not believe in Social Darwinism, which advocated for natural selection and survival of the fittest. *(Age of Revolution)*

Base your answer to Question 28 on the quotation below and on your knowledge of social studies.

   . . . The Communist party of the Soviet Union has been and remains a natural and inalienable part of social forces. Their cooperation will make it possible to attain the ultimate goal of Perestroika: to renew our society within the framework of the socialist choice, along the lines of advance to a humane democratic socialism. . . .

28. Which leader would most likely have made this statement?

  (1) Kwame Nkrumah
  (2) Mohandas Gandhi
  (3) Benito Mussolini
  (4) Mikhail Gorbachev

Correct Answer: (4) Mikhail Gorbachev believed in the sharing of new ideas in reforming Russia. His new economic policies, known as perestroika, called for limited capitalistic ideas in Russia. The policy of *glasnost,* or openness, led to the end of censoring of news media by the Russian government. *(Twentieth Century Since 1945)*

Base your answer to Question 29 on the graph below and on your knowledge of social studies.

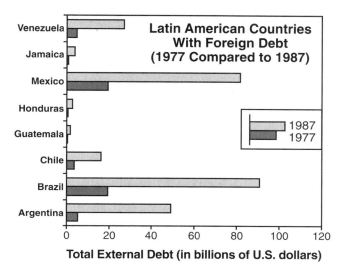

Latin American Countries With Foreign Debt (1977 Compared to 1987)

Total External Debt (in billions of U.S. dollars)

Sources: *World Bank Development Report, 1979* and *World Bank Development Report, 1989* (adapted)

29. According to information provided by the graph, which Latin American nation had the greatest ten-year increase in foreign debt in billions of U.S. dollars between 1977 and 1987?

(1) Brazil

(2) Argentina

(3) Mexico

(4) Venezuela

Correct Answer: (1) According to information provided by the graph, Brazil had the greatest ten-year increase in foreign debt in billions of U.S. dollars between 1977 and 1987. In order to industrialize, Latin American nations had to take out foreign loans in hope for a profitable return. When the demand and prices of goods dropped, countries had difficulties paying off their debts. (*Twentieth Century Since 1945*)

30. The terms cottage industries, mercantilism, guilds, and laissez-faire are most closely associated with

(1) political systems.

(2) social systems.

(3) economic systems.

(4) belief systems.

Correct Answer: (3) The terms *cottage industries, mercantilism, guilds,* and *laissez-faire* are most closely associated with economic systems. Under mercantilism, the purpose of colonies is to benefit the mother country. Colonies supply the mother country with raw materials and new markets for finished products. Laissez-faire capitalism as attributed to Adam Smith called for minimal government involvement in the economy. Adam Smith's economic theory of laissez-faire called for the hands-off approach of the economy by the government. Under laissez-faire capitalism, the government believed in minimal interference in addressing economic concerns. *(Age of Revolution)*

---

31. In a command economy, economic decisions are mostly influenced by

    (1) consumer demands.
    (2) government policies.
    (3) private investors.
    (4) banking practices.

Correct Answer: (2) In a command economy, economic decisions are mostly influenced by government policies. A command economy is an economy in which all decisions are made by the government. An economy driven by consumer demands, private investors, or banking practices would keep the market separate from the government, creating more of a private market or laissez-faire economy. *(Methodology of Global History/Geography)*

Base your answers to questions 32 and 33 on the diagram below and on your knowledge of social studies.

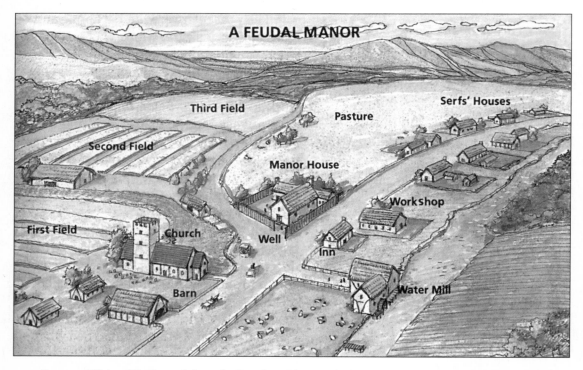

Source: Michael B. Petrovich et al., *People in Time and Place: World Cultures,* Silver, Burdett & Ginn, 1991

32. Most economic activities on this feudal manor were related to

(1) guilds.
(2) industry.
(3) banking.
(4) agriculture.

Correct Answer: (4) Most economic activities on the feudal manor shown were related to agriculture. The majority of the land shown was for farming, with many of the buildings designed to supply the farmers or refine the crops. There are very few economic activities dealing with industry or the guilds. There is nowhere on the manor that deals with banking, which was a limited activity, if it was used at all. *(Expanding Zones of Exchange)*

33. Which economic concept can be inferred from this diagram?

(1) self-sufficiency
(2) inflation
(3) trade embargo
(4) competition

Correct Answer: (1) The economic concept that can be inferred from this diagram is self-sufficiency. The fact that the manor had all the necessary components to life means that it could operate independent of anybody else, without the need for trade. There is no example of an embargo or competition, and inflation has nothing to do with the feudal manors. *(Expanding Zones of Exchange)*

34. Which statement best describes the concept of mercantilism?

(1) Universal suffrage leads to educated citizens.
(2) Controlling trade is a key to increasing power.
(3) Only the fittest deserve to survive.
(4) Strict social control prevents revolutions.

Correct Answer: (2) The concept of mercantilism is that controlling trade is the key to increasing power. The mercantilist position would be that the nation who controls trade routes could control an empire. Mercantilists care little for universal suffrage, survival of the fittest, or strict social control. The main focus of the mercantilists is to make money, and to do so by controlling trade. *(First Global Age)*

35. During the 1800s, reform legislation passed in Great Britain, France, and Germany led to

(1) formation of *zaibatsu,* greater equality for men, and establishment of a banking system.
(2) legalizing trade unions, setting minimum wages, and limiting child labor.
(3) government-owned factories, establishment of five-year plans, and limits placed on Immigration.
(4) bans on overseas trade, mandatory military service, and universal suffrage for women.

Correct Answer: (2) During the 1800s, reform legislation passed in Great Britain, France, and Germany led to legalizing trade unions, setting minimum wages, and limiting child labor. Western Europe was moving toward a period of social rights, away from the harshness of the early Industrial Revolution. Zaibatsu was a Japanese movement, while five-year plans were Soviet, and mandatory military service and universal suffrage was not a British policy. *(Age of Revolution)*

---

36. Karl Marx and Friedrich Engels encouraged workers to improve their lives by

    (1) electing union representatives.
    (2) participating in local government.
    (3) overthrowing the capitalist system.
    (4) demanding pensions and disability insurance.

Correct Answer: (3) Karl Marx and Fredrich Engels encouraged workers to improve their lives by overthrowing the capitalist system. Marx and Engels wanted to start an international communist revolution, overthrowing capitalists around the world. Marx and Engels did not encourage the election of union representatives, participation in government, or demanding pensions and disability services. These would be secondary, because the chief goal was to overthrow the government and create an international communist lifestyle. *(Age of Revolution)*

---

37. Which factor most helped Communist Party forces gain control of China after World War II?

    (1) The United States sent weapons to the Communists.
    (2) The Japanese gave economic aid to the Nationalists.
    (3) The Communists gained the support of China's peasant class.
    (4) The Chinese Nationalists set up their own government in Taiwan.

Correct Answer: (3) The factor that most helped the Communist Party forces gain control of China after World War II was that the Communists gained the support of China's peasant class. The Communists provided food and education to the peasants, whereas the Nationalist Party was distant and elitist. The United States did not send weapons to the Communists, so that did not help them gain control of China. Japan giving economic aid to the Nationalists did not help the Nationalists; the Japanese never gave aid to the Nationalists—they fought them during and before WWII—and the Nationalists setting up their own government in Taiwan was an effect of Communist forces controlling China. *(Twentieth Century Since 1945)*

---

38. One similarity between Mikhail Gorbachev's perestroika and Deng Xiaoping's Four Modernizations is that each

    (1) allowed elements of capitalism.
    (2) maintained the democratic process.
    (3) strengthened communism.
    (4) increased global tensions.

Correct Answer: (1) One similarity between Mikhail Gorbachev's perestroika and Deng Xiaoping's Four Modernizations is that each allowed elements of capitalism. Both of these policies began to allow private business in their respective nations and gave way to capitalism creeping into the nations. These policies did not allow for the democratic process, strengthen communism, or increase global tensions. All they did was reform the economy and allow capitalism to enter into the communist economy. *(Twentieth Century Since 1945)*

Base your answer to Question 39 on the graph below and on your knowledge of social studies.

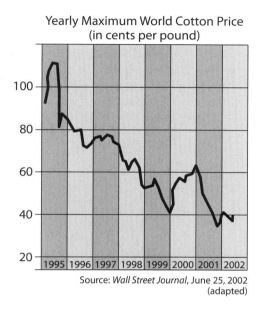

Yearly Maximum World Cotton Price
(in cents per pound)

Source: *Wall Street Journal,* June 25, 2002
(adapted)

Source: *Historical Maps on File,* Martin Greenwald Associates (adapted)

39. This graph suggests a potential problem for nations

    (1) with a favorable balance of trade.
    (2) with both industrial and agricultural exports.
    (3) that rely on a cash crop to support their economy.
    (4) whose economies have been diversified.

Correct Answer: (3) The graph suggests a potential problem for nations that rely on cash crops to support their economy. With the fall of the price of cotton, those who rely on cash crops will see less of a profit, putting more and more people into poverty. This doesn't affect nations with a favorable balance of trade, with both industrial and agricultural exports, or with diversified economies. Those nations can handle the fall of cotton prices. Nations that rely on cotton as a cash crop, however, will be in trouble. *(Global Connections/Interactions)*

40. The Silk Road was important because it allowed for the

(1) exploration of China by the Roman army.
(2) development of agriculture by the nomadic people of Central Asia.
(3) movement of Chinese armies through Southeast Asia.
(4) exchange of goods between Asia and the Middle East.

Correct Answer: (4) The Silk Road was important because it allowed for the exchange of goods between Asia and the Middle East. Because of the vast space between Asia and the Middle East, trade was not always an easy task. The European desire for silk, however, led the formation of a route in which goods could be transported from places like Constantinople to China, and back from China to Constantinople. *(Ancient World)*

41. A major reason that the Renaissance began in Italy was that

(1) Italian city-states had grown wealthy from trade between Europe and Asia.
(2) farmers produced great agricultural surpluses on vast plains.
(3) merchants supported the Green Revolution.
(4) many European scholars had migrated to this area.

Correct Answer: (1) A major reason that the Renaissance began in Italy was that Italian city-states had grown wealthy from trade between Europe and Asia. For a culture to place the focus on the arts that the Renaissance is known for, it needs money to support the artists. Surplus food and scholars are good, but the major reason that the Renaissance began comes back to the money provided by wealthy Italians such as the Medici family. *(Age of Revolution)*

42. Which statement describes an impact that the Columbian Exchange had on the lives of Europeans?

(1) The transfer of new products and ideas encouraged economic growth.
(2) New diseases were brought to Europe and resulted in massive deaths caused by a plague.
(3) Native Americans immigrated to Europe and competed with Europeans for jobs.
(4) Cross-cultural contacts between South America and Asia declined.

Correct Answer: (1) "The transfer of new products and ideas encouraged economic growth" describes an impact that the Columbian Exchange had on the lives of Europeans. The cross-cultural contacts between South America and Asia declining have no impact on the lives of Europeans, and the Native Americans did not immigrate to Europe in such large numbers that it would have an impact on the Europeans. New diseases coming to Europe were not so bad, leaving the new products and ideas as the impact that the Columbian Exchange had on Europeans. *(First Global Age)*

43. In Europe, joint stock companies, shareholders, entrepreneurs, and the bourgeoisie contributed to the

   (1) rise of capitalism.
   (2) development of feudalism.
   (3) decline of communism.
   (4) increase in power of the guilds.

Correct Answer: (1) In Europe, joint stock companies, shareholders, entrepreneurs, and bourgeoisie contributed to the rise of capitalism. Each of these examples, from joint-stock companies down to the bourgeoisie, has the overall goal of making more money, plain and simple. *(First Global Age)*

44. Which event had the greatest influence on the development of laissez-faire capitalism?

   (1) fall of the Roman Empire
   (2) invention of the printing press
   (3) Industrial Revolution
   (4) Green Revolution

Correct Answer: (3) The Industrial Revolution had the greatest influence on the development of laissez-faire capitalism. The Industrial Revolution led to the formation of vast factory systems, whose owners were concerned with making more and more money, and did not want government interference. The fall of the Roman Empire, invention of the printing press, and the Green Revolution do not fit into the development of laissez-faire capitalism, but the Industrial Revolution does. *(Age of Revolution)*

45. The main purpose of the North American Free Trade Agreement (NAFTA) and the European Union (EU) is to

   (1) increase the authority of the United Nations.
   (2) encourage increased economic development.
   (3) promote peace between nations.
   (4) establish and enforce military alliances.

Correct Answer: (2) The main purpose of NAFTA and the EU is to encourage increased economic development. NAFTA and the EU both serve as economic agreements aimed at furthering trade. Because neither comes under the authority of the United Nations or establishes any military alliances, these two cannot be the answers. Although it can be said that trade promotes peace between nations, the *main* purpose of NAFTA and the EU is still to encourage increased economic development, rather than achieve world peace. *(Global Connections/Interactions)*

Base your answer to Question 46 on the cartoon below and on your knowledge of social studies.

Source: Dan Wasserman, Tribune Media Services, Inc.

---

46. The concern expressed in this cartoon is most closely related to the consequences of

(1) rapid migration of animals to the Northern Hemisphere.
(2) further exploration of the Arctic Ocean.
(3) industrialization and the burning of fossil fuels.
(4) slow economic growth in developing nations.

Correct Answer: (3) The concern expressed in this cartoon is most closely related to the consequences of industrialization and the burning of fossil fuels. Global warming is not associated with rapid migration of animals, exploration of the Arctic Ocean, or even slow economic growth. When a question comes down to global warming, it can always be tied back to the burning of fossil fuels or other results of industrialization. *(Global Concerns/Interactions)*

---

47. The Commercial Revolution helped lead to the Industrial Revolution because during the Commercial Revolution

(1) the barter system was instituted.
(2) new forms of business were developed.
(3) socialism was introduced to Europe.
(4) subsistence agriculture was promoted.

Correct Answer: (2) The Commercial Revolution helped lead to the Industrial Revolution because during the Commercial Revolution, new forms of businesses were being developed. The Commercial

Revolution came during the Renaissance, and was made up of the new businesses that were forming alongside new trade routes, new technologies, and new influences on the lives of people. The barter system had already been in place, socialism was still in the future, and subsistence agriculture was on the fall. *(Age of Revolution)*

---

48. Venice in Europe, Mogadishu in Africa, and Canton in China emerged during the 13th century primarily as important centers of

(1) agriculture.
(2) trade.
(3) manufacturing.
(4) mining.

Correct Answer: (2) Venice, Mogadishu, and Canton emerged during the thirteenth century primarily as important centers of trade. Their strategic locations make them suited to be centers of trade, because they have access to all different kinds of trade. Venice, Mogadishu, and Canton are not important centers of agriculture, manufacturing, and mining. *(First Global Age)*

---

49. The major reason that Portugal and Spain established water routes to Asia's spice markets was to

(1) experiment with new technology such as the astrolabe and sextant.
(2) provide jobs for navigators, cartographers, and shipbuilders.
(3) avoid the overland routes that were controlled by Muslim traders.
(4) discover new continents, plants, and animals.

Correct Answer: (3) The major reason that Portugal and Spain established water routes to Asia's spice markets was to avoid the overland routes that were controlled by Muslim traders. By avoiding the overland routes, the Portuguese and Spanish traders could better guarantee safety and avoid the high tariffs charged by Muslim traders. Experimenting with new technologies, providing jobs, and discovering new continents all came second to the desire to maintain high profits and protect traders. *(First Global Age)*

---

50. Laissez-faire economists of the nineteenth century argued that

(1) the government should regulate the economy and foreign trade
(2) individuals should be allowed to pursue their self-interest in a free market
(3) governments should develop a state-run banking system to prevent instability
(4) anarchy would result if universal male suffrage was granted

---

Correct Answer: (2) Laissez-faire economists of the nineteenth century argued that individuals should be allowed to pursue their self-interest in a free market. Laissez-faire, or "hands-off" economics, creates the standard that government should leave the market alone, and the market can take care of itself. No laissez-faire economist would ever believe that the government should regulate the economy or develop a state-run banking system. Universal male suffrage had little to do with the economy, so lassez-faire economists would have little concern with that particular struggle. *(Age of Revolution)*

51. Where did Karl Marx predict a revolution of the proletariat would occur *first?*

    (1) industrial Europe
    (2) independent Latin America
    (3) colonial Africa
    (4) agricultural Russia

Correct Answer: (1) Karl Marx predicted a revolution of the proletariat would first occur in industrial Europe. Marx, in writing his manifesto, believed that the proletariat would rise as a result of the conditions resulting from the industrial revolution. Independent Latin America, colonial Africa, and agricultural Russia had no large-scale industrial society and, therefore, no proletariats who were being exploited by the factory owners. *(Age of Revolution)*

52. During the feudal period in Europe, power and position in society were based on the

    (1) amount of money earned.
    (2) level of education achieved.
    (3) number of slaves owned.
    (4) amount of land possessed.

Correct Answer: (4) During the feudal period in Europe, power and position in society were based on the amount of land possessed. Since society dissolved into a series of feudal manors, the amount of land possessed was the last true vestige of power in Europe. Education fell to the background of importance, while the amount of money earned or the number of slaves owned were not nearly as important as the land you owned and controlled. *(First Global Age)*

53. Much of the wealth of the West African kingdoms of Ghana and Mali was gained from the

    (1) sale of slaves to Europeans.
    (2) creation of colonies on the Mediterranean coast.
    (3) taxation on goods brought by Indian merchants.
    (4) control of the trans-Saharan trade in gold and salt.

Correct Answer: (4) Much of the wealth of the West African kingdoms of Ghana and Mali was gained from the control of the trans-Saharan trade in gold and salt. The history of West African kingdoms come down to the control of the gold and salt trade, because the ruler who could control salt and gold could control the main resources of the people and, thereby, the population. Mali and Ghana were kingdoms before the slave trade, before the creation of colonies on the Mediterranean coast, and before the taxation of goods brought by Indian merchants. *(Global Interactions)*

54. Under communism in the former Soviet Union, people were required to

   (1) reject modern technology.
   (2) limit the size of their families.
   (3) honor their ancestors and religious traditions.
   (4) put the interests of the state before individual gain.

Correct Answer: (4) Under communism in the former Soviet Union, people were required to put the interests of the state before individual gain. The very ideal of communism in Russia, that everything is subservient to the state, meant that everyone served the state in all aspects of life. People did not reject modern technology, limit the size of their families, or honor their ancestors and religious traditions any more or less, unless it was deemed in the best interest of the State. *(Crisis & Achievement (1900–1945)*

55. Which economic program was implemented by Joseph Stalin?

   (1) Four Modernizations
   (2) five-year plans
   (3) Great Leap Forward
   (4) perestroika

Correct Answer: (2) The economic program implemented by Joseph Stalin were his five-year plans. These plans were designed to modernize the Soviet Union and bring it to a state of prosperity. The Four Modernizations, Great Leap Forward, and perestroika are all economic plans, but only Joseph Stalin directly implemented the five-year plans. *(Crisis & Achievement (1900–1945)*

56. One reason the Chinese Communists were able to gain control of China was primarily due to the support of the

   (1) peasants.
   (2) landed elite.
   (3) foreigners.
   (4) warlords.

Correct Answer: (1) One reason the Chinese Communists were able to gain control of China was primarily due to the support of the peasants. During World War II, it was the Communists, who were fighting the Japanese, as well as feeding the peasants. The landed elite, foreigners, and warlords all stood to gain economically with the Chinese Nationalists and, thus, supported the Nationalists. However, the support of the peasants proved to be stronger, and the Chinese Communists gained control over China. *(Twentieth Century Since 1945)*

Base your answer to Question 57 on the cartoon below and on your knowledge of social studies.

Source: Ann Telnaes, Tribune Media Services, 2001 (adapted)

57. What is the main idea of this cartoon?

    (1) Traditional social and economic patterns are difficult to change.

    (2) Women have become outspoken supporters of the government in India.

    (3) The United Nations only holds conferences on problems that are easy to solve.

    (4) India is the most populated nation in the world.

Correct Answer: (1) The main idea of this cartoon is that traditional social and economic patterns are difficult to change. The cartoon points to the difficulties in India with the dismissal of the caste system, given that people still refer back to it. The cartoon does not discuss the role of women in India or the role of India in general. Rather, the cartoon discusses the difficulty of changing traditional patterns. *(Global Connections/Interactions)*

Base your answer to Question 58 on the passage below and on your knowledge of social studies.

. . . The history of all hitherto existing society is the history of class struggles. Freeman and slave, patrician [a person of high birth] and plebeian [common person], lord and serf, guild-master and journeyman, in a word, oppressor and oppressed, stood in constant opposition to one another, carried on an uninterrupted, now hidden, now open fight, a fight that each time ended, either in a revolutionary reconstitution of society at large, or in the common ruin of the contending [competing] classes. . . .

58. This passage expresses the ideas of

    (1) Napoleon Bonaparte.
    (2) Karl Marx.
    (3) Adolf Hitler.
    (4) Benito Mussolini.

Correct Answer: (2) This passage expresses the idea of Karl Marx. Any time you talk about class struggle, you automatically can shift over to the Communist ideals. Definitively, the second the article talks about the oppressor and the oppressed, Adolf Hitler and Benito Mussolini are removed as possible answers. The strong tones of proletariat power mean that the answer cannot be Napoleon, leaving Karl Marx as the author whose ideas are expressed. *(Age of Revolution)*

Civics, Citizenship, and Government

Multiple Choice

Directions: For each of the following questions, select the choice that best answers the question or completes the statement.

1. What was one cause of the development of many small independent city-states in ancient Greece?

   (1) Greece and Rome were often at war.
   (2) The mountainous terrain of Greece resulted in widely scattered settlements.
   (3) Military leaders found small Greek settlements easy to control.
   (4) The Greek people had many different languages and religions.

Correct answer: (2) The mountainous terrain of Greece resulted in widely scattered settlements. The mountains served as a barrier in spreading of new ideas. In addition, the sharp contrast between Athens and Sparta made cultural diffusion and unification difficult. Although the Greeks shared common languages and religions, these independent city-states often found themselves at war. Wars between the Greeks and the Romans did not lead to the development of small independent states. *(Ancient World)*

2. One way in which Iran's Ayatollah Khomeini and Afghanistan's Taliban were similar is that they each

   (1) established an Islamic state.
   (2) sponsored a United Nations Conference on Women's Rights.
   (3) joined the Organization of Petroleum Exporting Countries (OPEC).
   (4) incorporated communist doctrine into their government.

Correct answer: (1) One way in which Iran's Ayatollah Khomeini and Afghanistan's Taliban were similar is that they each established an Islamic state. Both Khomeini and the Taliban ruled their states under strict Islamic laws. Neither Khomeini nor the Taliban sponsored a United Nations conference on women's rights or incorporated communist doctrine into their government. Iran joined OPEC, but Afghanistan didn't. *(Twentieth Century Since 1945)*

3. Which statement best describes a result of the Glorious Revolution in England (1688)?

    (1) England formed an alliance with France.
    (2) The power of the monarchy was increased.
    (3) Principles of limited government were strengthened.
    (4) England lost its colonial possessions.

Correct answer: (3) The statement that best describes a result of the Glorious Revolution in England in 1688 is that principles of limited government were strengthened. The "revolution" is named "glorious" because no war was fought over the shift of power. Fueled by disdain over the absolute rule in England, the Parliament forced James II to give up the throne. Consequently, the power of the monarchy was limited. England and France were at war for much of the seventeenth and eighteenth centuries and were never allies. England did not begin to pursue its imperialistic goals until the eighteenth century. *(First Global Age)*

4. One reason Italy and Germany were *not* major colonial powers in the sixteenth and seventeenth centuries was that they

    (1) had self-sufficient economies.
    (2) lacked political unity.
    (3) rejected the practice of imperialism.
    (4) belonged to opposing alliances.

Correct answer: (2) One reason Italy and Germany were *not* major colonial powers in the sixteenth and seventeenth centuries was that they lacked political unity. To pursue its imperialistic goals, small independent states must unite for the common cause. Italy and Germany never rejected the practice of imperialism, as they became colonial powers after their unifications at the end of the nineteenth century. Neither Italy nor Germany had self-sufficient economies, which partly served as a motivation to colonize. *(Age of Revolution)*

5. The ideas of Rousseau, Voltaire, and Montesquieu most influenced

    (1) the growing power of priests in the Roman Catholic Church.
    (2) improvements in the working conditions of factory workers.
    (3) the rise of industrial capitalism.
    (4) movements for political reform.

Correct answer: (4) The ideas of Rousseau, Voltaire, and Montesquieu most influenced movements for political reform. Also known as the Age of Reason, the Enlightenment was an eighteenth century intellectual movement that promoted the importance of natural rights. Important documents such as the Declaration of Independence and the United States Constitution were derived from the work of these Enlightenment philosophers. These men focused on the movements for changes in the society, not the rights of factory workers or capitalism. *(Age of Revolution)*

Base your answer to Question 6 on the headlines below and on your knowledge of social studies.

"Gandhi Calls for Boycott of British Textiles"

"Gandhi and Followers Complete March to the Sea"

"Gandhi Begins Hunger Fast"

---

6. The above headlines reflect Gandhi's belief in

   (1) nonalignment
   (2) isolationism
   (3) appeasement
   (4) nonviolence

Correct answer: (4) These headlines reflect Mohandas Gandhi's belief in nonviolence. Gandhi was a nationalist leader of the independence movement in India. Believing in civil disobedience and nonviolence, Gandhi urged locals to boycott textiles and fasting as ways to free India from British rule. Nonalignment was a policy in which nations chose not to entangle with either the United States or the Soviet Union during the Cold War. By giving in to Hitler's demands, the French and the British adopted the policy of appeasement immediately before World War II. A nation adopts the policy of isolation when it chooses to not to involve itself in foreign conflicts. *(Age of Revolution)*

---

7. Which problem has faced both Cuba and North Korea under communist rule?

   (1) Their monarchs have been ineffective rulers.
   (2) Their governments have played a limited role in the economy.
   (3) Their workers have called many strikes.
   (4) Their command economies have been inefficient.

Correct answer: (4) Inefficient command economies have faced both Cuba and North Korea under communist rule. In a command economy, the government plays a dominant role in determining all important factors of production. Under the rule of communist dictators, strikes are not common in Cuba and North Korea. *(Global Connections/Interactions)*

Base your answer to Question 8 on the cartoon below and on your knowledge of social studies.

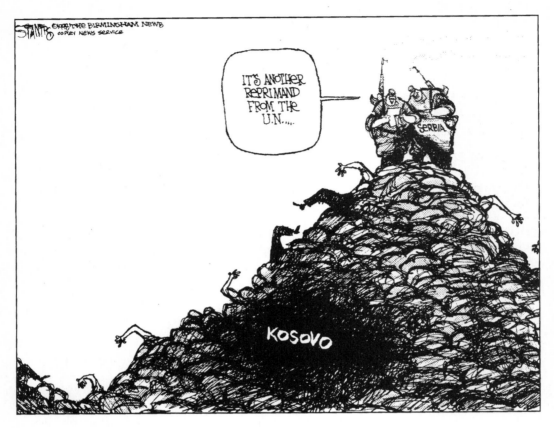

Source: Scott Stantis, *The Birmingham News,* Copley News Service

8. What is the main idea of this 1995 cartoon?

(1) The United Nations supported the Serbians in Kosovo.

(2) The United Nations was ineffective in its attempt to end genocide in Kosovo.

(3) Killing in Kosovo stopped because of United Nations reprimands.

(4) The Serbians lost the battle for Kosovo.

Correct answer: (2) The main idea of this 1995 cartoon is that the United Nations was ineffective in its attempt to end genocide in Kosovo. Led by President Milosevic, the Serbians did not stop their practice of ethnic cleansing of the Albanians in Kosovo. Efforts to end genocide in the region were unsuccessful despite reprimands from the United Nations. Finally, NATO troops were sent to stop the violence. *(Global Connections/Interactions)*

Base your answer to Question 9 on the statements below and on your knowledge of social studies.

Article 4: "No one shall be held in slavery or servitude; slavery and the slave trade shall be prohibited in all their forms."

—Universal Declaration of Human Rights, United Nations, 1948

". . . My best estimate of the number of slaves in the world today is 27 million. . . ."

—Kevin Bales, *Disposable People,* University of California Press, 1999

---

9. Based on an analysis of these statements, which conclusion is accurate?

(1) All governments have taken active steps to end slavery.
(2) The United Nations has solved the problem of slavery.
(3) The number of enslaved persons has increased dramatically since 1948.
(4) Slavery remains a problem in the modern era.

Correct answer: (4) Based on an analysis of these statements, the most accurate conclusion is that slavery remains a problem in the modern era. The number of enslaved persons has dropped, but the United Nations has not completely solved the problem of slavery. Common in developing regions of the world, women and children in parts of Asia and Africa were in constant danger of enslavement. *(Global Connections/Interactions)*

Base your answers to questions 10 and 11 on the quotation below and on your knowledge of social studies.

. . . Finally, gather together all that we have said, so great and so august [important], about royal authority. You have seen a great nation united under one man: you have seen his sacred power, paternal and absolute: you have seen that secret reason which directs the body politic, enclosed in one head: you have seen the image of God in kings, and you will have the idea of majesty of kingship. God is holiness itself, goodness itself, power itself, reason itself. In these things consists the divine majesty. In their reflection consists the majesty of the prince. . . .

—Jacques-Benigne Bossuet

---

10. Which concept is associated with this quotation?

(1) direct democracy
(2) imperialism
(3) socialism
(4) divine right to rule

Correct answer: (4) The concept is associated with this quotation is divine right. The passage emphasizes the importance of "royal authority," as the monarch was given the power to rule by God. The monarchs commanded total obedience from his subjects during the Age of Absolutism; therefore, this type of governance was neither a direct democracy nor socialism. Imperialism is control by a dominant nation over a weaker nation or region. *(First Global Age)*

---

11. Which individual most likely opposed the form of government described in this quotation?

    (1) Ivan the Terrible
    (2) Thomas Hobbes
    (3) John Locke
    (4) Louis XIV

Correct answer: (3) John Locke would most likely oppose the form of government described in this quotation. John Locke was an Enlightenment philosopher who wrote the *Two Treaties of Government.* Unlike Thomas Hobbes, Locke opposed absolute government. Instead, he believed that all people possessed natural rights. Both Ivan the Terrible and Louis XIV were examples of absolute rulers. *(First Global Age)*

---

12. One way in which the Magna Carta, the Petition of Right, and the Glorious Revolution are similar is that each

    (1) strengthened the power of the pope.
    (2) led to the exploration of Africa.
    (3) limited the power of the English monarchy.
    (4) settled religious conflicts.

Correct answer: (3) One way in which the Magna Carta, the Petition of Right, and the Glorious Revolution are similar is that each limited the power of the English monarchy. Beginning with the signing of the Magna Carta in 1215, royal powers such as lawmaking and taxation were limited by Parliament. *(Global Interactions)*

Base your answers to Question 13 on the quotation below and on your knowledge of social studies.

. . . I saw that the whole solution to this problem lay in political freedom for our people, for it is only when a people are politically free that other races can give them the respect that is due to them. It is impossible to talk of equality of races in any other terms. No people without a government of their own can expect to be treated on the same level as peoples of independent sovereign states. It is far better to be free to govern or misgovern yourself than to be governed by anybody else. . . .

    —Kwame Nkrumah, *Ghana: The Autobiography of Kwame Nkrumah,* Thomas Nelson & Sons, 1957

---

13. Which idea is expressed in this statement by Kwame Nkrumah?

    (1) free trade
    (2) collective security
    (3) self-determination
    (4) peaceful coexistence

Correct answer: (3) Self-determination is expressed in this statement by Kwame Nkrumah. In order to truly enjoy freedom, Kwame Nkrumah argued that the people must be able to make decisions about their own political affairs. To this end, Kwame Nkrumah led the Gold Coast, present-day Ghana, to independence in 1957. The passage does not suggest ideas such as free trade, collective security, or peaceful coexistence. *(Twentieth Century Since 1945)*

14. Which statement best describes a problem facing India today?

(1) Democracy has failed to gain popular support.
(2) Religious and ethnic diversity has continued to cause conflict.
(3) A decrease in population has led to labor shortages.
(4) Lack of technology has limited military capabilities.

Correct answer: (2) The statement that best describes a problem facing India today is that religious and ethnic diversity has continued to cause conflict. As an overwhelming majority, Hindus often clashed with minority groups such as the Sikhs and the Muslims in India. The conflicts resulted in political assassinations such as Indira Gandhi and terrorist activities. Lack of unity makes maintaining a democratic government more difficult for Indians. *(Twentieth Century Since 1945)*

15. Which heading best completes the partial outline below?

I. _____

   A. Centralized governments

   B. Organized religions

   C. Social classes

   D. Specialization of labor

(1) Economic Development in Ancient Egypt
(2) Cultural Diffusion in Mohenjo-Daro
(3) Features of the Old Stone Age
(4) Characteristics of Civilizations

Correct answer: (4) Characteristics of Civilizations best completes the partial outline. The development of agriculture was vital to the emergence of cities. Farming ensured the constant supply of food sources to sustain population growth. Without the need to constantly search for food, some people began to focus on other specialties. This led to the development of centralized governments, organized religions, and social classes. *(Ancient World)*

Base your answers to questions 16 through 18 on the speakers' statements below and on your knowledge of social studies.

Speaker A: Although I spread serfdom in my country, I tried to modernize our society by incorporating western technology.

Speaker B: I promoted culture with my support of the arts. Unfortunately, I drained my country's treasury by building my palace at Versailles and involving my country in costly wars.

Speaker C: I gained much wealth from my overseas empire in the Americas. I waged war against the Protestants and lost.

Speaker D: I inherited the throne and imprisoned my foes without a trial. I dissolved Parliament because I did not want to consult with them when I increased taxes.

16. Which speaker represents the view of King Louis XIV of France?

    (1) A
    (2) B
    (3) C
    (4) D

Correct answer: (2) Speaker B represents the view of King Louis XIV of France. Louis XIV was a French ruler during the Age of Absolutism. Believing in the divine right to rule, Louis XIV derived the power to rule from God. As the ruler of France, he promoted culture with strong support of the arts. This is evident in the building of the Versailles Palace. However, his costly wars with neighboring European nations such as Britain and Holland exhausted most of the nation's reserves. *(First Global Age)*

17. Which nation was most likely governed by Speaker D?

    (1) Russia
    (2) France
    (3) Spain
    (4) England ·

Correct answer: (4) England was most likely governed by Speaker D. In England, monarchs inherited the throne. Believing in the divine right to rule, English monarchs governed as absolute rulers. Since the 13th century, Parliament had taken steps to curtail the powers of the throne. This was evident in the battle between James II and Parliament in the seventeenth century. When Parliament tried to interfere with the new taxes levied by James II, he dissolved Parliament. This angered the people and led to the Glorious Revolution. *(First Global Age)*

18. Which type of government is most closely associated with all these speakers?

    (1) limited monarchy
    (2) absolute monarchy
    (3) direct democracy
    (4) constitutional democracy

Correct answer: (2) Absolute monarchy is most likely associated with all these speakers. These rulers most likely came from Russia, England, France, and Spain. These rulers believed in their absolute powers over the people. Although monarchs such as Louis XIV promoted learning and arts, he hurt the nation by engaging in costly warfare. *(First Global Age)*

Base your answer to Question 19 on the cartoon below and on your knowledge of social studies.

Source: Kim Song Heng, *Lianhe Zaobao*, 2002 (adapted)

19. The main idea of this 2002 cartoon is that East Timor is

(1) experiencing massive floods that might destroy the nation
(2) struggling with the arrival of large numbers of freedom-seeking refugees
(3) facing several dangers that threaten its existence as a new nation
(4) celebrating its success as an independent nation

Correct answer: (3) The main idea of this 2002 cartoon is that East Timor is facing several dangers that threaten its existence as a new nation. Since 1975, East Timor had been under the control of Indonesia. In 1999, the people voted for independence and achieved nationhood status in 2002. In 2002, Xanano Gusmao became the president of East Timor. The cartoon points out that East Timor still faces political and economic instabilities. *(Twentieth Century Since 1945)*

20. What was one similar goal shared by Simón Bolívar and Mohandas Gandhi?

    (1) ending foreign control

    (2) promoting religious freedom

    (3) establishing a limited monarchy

    (4) creating collective farms

Correct answer: (1) One similar goal shared by Simón Bolívar and Mohandas Gandhi was ending foreign control. The movement for Latin American independence from Spanish rule was primarily led by Simón Bolívar. Similar to Simón Bolívar, Mohandas Gandhi led a nationalist movement to free India from British rule in the twentieth century. He advocated the boycott of British goods, civil disobedience, and nonviolence. India attained independence from Great Britain in 1947. *(Age of Revolution)*

21. In a comparison of the ancient cities of Athens and Sparta, Sparta placed more emphasis on

    (1) education.

    (2) military service.

    (3) family order.

    (4) human rights.

Correct answer: (2) In a comparison of the ancient cities of Athens and Sparta, Sparta placed more emphasis on military service. The culture of Sparta placed major emphasis on the military. Athens, on the other hand, was home to the world's first democracy. Only citizens were able to participate in the decision-making process. This type of government is known as a direct democracy. *(Ancient World)*

22. One way in which the Twelve Tables and Justinian's Code were similar is that both provided

    (1) a standardized system of laws.

    (2) a means of achieving social equality.

    (3) the freedom to pursue their own religion.

    (4) the right to a public education.

Correct answer: (1) One way in which the Twelve Tables and Justinian's Code were similar is that both provided a standardized system of laws. The plebeians of Ancient Rome believed that a written law code was necessary to ensure justice. This belief gave birth to the Twelve Tables. Similarly, Emperor Justinian of Byzantine also commissioned legal scholars to compile a written set of laws based on the Roman law. This is known today as Justinian's Code. *(Ancient World)*

Base your answer to Question 23 on the map below and on your knowledge of social studies.

Africa: Ancient Kingdoms

Source: Sue Ann Kirne, et al., *World Studies: Global Issues & Assessments,* N & N Publishing, Inc. (adapted)

23. What is a valid conclusion that can be reached by studying this map?

(1) Africans had centralized governments during the age of European feudalism.

(2) African kingdoms did not exist before the Europeans arrived in Africa.

(3) African civilizations existed only in southern Africa.

(4) Africa's civilizations established many trade routes to India.

Correct answer: (1) According to this map, Africans had centralized governments during the age of European feudalism. The map shows ancient African kingdoms and their periods of existence, which take place during the European Middle Ages. African kingdoms were established prior to the Europeans' arrival in various regions of Africa. This map does not illustrate trade routes between Africa and India. *(Expanding Zones of Exchange)*

Base your answers to questions 24 and 25 on the quotation below and on your knowledge of social studies.

. . . Finally, let us put together the things so great and so august [exalted] which we have said about royal authority. Behold an immense people united in a single person; behold this holy power, paternal and absolute; behold the secret cause which governs the whole body of the state, contained in a single head: you see the image of God in the king, and you have the idea of royal majesty. God is holiness itself, goodness itself, and power itself. In these things lies the majesty of God. In the image of these things lies the majesty of the prince. . . .

—Bishop Jacques-Benigne Bossuet, 1679

---

24. This passage suggests that the authority to rule in seventeenth-century France was based on

(1) popular sovereignty.
(2) parliamentary consent.
(3) feudal obligation.
(4) divine right.

Correct answer: (4) This passage suggests that the authority to rule in seventeenth-century France was based on divine right. Within the passage, Bossuet discusses how the king derives his power from God. The king, as the representative of God, is revered by the people as God itself. Louis XIV was an example of a monarch who derived his powers from God. *(First Global Age)*

---

25. In this passage, Bossuet was describing the power held by

(1) Charlemagne.
(2) Joan of Arc.
(3) Louis XIV.
(4) Robespierre.

Correct answer: (3) In this passage, Bossuet was describing the power held by Louis XIV. Louis XIV, known as the "Sun King," derived his powers from God. Charlemagne ruled the Frankish Empire, while Robespierre took control of the Committee of Public Safety during the French Revolution. Joan of Arc was seen as a heroine for the Roman Catholic Church because of her claims to have seen visions of God. *(First Global Age)*

---

26. The writings of Jean Jacques Rousseau, Baron de Montesquieu, and John Locke were similar in that each supported the principles of

(1) a military dictatorship.
(2) an autocracy.
(3) a theocratic society.
(4) a democratic republic.

Correct answer: (4) The writings of Jean Jacques Rousseau, Baron de Montesquieu, and John Locke were similar in that each supported the principles of a democratic republic. During the Enlightenment, these philosophers sought to inform people of their natural rights and the benefits of democracy. Under a military dictatorship, the country is led by one powerful military leader. An autocracy is a form of governance in which one ruler retains complete control. A theocratic society has a government influenced by religious ideas. *(Age of Revolution)*

---

27. Which situation is an example of totalitarianism in Germany in the 1930s?

    (1) frequent meetings of the German Reichstag
    (2) decline of the German economy
    (3) strict government control of the press
    (4) negotiation of a nonaggression pact with the Soviet Union

---

Correct answer: (3) Strict government control of the press is an example of totalitarianism in Germany in the 1930s. Under totalitarianism, one party has total control of the government. If the government takes strict control of the press, censorship was used to prevent the opposing views of the government from publication. Frequent meetings of the German Reichstag (Parliament), a decline in the German economy or negotiating an agreement with the Soviet Union do not demonstrate total power of one group. *(Crisis and Achievement [1900–1945])*

---

28. Which situation existed under the policy of apartheid in South Africa?

    (1) All people were guaranteed suffrage.
    (2) The black majority held the most political power.
    (3) Society was controlled by the white minority.
    (4) Social inequality was eliminated.

Correct answer: (3) Under the policy of apartheid in South Africa, society was controlled by the white minority. Apartheid is defined as a system of government in South Africa where races were segregated. The white minority was the ruling power in South Africa. Social inequality and discrimination existed in South Africa limiting the rights of many black South Africans. *(Twentieth Century Since 1945)*

Base your answer to Question 29 on the chart below and on your knowledge of social studies.

Demographic Indicators for China	2000	2025*
Births per 1,000 population	16.0	12.0
Deaths per 1,000 population	7.0	8.0
Rate of natural increase (percent)	0.9	0.3
Life expectancy at birth (years)	71.4	77.4
Total fertility rate (per woman)	1.8	1.8

*projected

29. Which conclusion about the population of China between 2000 and 2025 can be drawn from the information provided by this chart?

(1) The fertility rate of Chinese women is expected to increase.
(2) Chinese life expectancy will likely decrease.
(3) The rate of population growth is expected to decline.
(4) By 2025, the birthrate in China will probably double.

Correct answer: (3) Based on the chart, the rate of population growth is expected to decline in China between 2000 and 2025. The chart shows a decrease in births per 1,000 people between the years of 2000 and 2025. The fertility rate has stayed the same, while the life expectancy will likely increase. *(Global Connections/Interactions)*

Base your answer to Question 30 on the statements below and on your knowledge of social studies.

■ Roman women could own property.
■ Roman women could make wills leaving their property to whomever they chose.

30. A valid conclusion drawn from these facts is that Roman women

(1) had the right to vote.
(2) enjoyed some legal rights.
(3) were equal to men.
(4) could hold political offices.

Correct answer: (2) A valid conclusion drawn from these facts is that Roman women enjoyed some legal rights. However, women were not equal in status to men. They could not hold offices or vote in general elections. Athens, a city-state of ancient Greece, was a direct democracy. *(Ancient World)*

31. In England the Magna Carta, the Puritan Revolution, the Glorious Revolution, and the English Bill of Rights led to the development of

(1) a dictatorship.
(2) an absolute monarchy.
(3) a theocracy.
(4) a limited monarchy.

Correct answer: (4) In England the Magna Carta, the Puritan Revolution, the Glorious Revolution, and the English Bill of Rights led to the development of a limited monarchy. For example, monarch powers such as lawmaking and taxation were limited by the Parliament as a result of the Magna Carta. Hence, the king could not rule as a dictator or an absolute monarch. *(Global Interactions)*

32. Many European monarchs of the 1600s maintained that they should have absolute power to rule because they

(1) needed to defend their nations against threats from the Western Hemisphere.
(2) thought that all people should have the right to a good ruler.
(3) had been given their power to govern from God.
(4) thought that communism was the superior political system.

Correct answer: (3) Many European monarchs of the 1600s maintained that they should have absolute power to rule because they had been given their power to govern from God. The authority to rule in seventeenth-century France was based on divine right, or power derived from God. The king, as the representative of God, is revered by the people as God itself. Louis XIV was an example of an absolute ruler who derived his powers from God. *(First Global Age)*

Base your answer to Question 33 on the passage below and on your knowledge of social studies.

. . . The key-stone of the Fascist doctrine is its conception of the State, of its essence, its functions, and its aims. For Fascism the State is absolute, individuals and groups relative. Individuals and groups are admissible in so far as they come within the State. Instead of directing the game and guiding the material and moral progress of the community, the liberal State restricts its activities to recording results. The Fascist State is wide awake and has a will of its own. For this reason it can be described as 'ethical'. . . .

—Benito Mussolini, *Fascism: Doctrine and Institutions,* Howard Fertig, 1932

33. Which statement expresses the main idea of the passage?

(1) The people have a right to overthrow ineffective governments.
(2) The state is more important than the individuals within it.
(3) The state gets its authority from the power of individuals.
(4) The establishment of an empire will cause division and chaos.

Correct answer: (2) According to the passage, the state is more important than the individuals within it. The poor conditions of many Italians gave rise to Benito Mussolini and Italian fascism after World War I. To gain public approval and support, Mussolini promised the people better economic conditions. To accomplish this goal, the Fascist Party took away individual rights, including the freedom of the press and free speech. Free elections stopped during the Fascist regime. *(Crisis and Achievement [1900–1945])*

34. The Justinian Code is considered a milestone because it

(1) preserved many ancient Chinese legal decrees in writing.
(2) served as a model for European legal systems.
(3) became the first democratic constitution.
(4) united Muslim and Roman thought.

Correct answer: (2) The Justinian Code is considered a milestone because it served as a model for European legal systems. The Justinian code of the Byzantine Empire provided for the basic rights that we protect today and led to many of the legal systems in Europe today. The Justinian Code did not base itself in Chinese legal decrees, unite Muslim and Roman thought, or even serve as a constitution. Rather, the code gave rights to people and created a system of law that is influencing legal systems today. *(Expanding Zones of Exchange)*

35. Which factor most influenced a person's social position in early Indian societies?

    (1) education
    (2) birth
    (3) geographic location
    (4) individual achievement

Correct answer: (2) The factor that most influenced a person's social position in early Indian societies was birth. The family to which you were born would lead to your caste, and your caste would cement your social position in society. Nothing in early Indian society—including education, location, or individual achievement—would overrule your status based on your caste. *(Expanding Zones of Exchange)*

36. The Magna Carta, the Petition of Right, and the English Bill of Rights were created to

    (1) limit the power of English monarchs.
    (2) establish laws protecting the rights of Protestants.
    (3) organize England's colonial empire.
    (4) abolish the role of Parliament.

Correct answer: (1) The Magna Carta, Petition of Right, and the English Bill of Rights were created to limit the power of the English monarchs. Before these bills, the English kings and queens had unlimited power with no checks or balances. These bills were designed to protect the subjects of England from unfair abuses of power by the crown. These bills were not designed to protect Protestants, organize the colonial empire, or abolish the role of Parliament. Rather, these bills *strengthened* Parliament, giving it power and oversight over the monarchs in Great Britain. *(Age of Revolution)*

37. The theory justifying a monarch's rule by God's authority is called

    (1) laissez faire.
    (2) totalitarianism.
    (3) predestination.
    (4) divine right to rule.

Correct answer: (4) The theory justifying a monarch's rule by God's authority is called the divine right to rule. Laissez faire is the theory that government should stay out of the market, while totalitarianism is the theory that advocates complete governmental control. Predestination is the theory that your fate is sealed upon birth, determining whether you go to heaven or hell. *(Age of Revolution)*

38. One similarity in the rule of Peter the Great, Suleiman I, and Louis XIV is that each leader

   (1) shared power with a legislature.
   (2) practiced religious toleration.
   (3) expanded his territory.
   (4) decreased the amount of taxes collected.

Correct answer: (3) One similarity in the rule of Peter the Great, Suleiman I, and Louis XIV is that each leader expanded his territory. Each of these leaders expanded his kingdom, building up empires. There is no universal sharing of powers with legislatures, religious toleration, or decrease of the amount of taxes collected. The only statement that applies to all the rulers is that they expanded their territories. Suleiman I was the only leader listed who practiced religious toleration. *(First Global Age)*

39. Totalitarian governments are characterized by the

   (1) elimination of heavy industry.
   (2) use of censorship, secret police, and repression.
   (3) lack of a written constitution.
   (4) support of the people for parliamentary decisions.

Correct answer: (2) Totalitarian governments are characterized by their use of censorship, secret police, and repression. The word *totalitarian* refers to the complete government control over the people, using the methods listed above. Totalitarian governments do not eliminate heavy industry, lack a written constitution, or support the people for parliamentary decisions. The only decisions made in a totalitarian government are by the leader. *(Methodology of Global History/Geography)*

Base your answer to Question 40 on the terms below and on your knowledge of social studies.

- Organization of American States (OAS)
- European Union (EU)
- North American Free Trade Agreement (NAFTA)

40. These organizations and agreements are examples of

   (1) political isolation
   (2) military alliances
   (3) regional cooperation
   (4) collective security

Correct answer: (3) The organizations and agreements are examples of regional cooperation. The OAS, EU, and NAFTA are all regional trade organizations, strengthening the areas that they represent. They do not represent political isolation, military alliances, or collective security. Instead, they are designed to provide cooperation amongst neighboring nations, leading to peace and profits for all. *(Global Connections/Interactions)*

41. In Iran, both the Revolution of 1979 and the rise of Islamic fundamentalism have caused

    (1) an increase in women's rights.
    (2) tension between traditionalism and modernization to continue.
    (3) foreign control of natural resources to expand.
    (4) the introduction of a communist form of government.

Correct answer: (2) In Iran, both the Revolution of 1979 and the rise of Islamic fundamentalism have caused tensions between traditionalism and modernization to continue. The Revolution of 1979, as well as the rise of fundamentalism, have caused two classes in Iran—the fundamental Islamic class and a more westernized class; tensions between the two continue to this day. There has not been an increase in women's rights or in foreign control of natural resources, nor has there been an introduction of communist government in Iran. *(Twentieth Century Since 1945)*

42. The caste system in India and the feudal system in Europe were similar in that both

    (1) provided structure for society.
    (2) developed concepts of natural rights.
    (3) established totalitarian governments.
    (4) promoted peace and prosperity.

Correct answer: (1) The caste system in India and the feudal system in Europe were similar in that both provided structure for society. Both systems did not provide individuals with great degree of social mobility. The feudal societies in Europe were not united; therefore they could not maintain peace or establish a totalitarian government. The caste system did not develop concepts of natural rights, as an individual's social status was largely determined by birth. *(Twentieth Century Since 1945)*

43. In his book *The Prince*, Niccolò Machiavelli advises that a wise ruler is one who

    (1) keeps taxes and food prices low.
    (2) encourages education and the arts.
    (3) allows advisors to speak their minds.
    (4) does what is necessary to stay in power.

Correct answer: (4) In his book *The Prince*, Niccolò Machiavelli advises that a wise ruler is one who does what is necessary to stay in power. Machiavellian politics will always come back to absolute rule, which should be upheld at all costs. Keeping taxes and food prices low, encouraging education and the arts, or allowing advisors to speak their minds may work, but Machiavelli primarily is concerned that a ruler should stay in power at all costs. *(Age of Revolution)*

44. King Louis XIV of France, Peter the Great of Russia, and Suleiman the Magnificent of the Ottoman Empire were all considered absolute rulers because they

    (1) broke from the Roman Catholic Church.
    (2) helped feudal lords build secure castles.
    (3) instituted programs that provided more power to their parliaments.
    (4) determined government policies without the consent of their people.

Correct answer: (4) King Louis XIV of France, Peter the Great of Russia, and Suleiman the Magnificent of the Ottoman Empire were all considered absolute rulers because they determined the government policies without the consent of their people. None of these leaders broke from the Catholic Church, and absolute rulers do not ever help feudal lords or give power to parliamentarians. Absolute rule means that the king makes decision alone, without concerns of input or consent from the governed. *(First Global Age)*

Base your answer to Question 45 on the passage below and on your knowledge of social studies.

    ". . . Men are born and remain free and equal in rights. Social distinctions may be founded only upon the general good. . . ."

        —Declaration of the Rights of Man and of the Citizen, 1789

45. Which principle of the Enlightenment philosophers is expressed in this quotation from the French Revolution?

    (1) natural law
    (2) nationalism
    (3) free trade
    (4) socialism

Correct answer: (1) The quotation from the French Revolution best expresses the Enlightenment principle of natural law. When quotes start talking about men being born free and equal in rights, this will always come back to natural rights. Free trade, socialism, and nationalism tie into the French Revolution, but they are not related to the principle that men are born and remain free. The quote leads to the only viable answer being natural rights. *(Age of Revolution)*

Base your answer to Question 46 on the statements below and on your knowledge of social studies.

- The people of Kashmir demand separation from India.
- The people of East Timor vote for independence from Indonesia.
- The Tibetans resent control of their country by China.
- The Kurds want to establish their own independent state of Kurdistan.

137

46. These statements are examples of the efforts of different peoples to achieve

(1) free-market systems.
(2) democratic governments.
(3) social equality.
(4) self-determination.

Correct answer: (4) These statements are examples of the efforts of different peoples to achieve self-determination. Each example listed—the people of Kashmir, East Timor, Tibetans, and Kurds—is an ethnic minority without a homeland. Before anything else, these ethnic minorities want control over themselves, the right to determine their own government. *(Global Connections/Interactions)*

47. The Twelve Tables, Justinian's Code, and the English Bill of Rights are similar in that each addresses the issue of

(1) social mobility.
(2) economic development.
(3) the individual and the state.
(4) the importance of religion.

Correct answer: (3) The Twelve Tables, Justinian's Code, and the English Bill of Rights are similar in that each addresses the issue of the individual and the state. Each of the legal codes deals with the role of people within the government, and where the people stand. Social mobility, economic development, and the importance of religion are not significant within these legal codes. *(Methodology of Global History/Geography)*

48. What is meant by Machiavelli's belief that "the end justifies the means"?

(1) Leaders may use any method to achieve what is best for the state.
(2) The general public always acts in its own best interest.
(3) Pleasing all of the people at any given time is possible.
(4) Leaders must always act for the common good.

Correct answer: (1) When Machiavelli said that "the end justifies the means," he meant that leaders may use any method to achieve what is best for the state. When the end justifies the means, the leaders may use any and all methods available to them to achieve their goals. The quote does not mean that the general public always acts in its own best interest, or that pleasing all the people at any given time is possible, or even that leaders must always act for the common good. *(Age of Revolution)*

49. The Magna Carta can be described as a

(1) journal about English feudal society.
(2) list of feudal rights that limited the power of the English monarchy.
(3) census of all tax-paying nobility in feudal England.
(4) statement of grievances of the middle class in England.

Correct answer: (2) The Magna Carta can be described as a list of feudal rights that limited the power of the English monarchy. In the 13th century, when the Magna Carta was written, it provided a basic series of rights for the English citizens, and limited the power of the king. It was in no way a journal about English feudal society or a census of all tax-paying nobility in feudal England. Though the middle class in England certainly had their share of grievances, the Magna Carta was a declaration of rights rather than a statement of those grievances. *(Age of Revolution)*

---

50. The success of the women's suffrage movement in twentieth-century Europe resulted in part from women

    (1) holding high political offices
    (2) working in factories during World War I
    (3) being encouraged to have large families
    (4) serving in combat positions during World War I

Correct answer: (2) The success of the women's suffrage movement in twentieth-century Europe resulted in part from women working in factories during World War I. With all the men going off to war, women took the role of producing necessary materials. When the men returned home, these same women who worked in the factories fought to keep their newfound rights, and be equal to the men returning from the front. Women didn't previously hold high political offices or serve combat positions in war, and encouragement to have large families would never lead to women's suffrage. *(Crisis and Achievement [1900–1945])*

Base your answer to Question 51 on the passage below and on your knowledge of social studies.

    . . . A free, open-minded, and absolutely impartial adjustment of all colonial claims, based upon a strict observance of the principle that in determining all such questions of sovereignty the interests of the populations concerned must have equal weight with the equitable claims of the government whose title is to be determined. . . .

    —President Woodrow Wilson's Fourteen Points, 1918

---

51. This statement held appeal for nationalists in areas under colonial control because it suggested

    (1) national self-determination.
    (2) economic development.
    (3) a system of alliances.
    (4) protection from terrorists.

Correct answer: (1) The statement held appeal for nationalists in areas under colonial control because it suggested national self-determination. President Wilson is suggesting that all colonies should have the right to decide who their rulers are and not be ruled by a foreign nation. Wilson is not talking about the economic development of these lands, a system of alliances for them, or protection from terrorists. *(Crisis and Achievement [1900–1945])*

52. In the 1920s and 1930s, Mustafa Kemal Atatürk changed the Turkish government by

    (1) introducing democratic reforms.
    (2) increasing the power of the sultan.
    (3) supporting absolutism.
    (4) incorporating religious teachings into civil law.

Correct answer: (1) In the 1920s and 1930s, Mustafa Kemal Atatürk changed the Turkish government by introducing democratic reforms. Atatürk turned Turkey from the predominantly Muslim-ruled nation it had been into a more Western democratic nation. Atatürk did not increase the power of the sultan, support an absolutist form of government, or incorporate religious teachings into civil law. *(Crisis and Achievement [1900–1945])*

53. Fascist leaders in Italy and Germany came to power in the 1920s and 1930s because they

    (1) supported the League of Nations.
    (2) exploited economic hardships to gain popular support.
    (3) resisted all forms of extreme nationalism.
    (4) maintained political traditions.

Correct answer: (2) Fascist leaders in Italy and Germany came to power in the 1920s and 1930s because they exploited economic hardships to gain popular support. The fascist leaders gave the peoples of their nations a reason why life was so bad and told them who was to blame. The fascist leaders did not support the League of Nations; quite the opposite, they railed against it. Fascist leaders used extreme nationalism to garner support rather than resist it, and they did not maintain political traditions. *(Crisis and Achievement [1900–1945])*

54. A common element in the movements for German unification, Italian unification, and Indian independence was the

    (1) support of the Catholic Church.
    (2) strength of nationalist leaders.
    (3) mediation of the League of Nations.
    (4) existence of democratic institutions.

Correct answer: (2) A common element in the movements for German unification, Italian unification, and Indian independence was the strength of nationalist leaders. People such as Bismarck, Cavour, and Gandhi have played major roles in their nations. German, and Italian unification as well as Indian independence did not have the support of the Catholic Church, the mediation of the League of Nations, or the existence of democratic institutions. Thus, the only possible answer comes back to the strong nationalist leaders. *(Age of Revolution)*

55. Totalitarian countries are characterized by

    (1) free and open discussions of ideas.
    (2) a multiparty system with several candidates for each office.
    (3) government control of newspapers, radio, and television.
    (4) government protection of people's civil liberties.

Correct answer: (3) Totalitarian countries are characterized by government control of newspapers, radio, and television. A totalitarian government is characterized by a sole dictator who controls every aspect of citizens' lives. Mao Zedong was an example of a totalitarian dictator. To suppress political dissidents, the Chinese government censored all forms of media. People's civil liberties were violated. *(Crisis and Achievement [1900–1945])*

56. Which leader is most closely associated with the use of civil disobedience in a struggle to end colonial rule?

    (1) Muammar Gaddafi
    (2) Saddam Hussein
    (3) Ho Chi Minh
    (4) Mohandas Gandhi

Correct answer: (4) The leader who is most closely associated with the use of civil disobedience in a struggle to end colonial rule is Mohandas Gandhi. Gandhi is one of the major figures in global history that used civil disobedience to achieve his ends. Mummar Gaddafi, Ho Chi Minh, and Saddam Hussein all used violence to achieve their goals, while Gandhi used nonviolence to achieve unity and independence for his nation. *(Twentieth Century Since 1945)*

Base your answer to Question 57 on the quotation below and on your knowledge of social studies.

. . . Finally, gather together all that we have said, so great and so august [important], about royal authority. You have seen a great nation united under one man: you have seen his sacred power, paternal and absolute: you have seen that secret reason which directs the body politic, enclosed in one head: you have seen the image of God in kings, and you will have the idea of majesty of kingship. God is holiness itself, goodness itself, power itself, reason itself. In these things consists the divine majesty. In their reflection consists the majesty of the prince. . . .

    —Jacques-Benigne Bossuet

57. Which philosophy of government is expressed by this quotation?

    (1) oligarchy
    (2) fascism
    (3) democracy
    (4) divine right to rule

Correct answer: (4) Divine right is the philosophy of government that is expressed by this quotation. The quote discusses the power that God has over the rulers, and how the power of rulers comes from God. Oligarchy is power contained in the hands of the few, fascism involves one absolute ruler, and democracy is power held by the people. *(Age of Revolution)*

Base your answer to Question 58 on the photograph below and on your knowledge of social studies.

Source: Pool Photo by Natalie Behring-Chisholm

58. What was a direct cause of the event illustrated in this photograph?

   (1) defeat of the Taliban-controlled government
   (2) rise of the Ayatollah Khomeini
   (3) signing of the Camp David Accords
   (4) withdrawal of Soviet troops from Afghanistan

Correct answer: (1) The direct cause of the event illustrated in this photograph is the defeat of the Taliban-controlled government. With this defeat, female delegates are allowed in the Afghan grand council and can participate in government. Ayatollah Khomeini was an Iranian ruler, not Afghani. The Camp David Accords dealt with Israel, and the withdrawal of Soviet troops led way for the Taliban to rise, not fall. *(Twentieth Century Since 1945)*

59. One similarity in the unification of Italy, the Zionist movement, and the breakup of the Ottoman Empire was that each was influenced by

   (1) humanism.
   (2) polytheism.
   (3) nationalism.
   (4) imperialism.

Correct answer: (3) One similarity in the unification of Italy, the Zionist movement, and the breakup of the Ottoman Empire was that each was influenced by nationalism. The desire of having one's own nation led to each of these movements. Humanism, polytheism, and imperialism do not factor into any of these movements, not nearly as much as the need for one's own nation and identity. *(Age of Revolution)*

Base your answer to Question 60 on the statements below and on your knowledge of social studies.

- The Nazi Party controls Germany.
- Khmer Rouge rules in Cambodia.
- The Sandinistas control Nicaragua.

60. Which statement describes a similarity in these situations?

   (1) Civil liberties were promoted.
   (2) Voting rights were extended to women.
   (3) Leaders won the support of all groups.
   (4) One group seized power and limited opposition.

Correct answer: (4) The statement that describes a similarity in these situations is that one group seized power and limited opposition. In all these statements, the group that seized power would violently keep that power, eliminating anyone in their way. Civil liberties were squelched, voting rights were revoked, and leaders often did not win the support of many of the groups, let alone all. *(Crisis and Achievement [1900–1945])*

Self-Evaluation Test with Answer Explanations

Answer Sheet

1 ① ② ③ ④		26 ① ② ③ ④	
2 ① ② ③ ④		27 ① ② ③ ④	
3 ① ② ③ ④		28 ① ② ③ ④	
4 ① ② ③ ④		29 ① ② ③ ④	
5 ① ② ③ ④		30 ① ② ③ ④	
6 ① ② ③ ④		31 ① ② ③ ④	
7 ① ② ③ ④		32 ① ② ③ ④	
8 ① ② ③ ④		33 ① ② ③ ④	
9 ① ② ③ ④		34 ① ② ③ ④	
10 ① ② ③ ④		35 ① ② ③ ④	
11 ① ② ③ ④		36 ① ② ③ ④	
12 ① ② ③ ④		37 ① ② ③ ④	
13 ① ② ③ ④		38 ① ② ③ ④	
14 ① ② ③ ④		39 ① ② ③ ④	
15 ① ② ③ ④		40 ① ② ③ ④	
16 ① ② ③ ④		41 ① ② ③ ④	
17 ① ② ③ ④		42 ① ② ③ ④	
18 ① ② ③ ④		43 ① ② ③ ④	
19 ① ② ③ ④		44 ① ② ③ ④	
20 ① ② ③ ④		45 ① ② ③ ④	
21 ① ② ③ ④		46 ① ② ③ ④	
22 ① ② ③ ④		47 ① ② ③ ④	
23 ① ② ③ ④		48 ① ② ③ ④	
24 ① ② ③ ④		49 ① ② ③ ④	
25 ① ② ③ ④		50 ① ② ③ ④	

What follows is a sample practice exam. It consists of actual Regents questions from previous tests set in a format similar to the actual exam. The Global History and Geography exam lasts for three hours. Set beginning and end times for yourself so that you can pace your progress.

This examination has three parts. You must answer all of the questions in all parts. On the actual exam you must use black or dark-blue ink to write your answers.

- **Part I** contains 50 multiple-choice questions.
- **Part II** contains one thematic essay question.
- **Part III** is based on several documents:

  Part III A contains the documents. Each document is followed by one or more questions.

  Part III B contains one essay question based on the documents.

Self-Evaluation Test

Part I: Multiple Choice

Directions: For each of the following questions, select the choice that best answers the question or completes the statement.

Base your answer to Question 1 on the passage below and on your knowledge of social studies.

. . . The Nazi holocaust, which engulfed millions of Jews in Europe, proved anew the urgency of the re-establishment of the Jewish state, which would solve the problem of Jewish homelessness by opening the gates to all Jews and lifting the Jewish people to equality in the family of nations. . . .

1. This statement is referring to the establishment of which nation?

1. Jordan
2. Poland
3. Israel
4. Ethiopia

2. Which set of historical periods in European history is in the correct chronological order?

A. Medieval Europe
B. Italian Renaissance
C. Golden Age of Greece
D. Enlightenment

1. C → A → B → D
2. A → B → D → C
3. C → B → D → A
4. B → A → C → D

3. Locke's *Two Treatises of Government,* Rousseau's *The Social Contract,* and Montesquieu's *The Spirit of the Laws* were works written during which time period?

1. Middle Ages
2. Renaissance
3. Enlightenment
4. Reformation

4. The activities of Mother Teresa are most closely associated with

    1. democracy and political freedom.
    2. industrialization and open markets.
    3. nationalism and independence movements.
    4. the needs of the poor and health care.

5. Which statement best describes an impact of the computer on the global economy?

    1. Countries can increase tariffs on imports.
    2. Companies now market more products worldwide.
    3. Wages have risen dramatically for most people in developing nations.
    4. Prices of oil and other resources have declined worldwide.

Base your answer to Question 6 on the cartoon below and on your knowledge of social studies.

Source: Steve Sack, *Minneapolis Star and Tribune*, 1983

6. What is the main idea of this political cartoon?

   1. Only the United States and Africa are affected by a lack of food.
   2. Pollution is often the cause of famine.
   3. The governments in Africa are unconcerned about the lack of food for their people.
   4. Reading about world famine is different from experiencing it.

7. Both Inca farmers and Japanese farmers adapted a geographic feature of their countries by

   1. engaging in overseas expansion.
   2. growing crops suited to desert climates.
   3. building terraces into the mountainsides.
   4. reclaiming land from the sea by building dikes.

8. What was a major cause of the civil wars in many Central American nations in the 1970s and 1980s?

   1. economic differences between social classes
   2. end of slavery in the encomienda system
   3. rapid economic reform
   4. oil production policies

Base your answer to Question 9 on the passage below and on your knowledge of social studies.

. . . The replacement of the bourgeois by the proletarian state is impossible without a violent revolution. The abolition of the proletarian state, i.e., of all states, is only possible through 'withering away.' . . .

   —V. I. Lenin, *State and Revolution,* 1917

9. This quotation is associated with the principles of

   1. imperialism.
   2. capitalism.
   3. communism.
   4. militarism.

Base your answers to questions 10 and 11 on the passage below and on your knowledge of social studies.

"From the beginning," says Marquis Ito, "we realized fully how necessary it was that the Japanese people should not only adopt Western methods, but should also speedily become competent to do without the aid of foreign instruction and supervision. In the early days we brought many foreigners to Japan to help to introduce modern methods, but we always did it in such a way as to enable the Japanese students to take their rightful place in the nation after they had been educated."

   —Alfred Stead, *Great Japan: A Study of National Efficiency,* John Lane Co., 1906

10. Which occurrence in Japanese history is described in the passage?

    1. The Meiji Restoration
    2. The Tokugawa shogunate
    3. The assimilation of Buddhism
    4. The adoption of Confucian practices

11. The author of the passage suggests that Japan

    1. remained isolated.
    2. accepted new technologies in order to modernize.
    3. became dependent on foreign nations.
    4. became militaristic.

12. The technology of papermaking traveled from China to Baghdad along the

    1. Saharan caravan trails.
    2. Trans-Siberian Railway.
    3. Silk Roads.
    4. Suez Canal.

13. A totalitarian society is one in which

    1. the government controls most aspects of life.
    2. the ruler of the government claims divine authority.
    3. the state is considered a servant of the citizens.
    4. citizens can publicly criticize the actions of the leaders.

14. Which statement about Greek civilization is an opinion rather than a fact?

    1. Boys in Sparta were trained to be soldiers.
    2. Athens had a better culture than that of Sparta.
    3. Socrates, Plato, and Aristotle were Greek philosophers.
    4. Many adults in Athens did not have the right to vote.

Base your answers to questions 15 and 16 on the woodblock print below and on your knowledge of social studies.

Ladies with western musical instruments

Source: Published by Omori Kakutaro, wood block print (detail), c. 1890, Museum of Fine Arts, Boston

15. This late nineteenth-century Japanese print illustrates

    1. isolationism.
    2. ethnocentrism.
    3. cultural diffusion.
    4. democracy.

16. During which period of Japanese history was this print most likely created?

    1. Tokugawa shogunate

    2. Meiji Restoration

    3. Russo-Japanese War

    4. post–World War II occupation

Base your answer to Question 17 on the illustration below and on your knowledge of social studies.

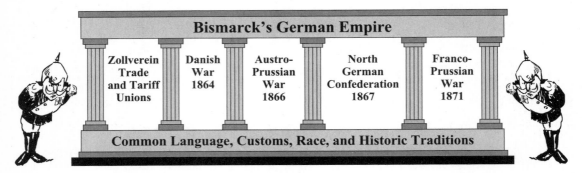

Source: Sue A. Kirne et al., *World Studies: Global Issues & Assessments,* N & N Publishing Co. (adapted)

17. All the elements identified in the illustration contributed to German

    1. interdependence.

    2. unification.

    3. imperialism.

    4. apathy.

18. Which set of events is in the correct chronological order?

    1. Renaissance → Middle Ages → Roman Empire

    2. Treaty of Versailles → World War II → Korean War

    3. Reformation → Crusades → European exploration of the Americas

    4. Bolshevik Revolution → French Revolution → American Revolution

19. What was one reason that some Italian cities developed into major commercial and cultural centers during the thirteenth and fourteenth centuries?

    1. unified central government

    2. isolationist economic policies

    3. geographic location

    4. system of social equality

Base your answer to Question 20 on the passage below and on your knowledge of social studies.

It took the Big Four just five hours and twenty-five minutes here in Munich today to dispel the clouds of war and come to an agreement over the partition of Czechoslovakia. There is to be no European war, after all. There is to be peace, and the price of that peace is, roughly, the ceding by Czechoslovakia of the Sudeten territory to Herr Hitler's Germany. The German Führer gets what he wanted, only he has to wait a little longer for it. Not much longer though—only ten days. . . .

—William Shirer, recording of CBS radio report from Prague, September 29, 1938

20. The policy that France, Britain, and Italy chose to follow at this meeting is known as

    1. appeasement.
    2. self-determination.
    3. liberation.
    4. pacification.

Base your answer to Question 21 on the cartoon below and on your knowledge of social studies.

Source: Cummings, *Winnipeg Free Press,* Cartoonists and Writers Syndicate

21. What is the cartoonist's view about democracy in India since 1947?

    1. India has become a democratic nation after fifty years.
    2. India has led Asia in democratic reforms.
    3. India is not a democratic nation and has not been for the last five decades.
    4. India's progress in becoming a democratic nation has been slow.

22. Which practice in medieval Europe was most similar to a Japanese warrior's *code of bushido?*

    1. indulgences

    2. serfdom

    3. chivalry

    4. tribute

Base your answer to Question 23 on the bullet points below and on your knowledge of social studies.

- Siberian Plain
- Sahara Desert
- Amazon Basin
- Mongolian Steppes

---

23. One characteristic common to these areas is that they all

    1. have a low population density.

    2. are located between major river valleys.

    3. are major religious centers.

    4. have large areas of valuable farmland.

24. Conflicts between Hutu and Tutsi, Ottoman Turks and Armenians, and Soviets and Ukrainian kulaks all resulted in

    1. establishment of new governments.

    2. international intervention.

    3. massacres or genocide.

    4. cultural interdependence.

25. Which statement about the European Union (EU) is most accurate?

    1. The European Union dissolved because of disagreements among its members.

    2. The goal of the European Union is to improve the economic prosperity of Europe.

    3. Some nations are now being forced to become members of the European Union.

    4. The European Union has recently expanded to include North African nations.

Base your answer to Question 26 on the cartoon that follows and on your knowledge of social studies.

Source: John Trever, *Albuquerque Journal,* Sept. 2001 (adapted)

26. What is the main idea of this 2001 cartoon?

   1. The main task in fighting terrorism is to eliminate nuclear weapons.

   2. The battle against terrorism will be long and difficult.

   3. New equipment is needed to eliminate terrorism.

   4. The methods of dealing with global terrorism have created consensus.

27. What was an important result of the Neolithic Revolution?

   1. Food supplies became more reliable.

   2. New sources of energy became available.

   3. People became more nomadic.

   4. Populations declined.

Base your answer to Question 28 on the passage below and on your knowledge of social studies.

   . . . Let the king and his ministers labor with a mutual sympathy, saying, 'We have received the decree of Heaven and it shall be great as the long-continued years of Hsia; yea, it shall not fail of the long-continued years of Yin.' I wish the king, through the attachment of the lower people, to receive the long-abiding decree of Heaven. . . .

   —Clae Waltham, ed., *Shu Ching, Book of History,* Henry Regnery Company, 1971

28. Which concept is being referred to in this passage?

1. dynastic cycle
2. matriarchal society
3. natural rights
4. monotheism

Base your answer to Question 29 on the bullet points below and on your knowledge of social studies.

- Maize and potatoes were grown in Europe.
- Millions of Africans suffered during the Middle Passage.
- Smallpox had devastating effects on indigenous peoples.
- Spanish language is used in much of Latin America.

29. Which global interaction is illustrated by these statements?

1. Silk Road trade
2. Crusades
3. Columbian Exchange
4. Scramble for Africa

30. How did geography affect both Napoleon's invasion and Hitler's invasion of Russia?

1. Deserts made invasion possible.
2. The climate created obstacles to success.
3. The tundra enabled the movements of troops.
4. Warm-water ports prevented the flow of supplies.

31. What was one effect of Alexander the Great's conquests?

1. expansion of Hellenistic culture
2. formation of the Christian church
3. decreased importance of the Silk Roads
4. increased support of the Mayan leaders

Base your answer to Question 32 on the cartoon that follows and on your knowledge of social studies.

Source: Jack Ohman, *The Oregonian*, 1995

32. This 1995 cartoon is suggesting that communism

    1. has no appeal in Russia.
    2. still dominates the Russian government.
    3. may return if democracy fails in Russia.
    4. is the best system for the Russian people.

33. Which innovation had the greatest impact on the Protestant Reformation?

    1. movable-type printing press
    2. Mercator map projection
    3. magnetic compass
    4. triangular sail

34. A study of Aztec, Maya, and Inca agricultural systems would show that these civilizations

    1. relied on mechanized agricultural techniques.
    2. carried on extensive food trade with each other.
    3. adapted to their environments with creative farming techniques.
    4. relied on a single-crop economy.

Base your answer to Question 35 on the passage below and on your knowledge of social studies.

. . . A place more destitute of all interesting objects than Manchester, it is not easy to conceive. In size and population it is the second city in the kingdom, containing above fourscore thousand [80,000] inhabitants. Imagine this multitude crowded together in narrow streets, the houses all built of brick and blackened with smoke; frequent buildings among them as large as convents, without their antiquity, without their beauty, without their holiness; where you hear from within, as you pass along, the everlasting din of machinery; and where when the bell rings it is to call wretches to their work instead of their prayers, . . .

—Robert J. Southey, *Letters from England,* 1807

35. The conditions described in this passage occurred during the

1. Age of Discovery.
2. Renaissance.
3. Industrial Revolution.
4. Green Revolution.

36. Which empire had the greatest influence on the development of early Russia?

1. Roman
2. Byzantine
3. Egyptian
4. British

37. Philosophers of the Enlightenment period believed that society could best be improved by

1. relying on faith and divine right.
2. borrowing ideas from ancient Greece and Rome.
3. applying reason and the laws of nature.
4. studying the practices of successful leaders.

38. Which heading best completes the partial outline below?

I. _____

A. Fall of Constantinople
B. Voyages of Columbus
C. Posting of Martin Luther's Ninety-five Theses
D. Collapse of communism in the Soviet Union

1. Importance of Revolution
2. War and Rebellion
3. Turning Points in History
4. Effects of Economic Change

Base your answer to Question 39 on the map that follows and on your knowledge of social studies.

Mongol Areas of Influence

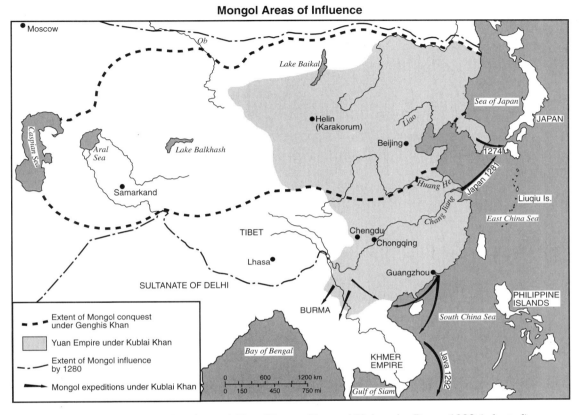

Source: John K. Fairbank, *China: A New History,* Harvard University Press, 1992 (adapted)

39. Which statement about the Mongols is supported by the information in the map?

1. The Yuan Dynasty kept China isolated from outside influence.
2. Most of the Chinese people lived in the river valleys.
3. Kublai Khan and Genghis Khan extended Mongol influence to other parts of Asia.
4. The city of Samarkand was part of the Yuan Empire.

40. The Treaty of Versailles angered many Germans after World War I because the treaty

1. divided Germany into Communist and non-Communist zones.
2. made Germany restore its emperor.
3. required all German-speaking Europeans to return to Germany.
4. forced Germany to pay large war reparations.

Base your answer to Question 41 on the passage that follows and on your knowledge of social studies.

. . . Our foundation rests upon trade, because, as you see, we have a large part of our capital invested [in it]. And therefore we shall have little for exchange operations, and we are forced to exert our ingenuity elsewhere. This, however, in my opinion, does not involve greater risk than one incurs in exchanges today, especially when no risks at sea are run [that is, when shipments by sea are insured]; nor does it bring smaller profits.

And [trade operations] are more legal and more honorable. In them we shall so govern ourselves that every day you will have more reason to be content; may God grant us His grace. . . .

—Letter to the home office of the Medici from the branch office at Bruges, May 14, 1464 (adapted)

41. This passage best illustrates circumstances that characterized the

　　1. Crusades.
　　2. Age of Reason.
　　3. Commercial Revolution.
　　4. Scientific Revolution.

42. The famine in Ukraine during the 1930s resulted from the Soviet government's attempt to

　　1. end a civil war.
　　2. implement free-market practices.
　　3. collectivize agriculture.
　　4. introduce crop rotation.

43. The Gupta civilization (fourth through sixth centuries) and the Maya civilization (third through tenth centuries) were similar in that both

　　1. built temple complexes and developed the concept of zero
　　2. eliminated standing armies and introduced an aristocracy
　　3. developed early democratic systems
　　4. were conquered by European imperialists

Base your answer to Question 44 on the bullet points below and on your knowledge of social studies.

- Egypt builds the Aswan Dam to control flooding and produce hydroelectric power.
- China builds the Three Gorges Dam to control flooding and improve trade.
- Brazil builds the Tucuruí Dam in the tropical rain forest to produce hydroelectric power.

44. Which conclusion can be drawn from these statements?

　　1. Societies often modify their environment to meet their needs.
　　2. Monsoons are needed for the development of societies.
　　3. Topography creates challenges that societies are unable to overcome.
　　4. Land features influence the development of diverse belief systems.

45. Which pair of belief systems share a belief that spirits reside in natural objects and forms?

  1. Hinduism and Confucianism
  2. Islam and Judaism
  3. Shintoism and Animism
  4. Christianity and Buddhism

46. Which statement most likely represents the view of a citizen of ancient Athens visiting Sparta?

  1. "The government and society in Sparta are so strict. The people have little voice in government."
  2. "I feel as though I have never left home. Everything here is the same as it is in Athens."
  3. "This society allows for more freedom of expression than I have ever experienced in Athens."
  4. "I have never heard of a society like Sparta that believes in only one God."

47. Which statement about the Tang Dynasty is a fact rather than an opinion?

  1. Technical advances would have been greater if the Tang Dynasty had lasted longer.
  2. China's best emperors came from the Tang Dynasty.
  3. The Tang emperors granted government jobs to scholars who passed examinations.
  4. The culture of the Tang Dynasty was superior to that of the Han Dynasty.

Base your answer to Question 48 on the diagram below and on your knowledge of social studies.

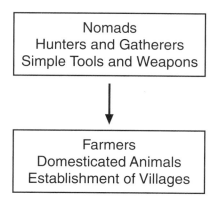

48. What is the best title for this diagram?

  1. Elements of Belief Systems
  2. Characteristics of Classical Civilizations
  3. Benefits of the Counter Reformation
  4. Changes during the Neolithic Revolution

49. During the fifteenth century, which two European countries began sea voyages of exploration?

1. Germany and Italy
2. Portugal and Spain
3. England and France
4. Russia and the Netherlands

50. During the late nineteenth century, which geographic factor helped attract European investors to southern Africa and Southeast Asia?

1. smooth coastlines
2. navigable rivers
3. natural resources
4. temperate climates

Part II

Thematic Essay Question

Directions: Write a well-organized essay that includes an introduction, several paragraphs addressing the task below, and a conclusion.

Theme: Change [Individuals Who Have Changed History]

> The beliefs and achievements of individuals have changed global history. These beliefs and achievements have had positive and negative effects on society.

Task:

> Identify *two* individuals who have changed global history and for *each*:
>
> - Explain *one* belief or achievement of that individual.
> - Discuss the positive and/or negative effects of the individual's belief or achievement.

You may use any individual from your study of global history *except* Nicholas Copernicus, Sir Isaac Newton, and Norman Borlaug. The individuals you identify must have had a major role in shaping global history and *must not be* **from the United States.** Some individuals that you might consider include Confucius, John Locke, Adam Smith, Simón Bolívar, Otto von Bismark, Vladimir Lenin, Mohandas Gandhi, Mao Zedong, Fidel Castro, Nelson Mandela.

You are *not* limited to these suggestions.

Guidelines:

In your essay, be sure to

- Address all aspects of the task
- Support the theme with relevant facts, examples, and details
- Use a logical and clear plan of organization
- Include an introduction and a conclusion that are beyond a simple restatement of the theme

Part III

Document-Based Questions

In developing your answer to Part III, be sure to keep this general definition in mind:

> **Discuss** means "to make observations about something using facts, reasoning, and argument; to present in some detail."

This question is based on the accompanying documents. It is designed to test your ability to work with historical documents. Some of the documents have been edited for the purposes of the question. As you analyze the documents, take into account the source of each document and any point of view that may be presented in the document.

Historical Context:

Throughout history, many different reasons for wars exist. These wars have led to both expected and unexpected outcomes.

Task:

Using information from the documents and your knowledge of global history, answer the questions that follow each document in Part III A. Your answers to the questions will help you write the Part III B essay in which you will be asked to

- Discuss the economic, social, and/or political reasons for wars
- Discuss the expected outcomes and the unexpected outcomes of wars

Part III A

Short-Answer Questions

Directions: Analyze the documents and answer the short-answer questions that follow each document in the space provided.

Document 1

. . . Though the great princes were apt to remain aloof, western knights responded readily to the appeal of the holy war. Their motives were in part genuinely religious. They were ashamed to continue fighting amongst themselves; they wanted to fight for the Cross. But there was also a land-hunger to incite them, especially in northern France, where the practice of primogeniture [eldest son inherited all] was being established. As a lord grew unwilling to divide his property and its offices, now beginning to be concentrated round a stone-built castle, his younger sons had to seek their fortunes elsewhere. There was a general restlessness and taste for adventure in the knightly class in France, most marked among the Normans, who were only a few generations removed from nomadic freebooters. The opportunity for combining Christian duty with the acquisition of land in a southern climate was very attractive. The Church had reason to be pleased with the progress of the movement. Could it not be applied also to the eastern frontier of Christendom? . . .

Source: Steven Runciman, *A History of the Crusades,* Cambridge University Press, 1951

1. According to this document, state *one* reason European knights and soldiers joined the Crusades.

_____

_____

Document 2

. . . One positive, undisputed result of the Crusades was a greatly expanded knowledge of geography gained by the West. With the coming of such vast hordes of invaders from all points of Europe, the veil of the "mysterious East" had been lifted for good. . . .

The Arab builders learned much about military masonry from the Crusaders who had brought this knowledge from Normandy and Italy. In constructing the famed Citadel of Cairo, Saladin had taken some of the features of Crusaders' castles he had observed up and down the Levant [lands of the Eastern Mediterranean]. Then, when the great cathedrals of Europe began to rise in a somewhat later period, their builders installed windows of stained glass made with a technique which had originated with the ancient Phoenicians of Syria and passed along by Syrian Arabs to Europeans living in the East. . . .

From a purely military point of view, the Crusades must be written off as a failure for the West, because, after changing hands so many times, the territory comprising the Christian Kingdom of Jerusalem reverted [returned] to the Moslems [Muslims] for good. But during that two-century struggle between East and West, it is plain now that each side made major contributions to the culture of the other. That vast interchange let in a few rays of light over a darkened Europe, and removed for good the wall of ignorance that had always existed between Europe and Asia. . . .

Source: "Legacy of the Crusades," *Aramco World,* VII, May 1956

2a. According to this document, what was *one* positive, unexpected outcome of the Crusades on Western civilization?

_____

_____

2b. According to this document, what was *one* positive, unexpected outcome of the Crusades on Muslim [Moslem] civilization?

_____

_____

2c. Based on this document, state *one* reason the West was disappointed with the outcome of the Crusades.

_____

_____

Document 3

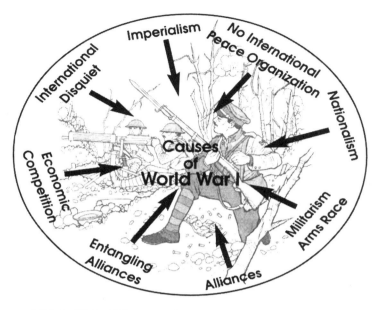

Source: Kirne and Stich, *Global History and Geography STAReview,* N & N, 2003

3. According to this diagram, what were *two* reasons for World War I?

_____

_____

_____

_____

Document 4

Selected Articles from the Treaty of Versailles (June 28, 1919)

Article 45:   As compensation for the destruction of the coal-mines in the north of France and as part payment towards the total reparation due from Germany for the damage resulting from the war, Germany cedes [gives] to France in full and absolute possession, with exclusive rights of exploitation, unencumbered and free from all debts and charges of any kind, the coal-mines situated in the Saar basin . . .

Article 119:   Germany renounces [surrenders] in favour of the Principal Allied and Associated Powers all her rights and titles over her oversea[s] possessions. . . .

Article 231:   The Allied and Associated Governments affirm [acknowledge] and Germany accepts the responsibility of Germany and her allies for causing all the loss and damage [for World War I] to which the Allied and Associated Governments and their nationals have been subjected as a consequence of the war imposed upon them by the aggression of Germany and her allies. . . .

Source: Versailles Treaty

4a. According to the document, how was France repaid for losses suffered during World War I?

_____

_____

4b. According to this document, what was a consequence of World War I for Germany?

_____

_____

Document 5

. . . State frontiers are established by human beings and may be changed by human beings. The fact that a nation has acquired an enormous territorial area is no reason why it should hold that territory perpetually [forever]. At most, the possession of such territory is a proof of the strength of the conqueror and the weakness of those who submit to him. And in this strength alone lives the right of possession. If the German people are imprisoned within an impossible territorial area and for that reason are face to face with a miserable future, this is not by the command of Destiny, and the refusal to accept such a situation is by no means a violation of Destiny's laws. For just as no Higher Power has promised more territory to other nations than to the German, so it cannot be blamed for an unjust distribution of the soil. The soil on which we now live was not a gift bestowed by Heaven on our forefathers. But they had to conquer it by risking their lives. So also in the future our people will not obtain territory, and therewith the means of existence, as a favour from any other people, but will have to win it by the power of a triumphant sword. . . .

Source: Adolf Hitler, *Mein Kampf*, Hurst and Blackett Ltd.

5. According to this document, what was *one* reason Adolf Hitler felt war was necessary?

_____

_____

Document 6

The Yalta Conference of the heads of the governments of the United States of America, the United Kingdom, and the Union of Soviet Socialist Republics (Soviet Union) which took place February 4–11, 1945, came to these conclusions.

DECLARATION ON LIBERATED EUROPE

. . . The establishment of order in Europe and the re-building of national economic life must be achieved by processes which will enable the liberated peoples to destroy the last vestiges [remains] of Nazism and Fascism and to create democratic institutions of their own choice. This is a principle of the Atlantic Charter—the right of all peoples to choose the form of government under which they will live—the restoration of sovereign rights and self-government to those peoples who have been forcibly deprived of them by the aggressor nations. . . .

POLAND

. . . A new situation has been created in Poland as a result of her complete liberation by the Red Army. This calls for the establishment of a Polish Provisional Government which can be more broadly based than was possible before the recent liberation of the Western part of Poland. The Provisional Government which is now functioning in Poland should therefore be reorganised on a broader democratic basis with the inclusion of democratic leaders from Poland itself and from Poles abroad. This new Government should then be called the Polish Provisional Government of National Unity. . . .

Source: *Protocol of the Proceedings of the Crimea (Yalta) Conference,* February, 1945 (adapted)

6. According to the Yalta Conference, state *two* ways Europe was expected to change as a result of World War II.

_____

_____

_____

_____

Document 7

. . . Our objectives in the Persian Gulf are clear, our goals defined and familiar:

- Iraq must withdraw from Kuwait completely, immediately, and without condition.
- Kuwait's legitimate government must be restored.
- The security and stability of the Persian Gulf must be assured.
- American citizens abroad must be protected.

These goals are not ours alone. They have been endorsed [supported] by the U.N. Security Council five times in as many weeks. Most countries share our concern for principle. And many have a stake in the stability of the Persian Gulf. This is not, as Saddam Hussein would have it, the United States against Iraq. It is Iraq against the world. . . .

Source: Speech by President George H. W. Bush, 1990

7. According to this document, what were *two* reasons President George H. W. Bush was concerned about the Persian Gulf region in 1990?

_____

_____

_____

_____

Document 8

Throughout the 1990s and before the United States went to war with Iraq in 2003, some people were concerned about the continuing actions of Iraq and Saddam Hussein.

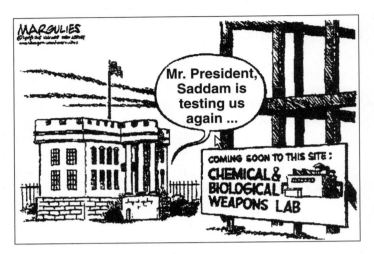

Source: Jimmy Margulies, *The Record,* 1998 (adapted)

8. Based on this 1998 cartoon, what was *one* unexpected outcome of the Persian Gulf War?

_____

_____

_____

_____

Part III B

Directions: Write a well-organized essay that includes an introduction, several paragraphs, and a conclusion. Use evidence from at least five documents in your essay. Support your response with relevant facts, examples, and details. Include additional outside information.

Historical Context:

Throughout history, many different reasons for wars exist. These wars have led to both expected and unexpected outcomes.

Task: Using information from the documents and your knowledge of global history, answer the questions that follow each document in Part A. Your answers to the questions will help you write the Part B essay in which you will be asked to

- Discuss the economic, social, and/or political reasons for wars
- Discuss the expected outcomes and the unexpected outcomes of wars

Guidelines:

In your essay, be sure to:

- Develop all aspects of the task
- Incorporate information from at least five documents
- Incorporate relevant outside information
- Support the theme with relevant facts, examples, and details.
- Use a logical and clear plan of organization, including an introduction and a conclusion that are beyond a restatement of the theme.

Answer Key

1. 3	**14.** 2	**27.** 1	**39.** 3
2. 1	**15.** 3	**28.** 1	**40.** 4
3. 3	**16.** 2	**29.** 3	**41.** 3
4. 4	**17.** 2	**30.** 2	**42.** 3
5. 2	**18.** 2	**31.** 1	**43.** 1
6. 4	**19.** 3	**32.** 3	**44.** 1
7. 3	**20.** 1	**33.** 1	**45.** 3
8. 1	**21.** 4	**34.** 3	**46.** 1
9. 3	**22.** 3	**35.** 3	**47.** 3
10. 1	**23.** 1	**36.** 2	**48.** 4
11. 2	**24.** 3	**37.** 3	**49.** 2
12. 3	**25.** 2	**38.** 3	**50.** 3
13. 1	**26.** 2		

Part I: Answer Explanations

1. **Correct Answer: (3)** This statement is referring to the establishment of Israel. The British were committed to setting up a permanent Jewish state in Palestine under the Balfour Declaration. With the support of the United Nations, the promise became reality at the end of World War II. The statement does not provide information on the creations of Jordan, Poland, and Ethiopia. *(Twentieth Century Since 1945)*

2. **Correct Answer: (1)** The correct chronological order of historical periods in Europe history is the Golden Age of Greece, Medieval Europe, the Italian Renaissance, and the Enlightenment. To be successful with this question type, always choose an item that must be first or last in the sequence. Then, use the process of elimination to come up with the answer. *(Global Interactions)*

3. **Correct Answer: (3)** Locke's *Two Treatises of Government,* Rousseau's *The Social Contract,* and Montesquieu's *The Spirit of the Laws* were works written during the Enlightenment. John Locke was *the* Enlightenment thinker, and he will always be associated with the Enlightenment. The Middle Ages had no big thinkers, and the Renaissance and Reformation were the periods that led to the Enlightenment and John Locke. *(Age of Revolution)*

4. **Correct Answer: (4)** The activities of Mother Teresa are most closely associated with the needs of the poor and health care. Mother Teresa worked hard to make sure that all people, regardless of wealth, had access to health care. Mother Teresa was not a nationalist working toward political freedom or independence, or an industrialist working toward open market, but rather focused on human rights issues she could fix. *(Global Connections/Interactions)*

5. **Correct Answer: (2)** The statement that best describes an impact of the computer on the global economy is that companies now market more products worldwide. The Internet provides companies around the world with reliable access to communication, which helps to promote international trade. On the other hand, tariffs on imports can have a harmful effect on international trade. Although the standard of living of some countries has benefited from the computer, wages have not risen dramatically for most people in developing nations. The prices of oil and other resources have not been affected by computers and continue to be high in most industrial nations. *(Global Connections/Interactions)*

6. **Correct Answer: (4)** The main idea of this political cartoon would be that reading about world famine is different from experiencing it. The cartoon shows two different boys asking for supper, one who obviously has no experience of famine and one who is living in it currently. The cartoon does not isolate the United States and Africa, nor does it blame pollution or the governments in Africa for world famine. *(Global Connections/Interactions)*

7. **Correct Answer: (3)** Both Inca farmers and Japanese farmers adapted a geographic feature of their countries by building terraces into the mountainsides. The mountain ranges that lay in these farmers' lands are used to their advantage, adapting the geography to suit the peoples. Inca and Japanese farmers did not engage in overseas expansion, grow crops in the desert, or reclaim land from the sea by building dikes. *(Global Connections/Interactions)*

8. **Correct Answer: (1)** A major cause of the civil wars in many Central American nations in the 1970s and 1980s was the economic differences between social classes. In many of the nations, those who were poor were very poor, and violence was their only resort to avoid starving. There had already been an end of slavery in the encomienda system, as well as rapid economic reform and oil production policies. None of these issues led to civil war the way that the economic differences did. *(Twentieth Century Since 1945)*

9. **Correct Answer: (3)** This quotation is associated with the principles of communism. In a pamphlet entitled the *Communist Manifesto,* Karl Marx and Friedrich Engels provided an argument for communism. Contrary to capitalism, communal ownership of property is critical in a classless society. They encouraged a class struggle between the "haves" and "have-nots" and believed that the poor would eventually revolt. Militarism is the build-up of the armed forces in preparation for war. Imperialism is a policy in which a powerful nation exerts extensive control over every aspect of life of a weaker nation. *(Crises and Achievement [1900–1945])*

10. **Correct answer: (1)** The Meiji Restoration is the occurrence in Japanese history described in the passage. The period refers to Japan's effort to modernize its social infrastructure during the late nineteenth century. Believing in militarism, Meiji rulers encouraged a massive buildup of the armed forces and military technology. Socially, the Japanese people benefited from the introduction of banking, public education, and new transportation systems. There were no mentions of the Tokugawa shogunate and absorption of other religions in the passage. *(Age of Revolution)*

11. **Correct Answer: (2)** The author of the passage suggests that Japan accepted new technologies in order to modernize. To avoid being a target of imperialism like China and India, Japan realized that modernization was necessary to stay competitive with other western nations. Japan began to exert its power on others by becoming more militaristic and less dependent on foreign nations. However, these ideas are not mentioned in the passage. *(Age of Revolution)*

12. **Correct Answer: (3)** The technology of papermaking traveled from China to Baghdad along the Silk Roads. Starting in China and moving westward, paper moved along the same trails that silk traveled in the same time period. The trail is too far north to be a Saharan caravan trail, too far south to be the Trans-Siberian Railway, and too far east to be the Suez Canal. *(Expanding Zones of Exchange)*

13. **Correct Answer: (1)** A totalitarian society is one in which the government controls most aspects of life. Whenever there is a question with the word *totalitarian* in it, look at the first part of this word, *total,* to remember that totalitarian rulers control every aspect of life in their country that they can. A government ruled by someone who claims divine authority would be a theocracy, while a state that is the servant of its citizens or a state where citizens can publicly criticize the actions of their leaders would be a democracy. *(Methodology of Global History/Geography)*

14. **Correct Answer: (2)** The statement that Athens had a better culture than that of Sparta would be an opinion rather than a fact about Greek civilization. There is no definitive way to prove that Athens had a better culture than Sparta. It is proven that boys in Sparta were trained to be soldiers and that Socrates, Plato, and Aristotle were Greek philosophers. It is false that many adults in Athens did not have the right to vote. Therefore, the only possible opinion is that Athens had a better culture than Sparta. *(Ancient World)*

15. Correct Answer: (3) The Japanese print illustrates cultural diffusion. The imagery, combining traditional Japanese garb with Western instruments (such as piano), shows how Japanese culture was incorporating Western cultures. This would be the opposite of isolationism or ethnocentrism, which would show prints in which Japanese women would be playing Japanese instruments. *(First Global Age)*

16. Correct Answer: (2) This print was most likely created during the Meiji Restoration. The ideals of cultural diffusion and incorporating Western technology into Japan was prevalent at this time period, and the Japanese government wanted people to incorporate Western culture and ideals into their lives, to bring Japan into a stage of world dominance. *(First Global Age)*

17. Correct Answer: (2) All the elements identified in the illustration contributed to German unification. The Prussian wars, as well as the North German Confederation, all tie into Bismarck and Prussian King Wilhelm seizing and solidifying power, creating a unified Germany. Interdependence was the pattern before the unification, and the various wars have nothing to do with imperialism or apathy. *(Age of Revolution)*

18. Correct Answer: (2) The set of events in the correct chronological order is the Treaty of Versailles → World War II → the Korean War. The Middle Ages occurred before the Renaissance, the Crusades occurred before the Reformation, and the French Revolution occurred before the Bolshevik Revolution. The only choice in correct order, the only choice that has the previous affecting the next choice, is choice two. *(Methodology of Global History/Geography)*

19. Correct Answer: (3) Geographic location was one reason that some Italian cities developed into major commercial and cultural centers during the thirteenth and fourteenth centuries. The major city-states such as Venice and Florence became important commercial links to Asia. Some Italian merchants, who benefited from enormous profits, became patrons of the arts. Their financial contribution was an important catalyst in the artistic and intellectual rebirth, referred to as the Renaissance. *(Global Interactions)*

20. Correct Answer: (1) The policy that France, Britain, and Italy chose to follow at the meeting in question is appeasement. During the Munich Conference, the quote says that the Big Four would give Czechoslovakia to Hitler in exchange for peace. This is the very definition of appeasement, where you give the aggressor what he wants in exchange for peace. Self-determination, liberation, or pacification did not fit into this quote. *(Crises and Achievement [1900–1945])*

21. Correct Answer: (4) According to the cartoonist, India's progress in becoming a democratic nation has been slow since 1947. Although India became an independent nation in 1947, India has not been successful in promoting democracy for its people. The cartoonist could point out that religious conflicts and the caste system have been barriers to democracy in India. *(Twentieth Century Since 1945)*

22. Correct Answer: (3) The practice in medieval Europe that was most similar to a Japanese warrior's *code of bushido* was chivalry. The code of chivalry defined the way in which a knight should act and how he should treat others, much like the code of bushido did for samurais. Indulgences, serfdom, and tributes, while all medieval terms, were not similar to the code of bushido. *(Ancient World)*

23. **Correct Answer: (1)** One characteristic common to these areas is that they all have low population density. The Siberian Plain, Sahara Desert, Amazon Basin, and Mongolian Steppes are all geographic landmarks that are difficult ones in which to maintain a civilization and, therefore, have few peoples living there. The areas are not all located between major river valleys, nor are they major religious centers, and not all of them have large areas of valuable farmland. *(Methodology of Global History/Geography)*

24. **Correct Answer: (3)** Conflicts between Hutu and Tutsi, Ottoman Turks and Armenians, and Soviets and Ukrainian kulaks all resulted in massacres or genocide. For example, Armenians were victimized by the Ottoman Turks through heavy taxation and ethnic discrimination. Armenians began to organize a nationalist movement in the early twentieth century. The suppression of this movement led to a massacre of Armenians. *(Global Connections/Interactions)*

25. **Correct Answer: (2)** The goal of the European Union is to improve the economic prosperity of Europe. Once called the European Economic Community (EEC) and European Community, the European Union was formed in 1992 to promote free trade by removing tariffs and other restrictions. The introduction of the euro, the official currency of the European Union, further promoted trade. The member nations also benefited from the universal banking system. *(Twentieth Century Since 1945)*

26. **Correct Answer: (2)** The main idea of the cartoon is that the battle against terrorists will be long and difficult. The cartoonist shows this by using the sewage system to symbolize terrorism. The exterminator is going in to clean out everything, which may take a while. The cartoon does not deal with nuclear weapons, equipment needed to fight terrorists, or methods for dealing with global terrorism and creating a consensus. *(Twentieth Century Since 1945)*

27. **Correct Answer: (1)** An important result of the Neolithic Revolution was that food supplies became more reliable. The Neolithic Revolution, also known as the Agricultural Revolution, led to the development of permanent settlements. The people became less nomadic as a result. The domestication of animals and cultivation of crops led to a significant increase in food supplies. Hence, humans no longer had to rely on hunting and gathering. *(Ancient World)*

28. **Correct Answer: (1)** The concept being referred to in this passage is the dynastic cycle. The rule of the king, receiving the decree of Heaven, refers to the dynastic cycle. Because the passage refers to a king and not a queen, it would not be a matriarchal society. *(Ancient World)*

29. **Correct Answer: (3)** The global interaction illustrated by these statements is the Columbian Exchange. The goods coming to Europe, such as maize (corn) and potatoes, as well as the Spanish language being used in Latin America is the definition of the Columbian Exchange. This definition would not fit the Silk Road, the Crusades, or the Scramble for Africa, because none of these events dealt with Latin America. *(Global Interactions)*

30. **Correct Answer: (2)** Geography affected both Napoleon's invasion and Hitler's invasion of Russia because the climate created obstacles to success. The Russian winter is exceptionally cold and difficult to transport large troops through, a lesson that both Hitler and Napoleon learned the hard way. No main deserts or warm-water ports exist in Russia, and the tundra hurt transport of troops, it didn't help it. *(Crises and Achievement [1900–1945])*

31. Correct Answer: (1) One effect of Alexander the Great's conquests was the expansion of Hellenistic culture. Alexander spread Hellenistic culture—the fusion of Greek, Persian, Egyptian, and Indian cultures—into the realms he conquered, creating a new trans-European culture. Alexander the Great predated the Christian church and the Silk Roads, and he had nothing to do with Mayan leaders. *(Expanding Zones of Exchange)*

32. Correct Answer: (3) This 1995 cartoon is suggesting that communism may return if democracy fails in Russia. Within the cartoon, a hammer and sickle, symbols of the USSR's flag, are shown. These icons are seen in a case saying "In Case of Emergency," which means that if all else fails, the ideas of the USSR, such as communism, will return. *(Crises and Achievement [1900–1945])*

33. Correct Answer: (1) The innovation that had the greatest impact on the Protestant Reformation was the movable-type printing press. The invention of the printing press led to more books being published, more people reading, and questions arising about the role of the Catholic Church. The Mercator map projection, magnetic compass, and triangular sail had a large impact on the Age of Exploration but had little to do with the Protestant Reformation. *(Age of Revolution)*

34. Correct Answer: (3) A study of Aztec, Maya, and Inca agricultural systems would show that these civilizations adapted to their environments with creative farming techniques. In order to farm on the hillsides, for example, the Incans used terraces rather than relying on planting crops on flat land. Similarly, the Aztecs met the challenges of geography by planting crops on their "floating garden." *(First Global Age)*

35. Correct Answer: (3) The conditions described in the passage occurred during the Industrial Revolution. By discussing Manchester, crowded streets, and smoke blackening everything, you can deduce that the Industrial Revolution is what is being discussed. The Age of Discovery, the Renaissance, and the Green Revolution all had different origins than Manchester or England. *(Age of Revolution)*

36. Correct Answer: (2) The Byzantine Empire had the greatest influence on the development of early Russia. The early Russians adopted the Eastern Orthodox religion, the Cyrillic alphabet, and different styles of art and architecture through extensive exchanges with Byzantine missionaries. This is an example of cultural diffusion. *(Global Interactions)*

37. Correct Answer: (3) Philosophers of the Enlightenment period believed that society could best be improved by applying reason and the laws of nature. The main belief of the Enlightenment was to apply reason to life, and understand the basics of human nature. Philosophers were moving away from relying on faith and divine right, as well as simply borrowing ideas from ancient Greece and Rome. While some Enlightenment philosophers, such as Machiavelli, were studying successful leaders, most did not. *(Age of Revolution)*

38. Correct Answer: (3) The heading that best completes the partial outline is Turning Points in History. Each of the events in the outline represents major points in history where events have caused a change in human history. Not all of the events are based on revolutions, war and rebellions, or economic change. Rather, the *best* choice is Turning Points in History. *(Methodology of Global History/Geography)*

39. Correct Answer: (3) The information on the map supports the statement that Kublai Khan and Genghis Khan extended Mongol influence to other parts of Asia. The influence of Kublai Khan and Genghis Khan spread over their realms, evident by the lines moving farther and farther out. None of the other choices fits into the map, such as the Yuan Dynasty keeping China isolated or that the Chinese mostly lived in river valleys. *(Global Interactions)*

40. Correct Answer: (4) The Treaty of Versailles angered many Germans after World War I because the treaty forced Germany to pay large war reparations. The Germans signed the Versailles Treaty, accepting sole responsibility for World War I. In addition to war reparations, the treaty forced the Germans to cede territories to other nations. The Versailles Treaty was in part to blame for the rise of the Nazi Party. The harsh treaty paved the road for World War II. *(Crises and Achievement [1900–1945])*

41. Correct Answer: (3) This passage best illustrates circumstances that characterized the Commercial Revolution. The increase in international trade created a need for an effective banking system. The Commercial Revolution marked the emergence of insurance and joint-stock companies. *(Global Interactions)*

42. Correct Answer: (3) The famine in Ukraine during the 1930s resulted from the Soviet government's attempt to collectivize agriculture. By creating collective farms, the Soviet leadership hoped to create an adequate supply of grain for everyone. The famine was not a result of the Soviets' attempting to end a civil war, implement free-market practices, or introducing crop rotation. These would have probably helped to feed the Ukrainian people, instead of the collectivization that led to a famine. *(Crises and Achievement [1900–1945])*

43. Correct Answer: (1) The Gupta civilization (fourth through sixth centuries) and the Maya civilization (third through tenth centuries) were similar in that both built temple complexes and developed the concept of zero. These two powerful civilizations saw advancements in art, literature, science, and mathematics. The development of the concept of zero led to advances in mathematics, particularly in the field of algebra. The temple complexes, built for religious purposes, demonstrated their architectural ingenuity. *(Expanding Zones of Exchange)*

44. Correct Answer: (1) A conclusion that can be drawn from these statements is that societies often modify their environment to meet their needs. Devastating floods often caused severe loss in property damages and human lives. To overcome challenges posed by a nation's topography, dams were being constructed to control flooding. In addition, dams were being used to generate electric power. *(Twentieth Century Since 1945)*

45. Correct Answer: (3) The two belief systems that share the belief that spirits reside in natural objects and forms are Shintoism and Animism. Both of these belief systems use natural objects and forms, such as animals, as homes for deities and other spirits. Hinduism, Confucianism, Islam, Judaism, Christianity, and Buddhism are belief systems in their own rights, but none of them is based in the belief that spirits reside in natural objects. *(Ancient World)*

46. Correct Answer: (1) The statement that would most likely represent the view of a citizen of ancient Athens visiting Sparta is, "The government and society in Sparta are so strict. The people have little voice in government." Athens, a Greek city-state, was home to the oldest democracy in the world. However, only citizens in Athens were able to participate in the decision-making process. This is known as a *direct democracy.* Sparta, another Greek city-state, lacked the privileges of democracy that the citizens of Athens enjoyed. Sparta, a military society, controlled every aspect of citizens' lives as they served the city-state. For example, all young boys were required to go through rigorous war training. *(Ancient World)*

47. Correct Answer: (3) The statement about the Tang Dynasty that is fact rather than an opinion is that the Tang emperors granted government jobs to scholars who passed examinations. This statement is a fact, because it can be and, in fact, is proven by records from the Tang Dynasty. The statements that technical advances would have been greater, or that China's best emperors came from the Tang Dynasty, or even that the Tang dynasty was superior to the Han Dynasty cannot be proven and, therefore, are opinions. *(Ancient World)*

48. Correct Answer: (4) The best title for this diagram is Changes during the Neolithic Revolution. Moving from one place to another, nomads during the Paleolithic Age were hunter-gatherers. Also known as the Agricultural Revolution, the Neolithic Age marked the discovery of farming. Instead of hunting and gathering, people began to plant crops and domesticated animals on permanent sites. *(Ancient World)*

49. Correct Answer: (2) During the fifteenth century, the two European countries that began sea voyages of exploration were Portugal and Spain. Partly due to economics and partly due to location, Portugal and Spain were both able to send ships overseas long before other nations had the resources. Germany and Italy were still divided, England and France weren't wealthy enough, and Russia and the Netherlands didn't have the resources necessary to lead to exploration. *(First Global Age)*

50. Correct Answer: (3) During the late nineteenth century, natural resources helped attract European investors to southern Africa and Southeast Asia. Unlike smooth coastlines, temperate climates and navigable rivers were desirable geographic factors to facilitate trade. However, European investors were only attracted by the regions' natural resources such as rubber, gold, and cotton. The investors used the natural resources to produce profitable manufactured goods during the Industrial Revolution. *(Age of Revolution)*

Part II: Key Points to Include

Person	Idea/Belief	How it changed nation/region
Confucius	Relationship between people divided superior/inferior	Provided emperors of China with Mandate of Heaven
	People are inferior to government; should accept emperor unquestioningly	Gave Chinese people a social hierarchy; created relationships
John Locke	Social Contract, government needs to provide basic human rights	British people began to believe they were entitled to these rights
	If government fails, you can overthrow it (two treatises on government)	Two treatises used as justification to overthrow James II (Glorious Revolution)
Adam Smith	Government has no role in business	English market runs without government
	Laissez-faire economy the best one	Survival of fittest in business sense
Simón Bolívar	South America should be free from colonial control	Fought to free Venezuela and others from Spanish control
	Strongly nationalist	Created independent nation of Venezuela
Otto von Bismarck	Germany should be unified under Prussia	Unified nation of Germany
	Germany united by 'blood and iron'	Created Germany into a modernized nation and European powerhouse
Vladimir Lenin	Communist, wanted Russia to be communist without czar	Entered Russian Revolution, led Bolshevik Revolution
		1st head of Soviet Union
Mohandas Gandhi	Independence for India	Led nonviolent battle for independence
	Nonviolent protest	Won independence for India from British
Mao Zedong	Communist leader in China	Sucessfully led Chinese communists to control China
	Believed in Maoist communism for China	Created the PRC that still exists today
Fidel Castro	Communist military leader, anti-Batista and corrupt government	Led Cuban Revolution, controlled Cuba
		Made policies for Cuba that affect world from Cuban Missile Crisis to today
Nelson Mandela	Leader of ANC, anti-apartheid	Once released, ran for president; won
	Arrested for belief, stuck in jail for decades	Mandela became 1st black president of South Africa

Part III A: Document Short Answers

Document 1:

1. One reason European knights and soldiers joined the Crusades is because they wanted to acquire land in a southern climate.

Document 2:

2a. One positive, unexpected outcome of the Crusades on Western civilization was a greatly expanded knowledge of geography.

2b. One positive, unexpected outcome of the Crusades on Muslim civilizations was increased trade with the West.

2c. One reason the West was disappointed with the outcome of the Crusades was because the Kingdom of Jerusalem was given to the Muslims.

Document 3:

3. According to the diagram, two reasons for World War I were entangling alliances and international disquiet. [There could be many answers to this particular question.]

Document 4:

4a. France was repaid for losses suffered during World War I by reparation payments from Germany.

4b. A consequence of World War I for Germany was that it had to renounce its colonial empire.

Document 5:

5. One reason Adolf Hitler felt war was necessary was to gain territory so as to provide a better future for the German people.

Document 6:

6. According to the Yalta Conference, two ways Europe was expected to change as a result of World War II by putting new democratic governments in place and by getting rid of Nazism and Fascism.

Document 7:

7. Two reasons that President George H. W. Bush was concerned about the Persian Gulf region in 1990 were that Iraq had invaded Kuwait, and that American citizens abroad needed protection.

Document 8:

8. One unexpected outcome of the Persian Gulf War was that it did not put an end to the problem of Iraq and Saddam Hussein for the United States.

Part III B: Key Points to Include

	Reasons for Wars	Expected Outcomes	Unexpected Outcomes
The Crusades	Gaining land (Document 1) Spreading Christianity (Document 1)	Control of Jerusalem (Document 2)	New products, techniques of building (Document 2) Military failure for the West (Document 2)
World War I	Economic competition, imperialism (Document 3) Nationalism (Document 3) Militarism, alliances (Document 3)	Land given to French (Document 4) Germany held responsible for starting war, paying for damages (Document 4)	Loss of Germany's colonies/ land to France (Document 4)
World War II	Survival (Document 5) Nationalism (Document 5) Obtaining land (Document 5)	Replacement of Nazis and Fascists in Europe (Document 8) Right of self-government (Document 8)	Liberation of Poland by Soviets (Document 6) Destruction of Nazism and Fascism in Europe (Document 6)
Persian Gulf War	Stability in the Persian Gulf region (Document 7) Withdrawal of Iraqis from Kuwait (Document 7)	Restoration of Kuwait's government (Document 7)	Continued threat from Saddam Hussein (Document 8)

How to Write an Essay

The Global History and Geography Examination requires you to write two essays. The first is the Thematic Essay Question, which is worth 15 percent of the exam. You are presented with a specific overall theme and then a task. Over the years, these themes have covered such topics as Economic Systems, Global Problems, and Change. These essays require you to use your knowledge and study of global history and geography to write the essay, and they usually offer you suggestions on which you can base your writing.

The second essay is the Document-Based Essay. You are presented with a series of short documents, diagrams, cartoons, and so on, followed by a series of short-answer questions and then the essay. You will be given the historical context of the essay, the specific task that outlines what should be covered, and guidelines to make sure you've written a cogent essay. You are required to write a well-organized essay that includes a proper introduction, the basic content, and a conclusion.

To that end, this section will give you an overview on the basics of clear and effective writing. During the examination, you will not necessarily have time for all of the steps that we've provided here, but you will at least know the basics, and many of these steps can be done in your head—without actually writing them down. Once you have the preliminaries out of the way, it is then time to tackle the specific writing assignments.

In addition, at the end of this writing section, we have provided sample Thematic Essays that have appeared on earlier Regents exams, so you can have an idea of the wide range of topics that might be covered on your exam. While it is not necessary to actually write these essays here, you will be well-served to look them over, think about them, and see if you can visualize how you might approach each one. These cover a wide range of subjects and if you are unclear about the topics presented here, these will help you focus on the areas that you might want to review.

Prewriting: How to Begin a Writing Assignment

Writing is a process. The formula good writers follow consists of prewriting, writing, and rewriting, or revising and editing. This allows their work to emerge in a series of small manageable steps.

Your main purpose in writing is to inform, persuade, or entertain. Defining your purpose or goal is the first step. Select a topic that is narrow enough to be explained within your page limitations. A thesis, unlike a topic, is a single statement that makes an assertion about a topic. It is usually placed somewhere in the introduction of an essay. Often, a thesis sentence will give the reader a clear overview of the essay by stating the main ideas. Generally, if you choose a topic that is interesting to you, then your reader will find it interesting too.

The Steps in Writing

Although it is a process, writing doesn't progress as neatly from one step to the next as does, for example, baking a cake or changing a tire. Roughly speaking, when you write, you:

- Decide on a topic (or have a topic assigned to you)
- Explore ideas about the topic through thinking, reading, listening, and so on
- Formulate a thesis or main idea and decide what points you want to make to support it
- Select details and examples (from reading, research, personal experience)
- Decide on the order in which you'll present your ideas and examples
- Write a first draft; edit and revise for content, style, and writing mechanics; write a final draft

At any time during this process, you may need to stop and go back several steps. For example, when you're selecting details and examples, you may realize your topic is too broad or your thesis statement weak. Or when you're organizing your points, you may see that the thesis you *thought* you were developing isn't the one that you are developing. Often the act of writing itself generates new ideas you may want to pursue. Even as late as your final draft you may decide that the organization isn't working, or you may spot a flaw in your argument that causes you to throw out much of what you've written and rework the rest. The most realistic way to view writing is not as a straight line but as a back-and-forward movement. Take that into account when deciding how long you'll need to finish a writing assignment.

Types of Writing

The writing you're required to do in your lifetime varies-for example, timed writings and essay questions on exams (like the Global History and Geography examination; autobiographical essays for college applications; high-school and college papers on a variety of subjects; business letters, proposals, and reports related to your work. In most of your writing you'll be doing one of the following:

- Describing a person, place, or thing
- Telling a story or recounting an incident
- Reporting information

- Providing instructions or explaining a process
- Arguing a position or proving a point
- Analyzing something-a text, a theory, an attitude, or an event
- Comparing various documents

The techniques you use will overlap. For example, if you're writing a descriptive essay about your Uncle Mark, you might narrate an incident that reveals his personality.

Most—though not all—writing assignments focus on argument and analysis. But within an essay arguing a position, you might use descriptive and narrative techniques. In a paper taking a stand against capital punishment, you might include a vivid description of a gas chamber, or recount the steps of an execution, or even narrate an incident. In choosing your approach to any writing task, be guided by your purpose and the best way to fulfill it.

Understanding Your Assignment

If you're given a writing assignment, fulfilling it is your main purpose. Understand what you are asked to do. In an examination question, for example, if you're asked to analyze how an author's techniques contribute to his theme, and if you describe the theme thoroughly but don't discuss the techniques, then you've failed to fulfill the assignment. Or if in a psychology class you're asked to compare and contrast two recent theories about selective amnesia, and you write five pages on one of the theories and only half a page on the other, you probably haven't done what is required.

Writing on the job is no different. For example, if you need to write a testing protocol for a new product, you should include such things as a detailed description of the testing samples and the control group, the conditions of testing, materials and equipment, all the steps of the tests, relevant formulas and equations, and the methods to be used in evaluating results. If after the testing your manager asks for a summary of the results, you should provide them as clearly, honestly, and succinctly as you can. You may need to include a brief explanation of the tests, but you won't want to give a blow-by-blow account.

Whether you're writing in school or at work, make sure that you understand your task. Then, in planning what you'll write, aim everything you say at achieving that purpose.

Understanding Your Audience

For whom are you writing? Before you begin, think about your **audience.** A reader is at the other end of your writing, and you should keep that reader in mind.

Student writers sometimes think that their audience is a stuffy instructor who will be impressed by big words and long sentences. But most teachers know good, clear writing when they see it. Most can distinguish between solid content and inflated trivia. If you have little to say but dress it up in overblown prose with commas in all the right places, you won't fare as well as someone who has something to say and says it clearly, even with a few mechanical errors.

The reason you're writing and the audience you're writing for are closely related, so be realistic. If you're writing a letter to a surfing magazine praising a new board, you'll use different language and a different tone than you will in an essay on Mikhail Gorbachev's success in attempting to modernize Russia in the late 1980s. Though both audiences want to understand and be interested in what you write, they'll expect and respond to different styles. Changing your language, style, or tone to meet specific circumstances is fine. But don't make the mistake of thinking that you can be straightforward in the letter to the surfing magazine while you should strive to sound important in the paper on Gorbachev.

Ask yourself some specific questions about your audience before you begin. Among some things to consider:

- **Are you writing for people in a particular field, such as social studies, English literature, or biology?** Can you assume knowledge of the terminology and concepts you'll be using, or do you need to define them in the paper? Will you need to provide extensive background information on the subject you plan to discuss, or will a brief summary be enough?

- **What expectations does your audience have?** An audience of marine biologists will have different expectations from an article on marine biology than will a general audience, for example.

- **Are you writing for someone who insists on certain writing practices or who has pet peeves?** One instructor may require a five-paragraph essay, or another may forbid the use of intentional sentence fragments. Be aware of any requirements or restrictions. On grammar, punctuation, and usage questions, if you aren't sure about a particular instructor, you're safest taking a conservative path.

- **What is the reading level of your audience?** Instructions and explanations written for fourth graders shouldn't include college-level vocabulary, for example.

- **Are you writing for an audience that is likely to agree or disagree with your point of view?** Consider this question if you're writing an argumentative or editorial piece. It can make a difference in the language you select, the amount of proof you offer, and the tone you use. An editorial for a small-town paper on the importance of family values, for example, is less likely to encounter resistance from the audience than an editorial on legalizing drugs.

Guidelines for Choosing a Topic

Often you're assigned a topic to write about or asked to choose among several. When you must create your own, keep in mind these points:

- **Choose a topic appropriate to the length of your paper.** Generally, students pick topics that are too broad to be adequately covered. Narrow topics lead to close observation, while broad topics lead to generalizations and sketchy development. If you're writing a five-page paper, don't write on the history of women's rights; instead, write about one incident in the history of women's rights. Even a personal or descriptive essay will be better if you choose a narrow topic—my childhood in a small town, for example, rather than my childhood, or my uncle's barn, rather than the Midwest.

- **Avoid a topic that will tempt you to summarize rather than to discuss or analyze.** Don't choose *the plot of Macbeth* but how *the final scene of Macbeth illustrates the play's theme.* The second topic is narrower and less likely to lead to summary. When considering a topic, ask yourself if it can lead to a reasonable thesis.

- **Choose a topic that interests you.** If you don't care about limiting cigarette advertising, don't select it as a topic for a persuasive essay. You'll have more to say and write better on something you care about.

- **If your assignment requires research, choose a topic on which you can find material.** Even when you aren't writing a research paper, make sure that you've picked a subject that you can develop with sufficient details.

- **After you've picked a topic, don't be afraid to change it if it isn't working out.** Instructors would rather you write a good essay than that you grind out pages on something you realize was a bad choice.

Topic versus Thesis

Don't confuse a topic with a main idea or thesis. The topic provides the subject; the thesis makes an assertion about that subject. Here are a few examples of topics that you might be assigned in school or on an exam:

- Compare and contrast X's poem "To *a Wolf*" with Y's poem *"The Happy Meercat."* Consider both theme and technique.

- Discuss the following statement: "No matter how much we may deplore human rights violations in China, the United States should not impose sanctions on the Chinese government." Do you agree or disagree? Support your opinion.

- Analyze Shakespeare's use of clothing imagery in *King Lear.*

- Describe an incident in your life that caused you to change an opinion or attitude.

- "The Civil War had much more to do with economics than with morality." Do you agree or disagree with this statement? Support your opinion.

Two of these topics (the second and fifth) ask the writer to argue a position. A sentence expressing that position is a **thesis** statement. A thesis statement for the second topic might be: *Imposing sanctions on China would be a mistake because it would hurt the American economy, because sanctions are notoriously unsuccessful as a way to force change, and because the United States should not interfere in the internal policies of other countries.*

While the remaining three topics don't ask the writer to take a position, for a good essay on any of these topics, the writer should formulate a thesis. A thesis statement for the first might be, *Although both poet X and poet Y show appreciation for their subjects, poet X's Wolf symbolizes the separation between humans and other animals, while poet Y's Meercat symbolizes the connection between all living things.* With this thesis statement, the writer makes a point about the topic and sets up a direction for the essay.

Writing a Thesis Statement

Whenever you write a paper analyzing, discussing, comparing, identifying causes or effects, or arguing a position, you should be able to write a thesis statement. You can refine and improve it as you go along, but try to begin with a one-sentence statement. A thesis statement can help you steer a straight course, avoiding the danger of digression.

Make your thesis statement say something. Don't be satisfied with weak generalities that fail to zero in on your main point. The following are examples of pseudo-thesis statements:

> Poets X and Y make important points about animals in their poems *"To a Wolf" and "The Happy Meercat."*

> People hold different opinions as to whether it is wise to impose sanctions on China because of their human rights violations.

> Shakespeare uses quite a bit of clothing imagery in *King Lear.*

None of these statements provides a clear direction for an essay because the assertions they make are so vague, they are useless. A better thesis statement for the third example might be, *Clothing images in King Lear reflect the development of Lear from a man blinded by appearances to a man able to face the naked truth.* Remember that the creation of a thesis statement is important to the way you approach your topic, helping you direct your thinking as well as your writing.

Avoiding Fallacies

As you write be careful to avoid logic fallacies and ideological reasoning. *Logic fallacies* are problems in thinking or connecting ideas. Common fallacies include:

- **Ad Hominem:** Also called name-calling, this fallacy is an attack either directly or indirectly on a person.
  Bob can't be right because he is an idiot.
- **Bandwagon/Celebrity Appeal:** This is a fallacy that implies the reader should agree with a premise because a majority or a particularly significant person agrees with the premise.
  As everyone knows, this bill will help our children.
- **Either/Or Reasoning:** Assuming that there can be only one cause or one solution in an issue.
  The only way to keep our children safe is to ban video games.
- **Slippery Slope:** Assuming that because one minor fact is true, then a larger premise must be too, despite any further proof.
  Congressman Smith voted against tax increases last week; therefore, Congressman Smith will always be against tax increases.
- **Ad Populum:** Arguing based upon emotional appeals rather than facts.
  All true Americans want to ban this book.
- **Circular Reasoning:** Presents as reasons a restatement of the problem.
  There are not enough parking spaces because there are too many cars.

Ideological reasoning is the use of cultural, religious, or moral values and beliefs to prove a position. While there is nothing wrong with making personal judgments in this way, you should always be aware that your audience might not share your ideological views. To reach the greatest number of individuals you should avoid making ideological reasons the foundation of your arguments.

The Main Idea in Narratives and Personal Essays

Narrative and personal essays also require a main or controlling idea to help you focus and direct your writing. For example, consider this topic:

Describe an incident in your life that caused you to change an opinion or attitude. Before you begin writing, create a sentence that will both identify the incident you plan to narrate and describe the change it caused. Below are some examples of main idea statements.

- The divorce of my parents when I was seven changed my view that adults were infallible and always in control of their own lives.
- When I was six, my cat Edward died; and I began to mistrust the reassurances of doctors, a mistrust that has remained with me ever since.
- Changing high schools when I was fifteen made me realize for the first time that the fear of an experience is often worse than the reality.

When you write your paper, you may decide to suggest your main idea indirectly rather than state it. But making yourself create a statement is still a good idea.

Prewriting: How to Research and Organize

Once you have narrowed your topic and established a working thesis, you can start researching your essay. You may want to begin by writing what you know about the topic before you head to the library or the Internet. Generally, information that is assumed to be common knowledge does not have to be identified. However, you should identify, either by quote or citation, all specific phrasing that comes from another writer. Paraphrasing is a valuable way to summarize long passages or ideas from other writers.

Write an outline to focus and develop the main ideas that support or explain your thesis. You can organize your ideas in a variety of spatial or chronological ways. If you make your outline detailed, then the body of the essay should be easy to write. While a written outline can seem like extra work, it is a valuable, almost essential, key to writing a good first draft.

Finding Examples and Evidence

When you have a topic, you begin thinking of what you'll say. Write a thesis statement to organize your thinking. Before you start writing, take notes. For personal essays, write down your thoughts, observations, memories, and experiences. When analyzing a text, take notes on the significant sections or underline them. For most other essays, read materials with an eye to finding details, examples, and illustrations to support your main idea.

If you want to use quotations, write them down accurately. Remember that you'll need to footnote tiny facts, ideas, or quotations you borrow from other sources, so be sure to include bibliographical information in your notes. Some of what you write down will probably never appear in your essay. Your notes might even include questions that occur to you as you read, possibilities you want to explore, warnings to yourself, or reminders to check further on certain points. This stage of preparing a paper is not only to ensure that you have examples and evidence but also to help you think in more detail about your topic and thesis.

Brainstorming, Taking Notes, and Outlining

Begin the process by trying free writing on the computer. You can get ideas down quickly and legibly and save them as a brainstorming file; later, you can import parts of this file into your first draft. Take notes on the computer too, being sure to include the information you'll need to cite references. Word-processing programs can format and place footnotes when you're at the point of preparing your final draft, but of course you are responsible for accurately recording the sources of your information. If your writing project requires a bibliography, start a list of your references. Later you can easily add to and rearrange the list.

Most programs have a feature that allows you to create a formal outline according to a style you choose, such as roman numerals for headings, alpha characters for first-level subheadings, and so on. If you go back into your outline to add a heading or subheading, the program will automatically update your outline designations. Changing an outline on your computer is so simple that, you can experiment with different organizational plans.

Using the Computer for Research

With a computer, you can gain access to thousands of documents and databases, some in portable form on CD-ROMs (disks that store large amounts of information) and some directly online. You can call up journal and newspaper articles, abstracts, a variety of encyclopedias and dictionaries, and much more. Through the Internet (which includes the World Wide Web), you can view databases on many subjects and have access to library archival materials. The challenge is to know what there is and how to search for it. So much information is available online that you may feel overwhelmed and frustrated. Before you use the Internet to do serious research, it's a good idea to get some training. How-to books and classes are available, as are Internet directories that steer you in the right direction. Once you are online, search systems (or search engines)—to which you enter key words-help you navigate. When you use information from electronic sources in a paper, consult a current style guide (such as the *MLA Handbook for Writers of Research Papers,* Fourth Edition) on the correct forms for citing it in footnotes and a bibliography.

The Importance of Specific Details

A frequent mistake in writing is failing to provide specific examples, evidence, or details to support an idea or thesis. In an essay about a poem, for example, it isn't enough to say that the author's language creates a dark, gloomy atmosphere; you must cite particular words and images that demonstrate this effect. In an essay arguing that magnet schools in cities improve education for minority students, you must provide some evidence-statistics, anecdotes, and so on. In a timed writing on the statement, *We learn more from our failures than our successes,* you shouldn't merely reflect on the statement; you should cite examples from your life, or from the news, or from history.

Remember that essays filled with general unsupported statements are not only unconvincing, but also uninteresting.

Plagiarism

As you take notes, be aware that when you write your paper you must cite any sources you use, so record the information you'll need for footnotes. Consult a style guide for proper footnoting and preparation of a bibliography. You'll be guilty of **plagiarism** if you don't properly give credit for words or ideas that you borrow from others.

Most people understand that they can't steal exact words from a source, but some believe that paraphrasing—simply borrowing an idea—is acceptable. Generally, it isn't. While you don't need to footnote well-known ideas such as evolution or easily accessible facts such as the date of the first moon landing, you should document less generally known ideas or opinions (for example, a news analyst's assessment of a Supreme Court decision), and less accessible facts (such as the number of motorcycles sold in the United States in a given year). Deciding what to footnote is sometimes a gray area, but play it safe. If you have doubts, cite your source.

Quoting and Paraphrasing

When should you use quotations in a paper, and when should you paraphrase information instead? If you want to make a point about an author's language or style—as in the analysis of a literary work—use quotations.

But don't quote an entire stanza if you are going to comment on only two words, and don't give up your responsibility to discuss a character simply by quoting a descriptive passage from a novel.

If your interest is in the information a source conveys rather than in the author's expression, consider paraphrasing (putting the information in your own words) rather than quoting, particularly if the relevant passage is long and includes material you don't need. The question to ask is, "Why am I choosing to include this quotation?" If you have a good reason—an author's language or tone, for example, or a particularly apt expression go ahead. But often you're after only the information or part of the information.

Consider the following passage:

> Community-based policing has given rise to several important questions, among them the following: Should police officers address social problems that extend beyond particular crimes? Some experts on police reform say yes, while others say no. Although there is agreement that having police officers walk regular beats can decrease community suspicion and deter lawbreakers, the experts who are against greater involvement feel that giving police a broader responsibility by expecting them to deal with problems such as urban decay and irresponsible parenting is unrealistic and ultimately undesirable.

If you're writing about attitudes towards police reform, why not paraphrase the point that relates to your topic as shown in the following paragraph?

> Police-reform experts disagree about many issues, including whether or not police should involve themselves in social issues that go beyond their direct responsibility to deter crime and apprehend lawbreakers.

Don't pad a paper with quotations to add to its length (you'll irritate the instructor) and don't quote heavily to prove that you've read a source and have evidence for your points. Paraphrasing works just as well. One caution, however. Paraphrasing a source requires correct citation (footnoting) just as quotation does.

The Writing Assignment

All assignments are not identical, and you can use different strategies as you approach each writing task. The main purpose of your project may be research, argument, analysis, or narrative. In each of these areas you can learn some basic skills that will make the work easier.

The Research Paper

Don't regard a research paper as unlike other writing assignments. As in other essays, you should have a topic, a thesis, an introduction, good organization, unified and coherent paragraphs, transitions, and so on. A research paper should *not* consist of footnoted facts loosely strung together.

However, unlike other essays, a research paper depends on the use and citation of several sources of information, such as reference books, books related to your subject, relevant journal and magazine articles, speeches, and lectures. During the information-gathering period, get to know your library well. If available, check electronic databases. Learn how to locate a variety of materials that will give you a thorough (not one-sided) view of your topic. (See "Using the computer for research.") When you do find information, take careful notes that include bibliographical information about your source.

Practices for footnoting and preparing a bibliography vary. Therefore, when you're assigned a research paper, ask your instructor to recommend a style guide. Several general guides are available, as well as more specific ones designed for particular fields, among them language and literature, biology, business, history, and law.

Essays Arguing a Position from a Single Text

If your assignment is to write about a single text—for example, to take a position on an article in favor of regulating the Internet—read the text more than once. Look up terms you're uncertain about. Mark points that seem unclear or issues that may require research, and include outside research if is allowed by the assignment. (If you do use material from other sources, be sure to cite them, just as you would in a research paper.)

Determine the strongest and weakest arguments in the article. After studying the text carefully, decide whether you agree or disagree with the author's position. Remember that when you write your paper, you should provide a brief, fair summary of that position, whether you're agreeing with it or not. In an argumentative essay you must support your own viewpoint *and* answer the opposition.

Essays Analyzing a Literary Work

When you're asked to analyze a literary work, or one aspect of a literary work, stay close to the text. Read it and, if possible, reread it. Your first job is to interpret meaning, which can take some time. Once you feel comfortable with your interpretation, take notes or mark the text with an eye to finding support for your topic and thesis. You'll be using quotations in your paper, so indicate those passages or lines that might be particularly effective.

Generally, when you write an essay on a nonliterary text, you focus on content, concentrating on the author's information and the quality of his or her arguments. When you write about a literary text, however, you must also pay close attention to the author's technique. If you don't already know such terms as *meter, image, metaphor, simile, diction, flat character,* and *irony* check a glossary of literary terms. In your notes include specific words and images from the text, observations about structure (a poem's rhyme scheme, for example, or a novel's subplot), point of view, and tone. Remember, however, that when you discuss formal features like these in your essay, you should relate them to a point you are making, usually about the author's theme or purpose. Don't risk having your reader ask, "So *what if* the rhyme scheme changes in the last stanza?"

Narrative, Descriptive, and Autobiographical Essays

For some essays, you'll use your own thoughts, observations, and experiences, without reference to a text. But as with essays of argument and analysis, you need to gather information to develop your main ideas, and taking notes is a good way to do it. Before beginning an essay describing your Aunt Gladys, for example, write down all the details you can about her, including any anecdotes that reveal her characteristics. At this point don't worry about organizing your observations. Remember that you're gathering information. If you haven't yet written a sentence stating a main idea, try to do so now. (For example, *Although Aunt Gladys prides herself on being no trouble to anyone, she finds ways to get everyone in the family to do what she wants,* or *Aunt Gladys looks like a little old lady, but she acts like a teenage girl.*) Without a controlling idea, your essay will be a list of details with nothing to unify them or give them purpose.

Soon you'll be filling out college applications. When it asks for an essay about yourself, your purpose will be to describe the traits, experiences, interests, achievements, and goals that show you're a good candidate for college admission. First, take notes about yourself—whatever you can think of. Be sure to consider things that emphasize your individuality. In going over your notes later, you may decide not to include the no-hit Little League softball game you pitched when you were nine, or every fast-food job you've ever had; but by making a complete list, you can look for patterns that will help you organize your essay. When it comes time to put your points in order, throw out unnecessary details, consolidating and summarizing—for example, mentioning that you held five fast-food jobs (but not specifying each employer) while attending high school and becoming class valedictorian.

Writing

A common misconception about writing is that the first draft must be perfect. However, even excellent writers create multiple drafts before they feel content with their writing. In the first draft, focus on introductions, connecting ideas within paragraphs, and conclusions.

A good introduction catches the reader's attention and then provides a general orientation to the topic. You can interest the reader by using quotations, anecdotes, questions or addressing the reader directly. Paragraphs develop a single idea in a series of connected sentences. A unified paragraph stays focused on a single idea and is coherent and well developed. Your final statement should bring all of your points to their logical conclusion. You can leave the reader pondering your essay by using a quotation, a reference back to a point or question made in the introduction, or a story that emphasizes your thesis.

Working from a Thesis Statement

The first thing to look at when you're ready to organize your paper is your main idea or thesis statement. Putting yourself in a reader's place, imagine how you would expect to see the main idea developed. Then look at the notes you've taken. If you used your thesis statement as a guide in gathering information, you should see a pattern.

Look at the following thesis statement:

> Imposing sanctions on China would be a mistake because it would hurt the American economy, because sanctions are notoriously unsuccessful as a way to force change, and because the United States should not interfere in the internal policies of other countries.

This statement suggests that the paper will be divided into three main parts; it even indicates an order for those sections. When you go through your notes, decide where each note most logically fits. For example, a note about U.S. clothing manufacturers' increasing use of Chinese labor would fit into section one, and a note about the failure of sanctions in the Middle East in section two.

Of course, things aren't usually this neat. Your thesis statement might not be this precise, or the kind of essay you're writing might not lend itself to such an easy division. But starting from the moment you look at your topic and decide on your main idea, you should be thinking about ways to develop it. This thinking leads you to your organizing principle.

A review of some common methods of organization will help you. Remember, however, to avoid an overly rigid approach. After you begin to write, you may realize that your plan needs to be changed. Writing itself, often generates new ideas, or suggests a different direction.

Spatial or Chronological Organization

Some topics lend themselves to organization based on space or time. A descriptive essay might work well if you begin with a distant view and move closer—first describe how a barn looks from the road, for example, then describe the view you see when you stand directly in front of the barn, then describe the view (and smell and sounds) when standing inside the barn door, and completing your description with what you see when you climb the ladder into the loft.

In the narration of an event and in some kinds of technical writing (describing a process, for example) you write about events in the order they occur. Often dividing your material into stages avoids the "and then, and then, and then!" effect. If you were writing about making a ceramic vase, you could divide the process into three main stages—selecting and preparing the clay, forming and refining the shape of the vase on the potter's wheel, and glazing the piece and firing it in a kiln. The detailed steps in making the vase could then be organized sequentially under these sections.

Dividing a Subject into Categories

Just as you can divide a process into stages, you can divide a subject into categories. When you look over your notes, and using your thesis statement as a guide, see if logical groupings emerge. Look at the following topic and thesis statement, written by a fictional student.

TOPIC   Write a paper addressing an environmental concern and suggesting ideas for a solution.

THESIS   The United States is losing its forests, and the solution is everyone's responsibility.

Note that the second half of this thesis statement is weak: *the solution is everyone's responsibility is* a vague assertion.

In looking over his notes, the student quickly identifies those that relate to the first part of the thesis statement (*Less than 1 percent of U.S. old-growth forests remain, U.S. consumption* of *wood is up 3 percent since 1930, and so on*). However, when he looks at the rest of his notes, he finds he has everything from *Logging bans have been effective in many areas* to *Don't use disposable diapers,* to *Agricultural waste can be effectively processed to make building materials that provide excellent insulation.*

At this point he decides to create categories. He finds that many notes are related to simple, everyday actions that can help reduce wood and paper consumption (*no disposable diapers, e-mail instead of memos, cloth bags instead* of *paper bags, recycling newspapers, etc.*). Still others cover alternatives for wood, such as *agricultural waste, engineered wood manufactured by the forest products industry, the use of steel studs in construction rather than wooden ones, a method of wall forming called "rammed earth construction,"* and so on. Then he notices that several notes relate to government actions such as *logging bans, wilderness designations, Forest Service reforms,* etc. He decides to use three general classifications as a principle of organization:

    I. Problem

        A. Old-growth forests have virtually disappeared.

        B. U.S. consumption of wood up 3 percent since 1930.

    II. Solutions

        A. Consumer actions

        B. Alternatives to wood

        C. Government regulations

He may decide to change the order of the classifications when he writes his paper, but for now he has a principle of organization.

If some notes don't fit into these classifications, he may want to add another category, or add some subsections. For example, if several notes deal with actions by major conservation groups, he may want to add a division under *Solutions* called *Conservation group activities.* Or, if he finds some notes relating to disadvantages of wood alternatives, he may add some subtopics under B, for example, *price, stability, public perception.*

Dividing material into categories is one of the most basic forms of organization. Make sure the categories are appropriate to the purpose of your paper and that you have sufficient information under each one.

Organizing Essays of Comparison

Sometimes students have problems with topics that ask them to compare and contrast two things. After gathering information on each thing, they fail to focus on the similarities and dissimilarities between them.

When your topic involves comparison, you can organize in either of two ways. First, you can discuss each thing separately and then include a section in which you draw comparisons and contrasts between them. With this organization, if you were comparing and contrasting two poems, you would write first about one—covering, for example, theme, language, images, tone, and rhyme scheme—and then about the other, covering the same areas. In a third section you would make a series of statements comparing and contrasting major aspects of the poems. If you choose this method, make your separate discussions of the poems parallel—that is, for the second poem, address points in the same order you used for the first poem. Also, in the third section of the paper, avoid simply repeating what you said in sections one and two.

A second way of organizing requires you to decide first which aspects of the poems you want to compare and contrast (theme, language, and imagery) and then to structure your essay according to these. For example, if you begin with theme, you state the themes of both poems and compare them. Then you compare the language of the two poems, then the imagery, then the tone, and so on. Two advantages of this type of organization are, first, you are forced to focus on similarities and dissimilarities and less likely to include material that isn't pertinent and, second, you avoid repetition by eliminating a separate compare-and-contrast section.

You can also combine these two types of organization. For example, you may want to discuss each poem's theme separately, and then move into a point-by-point comparison of the other aspects of the poem (language, imagery, tone, and so on).

Inductive or Deductive Patterns of Organization

In a logical argument, the pattern in which you present evidence and then draw a general conclusion is called *inductive.* This term can also be used to describe a method of approaching your material, particularly in an essay presenting an argument. You are using this method in an essay even when you state the general conclusion first and present the supporting evidence in successive paragraphs. In fact, in essays it is customary to begin with the general conclusion as a thesis statement:

EVIDENCE   The student action committee failed to achieve a quorum in all six of its last meetings.

During the past year, the student action committee has proposed four plans for changing the grievance procedure and has been unable to adopt any of them.

According to last month's poll in the student newspaper, 85 percent of the respondents had not heard of the student action committee. Two openings on the committee have remained unfilled for eight months because no one has applied for membership.

CONCLUSION   The student action committee is an ineffective voice for students at this university.

(Note: In an essay, this would be a thesis statement.)

Another type of organization borrowed from logical argument is called *deductive*. With this pattern you begin with a generalization and then apply it to specific instances. In a timed writing, you might be given a statement such as *it's better to be safe than sorry* or *beauty is in the eye of the beholder* and then asked to agree or disagree, providing examples that support your view. With such essays, you aren't proving or disproving the truth of a statement, but offering an opinion and then supporting it with examples. For example, if you begin with a generalization such as *beauty is in the eye of the beholder, you* could cite instances such as different standards for human beauty in different cultures, or different views of beauty in architecture from era to era. You could also use examples from your own experience, such as your brother's appreciation of desert landscapes contrasted to your boredom with them.

Order of Examples and Evidence

Within any overall pattern of organization, you must decide on the specific order of your examples and evidence. The best plan is to save your most important point or most convincing piece of evidence for last. The last position is the most emphatic, and a reader will expect you to build to your strongest point. Saving the best for last isn't a rule; you must decide, based on your thesis and the evidence and examples you've collected, which order works best. But do remember that you want to avoid having your essay trail off with a trivial example or weak argument.

Outlining

Creating an outline, either a formal or an informal one, helps you stay with your organizational plan. Sometimes an outline helps you see problems in your original plan, and you can eliminate them before you've spent time writing.

If you prefer writing papers without an outline, try an experiment. Create an outline *after* a paper is finished to see if your organization is clear and logical. This exercise may make you decide that outlining is a good idea.

Informal Outlines

An *informal outline* can be little more than a list of your main points. You can refine it by following each main point with notations of the evidence or examples that support it. You are, in effect, grouping your notes. A simple outline like this is often all you need. It is especially valuable for timed writings or essay exams. Thinking your approach through before you begin—and jotting your thoughts down—will help you avoid rambling and moving away from the assignment.

Formal Outlines

You may want to prepare a more *formal outline*. Sometimes you may even be asked to submit an outline with a writing assignment. Following are a few guidelines:

Use roman numerals for main topics, alternate letters and Arabic numerals for subtopics. Indent subtopics.

I.
  A.
  B.
    1.
    2.
      a.
      b.

Make outline topics parallel in form. Make subtopics parallel in form also.

For example, if you use a sentence for the first topic, use sentences for all subsequent topics, but if you use a noun for the first subtopic, use a noun for the following ones.

Watch the logic of your outline. The main topics generally indicate the basic structure of your essay. The second level of your outline (A, B, C) covers the major ideas that contribute to the larger units. The next level of subtopics is for narrower points related to these ideas. Don't stick irrelevant ideas in your outline under the guise of subtopics. Make sure each element logically fits under its heading or you're defeating the purpose of an outline.

Each topic and subtopic should have at least one mating topic or subtopic, that is, no I without a II, no A without a B, and so on. Remember that topics and subtopics are divisions of your subject, and you can't divide something into one part. If your outline shows solitary topics or subtopics, re-evaluate to see whether you are misplacing or poorly stating your headings. The information should perhaps be worked into an existing larger category or divided into two topics or subtopics.

Sentence Outlines and Topic Outlines

In a *sentence outline,* all elements are stated in complete sentences. In a *topic outline,* the elements may be presented as single words or as phrases. Study the following examples.

Sentence Outline

I. Many high school classes do not prepare students for large university classes.

    A. Nontracked high school classes don't challenge more able students to achieve at the highest level.

        1. Less competition leads some students to "get by" rather than excel.

        2. Inflated grading of good students in nontracked classes can lead to false expectations.

    B. High school classes are not designed to encourage individual responsibility, which is required in large university classes.

        1. Required attendance in high school may lead students to react to less rigid attendance requirements by cutting classes.

        2 High school teachers assign daily homework and reading assignments, whereas university professors generally make long-term assignments.

        3. High school teachers frequently spend more time with individual students than do professors in large universities.

II. Some high schools offer programs to help students prepare for university classes.

Topic Outline

I. Lack of preparation of high school students for university classes

    A. Nontracked high school classes

        1. Less competition

        2. Mated grades

    B. Less individual responsibility in high school classes

        1. Required attendance

        2. Homework and daily assignments

        3. Individual attention from teachers

II. Programs to prepare high school students for university classes

Getting Started

The first thing to remember when beginning to write is that you don't have to create a perfect first draft. Count on rewriting. Your first draft may well be a mixture of planning and improvising—letting yourself move in a direction you hadn't originally intended. Remember that writing is not a straightforward process, that even when you begin a first draft you may make changes in your thesis statement or in your organizational plan.

The exception to the rule about first drafts is in timed writing assignments, for which you may have time for only one draft. Spend a few moments planning your answer, noting examples you intend to use, and then move ahead. Graders of these assignments are looking for substance, support for your thesis statement.

Suggestions for Introductions

An **introduction** should lead naturally into the rest of your paper and be appropriate to its subject and tone. Some suggestions for openings follow, but use judgment in applying them. Although beginning with an anecdote can be effective for some papers, don't force one where it doesn't belong. A story about your indecisive father is not the best way to begin a paper analyzing the character of *Hamlet*.

- Use a relevant quotation from the work you are discussing.

  "I am encompassed by a wall, high and hard and stone, with only my brainy nails to tear it down. And I cannot do it." Kerewin Holmes, one of the main characters in Keri Hulme's novel *The Bone People,* describes herself as both physically and emotionally alone in a tower she has built by the New Zealand Sea. Throughout the novel Hulme uses concrete images—the tower, muteness, physical beatings, the ocean-to suggest her characters' isolation from each other and the community around them.

- Provide background or context for your thesis statement.

  Until the second half of this century, Americans spent the country's natural resources freely. They mined for minerals, diverted rivers, replaced wilderness with cities and towns. In the process they cut down forests that had been in place for thousands of years. Now, as the twenty-first century approaches, the reality that progress has its price is obvious to almost everyone. Only ten percent of old-growth forests in the United States remain intact, with demand for wood products expected to grow by fifty percent in the next fifty years. The country is in danger of losing its forests altogether unless citizens pursue solutions from everyday recycling to using wood alternatives to actively supporting government regulations.

- Ask a question that leads to your thesis statement.

  Is the United States still a country where the middle class thrives? Strong evidence suggests that the traditional American view of a successful middle class is fading. At the very least, the prospects for someone who stands in the economic middle have significantly changed since the 1970s. Twenty-five years ago middle-class people expected to own their own homes in the suburbs and send their children to college. Today, for many people, these expectations have become more like distant dreams. Two factors—a growing disparity in wages within the labor force and rising prices for real estate and goods—suggest that the middle class is a less comfortable place to be than it was for the previous generation.

- Begin with a relevant anecdote that leads to your thesis statement.

  Doug was the star in my high school senior class. He captained the football team, dated the best looking girls, charmed the teachers, and managed to get A's and B's seemingly without studying. When he headed off to a big Midwestern university, we weren't surprised. But when he was home again a year later on academic probation, many of us wondered what could have happened. Doug told me candidly that his year at the university was far removed from anything he'd experienced in high school. Quite simply, his small, noncompetitive high school classes hadn't prepared him for a large, impersonal university where the professors didn't know his name, let alone his role as a big man on campus. I believe programs to help students like Doug make the transition from high school to college could help reduce the high failure rate among college freshmen.

- Speak directly to your readers. Ask them to imagine themselves in a situation you create.

  Imagine being escorted into a room and asked to disrobe every time you want to take an airplane trip. Picture someone in a uniform grilling you about your background or even hooking you up to a lie detector. Such scenarios seem impossible in America, but experts agree that the United States may be forced to take extreme measures to combat increasing domestic terrorism.

- In your opening, avoid definition of a term that doesn't require defining or that leads nowhere.

  The novel *Silas Marner* by George Eliot is about a man who is a miser. What is a miser? According to the definition in *Webster's New World Dictionary,* a miser is "a greedy, stingy person who hoards money for its own sake."

  This opening does not make a reader want to continue reading.

Your own particular topic may suggest to you any number of creative beginnings. Try to go beyond the obvious. For example, which of the following two openings for an essay on the qualities of a good mate is more likely to catch a reader's interest?

STUDENT 1   It is important to look for many qualities in the person you choose to spend your life with.

STUDENT 2   Finding a mate is hard enough. Finding a mate you're happy with may seem close to impossible.

The Paragraph

A **paragraph** develops one idea with a series of logically connected sentences. Most paragraphs function as small essays themselves, each with a main topic (stated or implied) and several related sentences that support it.

How many paragraphs do you need in your paper? That depends on what you have to say. The idea that an essay should consist of five paragraphs—an introduction, three paragraphs of examples, and a conclusion—is much too rigid, though students first learning to write are sometimes taught this. You may well have more than three examples or points to make, and you may have an example or point that requires several paragraphs of development in itself. Don't limit yourself. Let your particular topic and supporting points guide you in creating your paragraphs.

Paragraph Length

Paragraphs vary in length. For example, short paragraphs (one to three sentences) are used in newspaper stories where the emphasis is on reporting information without discussion, or in technical writing where the emphasis is on presenting facts such as statistics and measurements without analysis. Written dialogue also consists of short paragraphs, with a new paragraph for each change of speaker. In an essay, a short paragraph can also be effectively used for dramatic effect or transition.

But the reconciliation was never to take place. Her grandmother died as Jane was driving home from the airport.

Generally, however, avoid a series of very short paragraphs in your essays. They suggest poor development of an idea.

On the other hand, paragraphs a page or more in length are difficult for most readers, who like to see a subject divided into shorter segments. Look carefully at long paragraphs to see whether you have gone beyond covering one idea or are guilty of repetition, wordiness, or rambling. Don't arbitrarily split a long paragraph in half by indenting a particular sentence, however. Make sure that each paragraph meets the requirement of a single main idea with sentences that support it.

Paragraph Unity

A **unified paragraph** is one that focuses on one idea and one idea only. Look at the following example of a paragraph that *lacks* unity.

> Identification of particular genes can lead to better medicine. For example, recently scientists identified a defective gene that appears to cause hemochromatosis, or iron overload. Iron overload is fairly easily cured if it is recognized and treated early, but currently it is often misdiagnosed because it mimics more familiar conditions. The problem is that when not treated in time, iron overload leads to a variety of diseases, from diabetes to liver cancer. The identification of the faulty gene can prevent misdiagnosis by allowing physicians, through a screening test, to identify patients who carry it and treat them before the condition becomes too advanced. *It is interesting that most people don't realize the exact role of iron in the body.* They know that it is important for their health, but few are aware that only about ten percent of the iron in food is normally absorbed by the small intestine. Most of the rest is tied up in hemoglobin, which carries oxygen from the lungs.

The first sentence of the paragraph presents the main idea that identification of genes leads to improved medical care. This idea is developed by the example of how the identification of a gene causing iron overload can lead to better diagnosis and early treatment. In the italicized sentence the Paragraph begins to wander. It is a topic sentence for a different paragraph, one about the role of iron in the body and not about a benefit of genetic research.

Sometimes a sentence or two buried in the middle of a paragraph can break its unity, as in the following example.

> Moving out of my parents' house and into an apartment didn't bring me the uncomplicated joy that I had expected. First of all, I had to struggle to make the rent every month, and the landlord was much less understanding than my parents. Then I realized I had to do my own laundry, clean up the place now and then, and fix my own meals. *One nice thing about my mother is that she is an excellent cook. She even attended a French cooking school before she married my father.* It's true that I liked the greater freedom I had in my apartment—no one constantly asking me what time I'd be home, no one nagging me about cleaning up my room or raking the front lawn—but I wasn't thrilled with spending most of a Saturday getting rid of a cockroach infestation, or Sunday night doing three loads of smelly laundry.

Notice how the italicized sentences interrupt the flow of the paragraph, which is really about the down side of leaving home and not about the writer's mother.

To test the unity of your paragraphs, locate your topic sentence (if you have left it unstated, be clear on your paragraph's main idea) and then test the other sentences to see if they are developing that particular idea or if they are wandering off in another direction.

Paragraph Coherence

Along with developing a single idea, a paragraph should be well organized. You can use many of the same principles—chronology, inductive and deductive patterns, and so on—that you use to organize complete essays.

Once you've decided on the order of your details, make sure the connections between sentences in the paragraph are clear. The smooth, logical flow of a paragraph is called **paragraph coherence.** Write each sentence with the previous one in mind.

Connecting Sentences through Ideas

Connect your sentences through their content, by picking up something from one and carrying it into the next.

Follow a sentence that makes a general point with a specific, clear illustration of that point. Look at the following example.

> The gap in pay between people with basic skills and people without them seems to be widening. In one comparison, the pay difference between women of varied mathematical skills had grown from $.93 an hour in 1978 to $1.71 an hour in 1986.

Here, the second sentence is a clear illustration of the point made in the first sentence. But look at how coherence can be lost in a paragraph.

> The gap in pay between people with basic skills and people without them seems to be widening. Women are now playing a more important role in the work force than they have since World War II, when many had to fill the positions of men who were overseas. The pay difference between women of varied mathematical skills has grown considerably, from $.93 an hour in 1978 to $1.71 an hour in 1986.

In this example, the second sentence is not clearly connected to the first. Sentence three returns to the subject, but the continuity of the idea has been weakened.

You can also use one sentence to reflect or comment on the previous sentence, as in the following example.

> The idea that in America hard work leads to financial success has been one of our most successful exports. For decades immigrants have arrived on American soil with a dream that here they can have what was impossible in their home countries, where they were limited by class structure or few opportunities.

Be sure in reviewing your paragraph that such reflections logically follow from the previous statement. Here, immigrants arriving with the preconceived notion that they will succeed, is tied to the point in the first sentence that the American dream has been a successful export.

You can also connect sentences by asking a question and following it with an answer or making a statement and following it with a question.

> Why should the government invest in research? Research leads to technological advances that create employment, as was shown in the years following World War II.

> Polls indicate that many Americans favor regulation of the Internet. Are they willing to pay both with their tax dollars and their freedoms?

The sentences in these two examples are linked by words as well as by ideas. In the first example, the word *research* has been picked up from the question and repeated in the answer. In the second example, the pronoun *they* in the question has its antecedent *(Americans)* in the previous statement.

Connecting with Words and Phrases

Achieving paragraph coherence by connecting ideas is your first step. But as indicated in the last two examples, words and phrases can help strengthen the connection between sentences.

- Use a pronoun whose antecedent appears in the previous sentence.

  Gabriel Garcia Marquez suspends the laws of reality in his novels. *He* creates bizarre and even magical situations that reveal character in surprising ways.

- Repeat a key word or phrase.

  The idea of a perfect society, though never realized, continues to intrigue political *philosophers.* None of *these philosophers* seem to agree on where perfection lies.

- Use a synonym.

  According to my research, *physical beauty is* still considered a more important asset for women than for men. *Looks* are everything, according to several girls I spoke to, while the boys I interviewed felt that their athletic prowess and social status were at least as important as their appearance.

- Use word patterns, such as *first, second, third,* and so on.

  The reasons for the dean's announcing his decision today are clear. *First,* students will recognize that he is listening to their concerns. *Second,* faculty will applaud the end of a disruptive period of indecision. *Third,* wealthy and influential alumni though not particularly pleased by all the details of the plan will be overjoyed that the controversy will be off the front page of the paper.

- Use transitional words and phrases. Many words and phrases signal connections between sentences in a paragraph or between paragraphs in a paper. Look at the italicized words in the following sentences.

  The main character worships her. *Later,* his adoration turns to hatred.

  The church stood at the top of the hill. *Below* stretched miles of orchards.

  She treated him well. *For example,* she bought him a car and new clothes.

  The product promised he'd grow new hair. *But* all he grew was a rash.

207

Hamlet disdained Ophelia. As *a result,* she killed herself.

Elizabeth was angry at Darcy. *In fact,* she wanted nothing to do with him.

The plan is too expensive. *Furthermore, it* won't work.

No one volunteered to help. *In other words,* no one cared.

In the preceding examples, the italicized words or phrases explicitly connect the second sentence to the first by creating a particular relationship.

- Vary the transitional words you use.

Following is a list of words classified according to the relationships they suggest.

Time or place: above, across from, adjacent to, afterward, before, behind, below, beyond, earlier, elsewhere, farther on, here, in the distance, near by, next to, opposite to, to the left, to the right

Example: for example, for instance, specifically, to be specific

Contrast: but, however, nevertheless, on the contrary, on the other hand

Similarity: similarly, in the same way, equally important

Consequence: accordingly, as a result, consequently, therefore

Emphasis: indeed, in fact, of course

Amplification: and, again, also, further, furthermore, in addition, moreover, too

Restatement: in other words, more simply stated, that is, to clarify

Summary and conclusion: altogether, finally, in conclusion, in short, to summarize

Connecting Paragraphs in an Essay

Your essay should move from paragraph to paragraph smoothly, each point growing out of the preceding one. If you are shifting direction or moving to a different point, prepare your reader with a transition. Achieving continuity in your essay is similar to achieving continuity in a paragraph.

Conclusions

How should you end your paper? Writing a proper **conclusion** is like tying a ribbon around a gift package. It's the last thing you do, but it also gives your final effort a finishing touch. If your ending works, your reader will feel satisfied.

What to Avoid

Before you can write your conclusion you should know what to avoid. Here are some common errors.

- Don't introduce a new topic. For example, if your essay has been about the loss of forests and possible solutions for the high consumption of wood products, don't end with a paragraph about another environmental concern, such as the disappearance of the California condor.

- Don't trail off with a weak statement or a statement leaving your reader up in the air.

  The Internet, free of regulation, has opened a world of information and ideas to everyone. Children enjoy learning at the computer.

- Don't simply repeat your thesis or main idea in the same words.

  Thus, as stated earlier, clothing imagery shows the changes in King Lear throughout the play.

- Don't apologize for or suggest doubts about your thesis.

  For a variety of reasons, middle-class expectations in the 1990s differ from those in the 1970s. It is possible, however, that the difference is not particularly illuminating about life in the United States.

You may use a brief concluding sentence instead of a formal conclusion in a simple or short paper (up to five pages, for example). Formal conclusions can sometimes be superfluous and even insulting to the reader's intelligence, particularly if the conclusion is a long summary of what he or she just read. Instead, end your paper with your best point, using a strong final sentence.

Suggestions for Conclusions

The two most important things a conclusion should do is give your readers a sense of completion and leave them with a strong impression. You can do this with a single statement or with a paragraph. If you do write a concluding paragraph, consider these possibilities.

- End with an appropriate quotation:

  Throughout the novel the characters suffer both from their isolation and from their attempts to end it. Kerewin burns her tower, Joe beats his son and goes to prison, and Simon—who barely survives the beating—must painfully find his way back to those he loves. Recurring images dramatize their journeys, which end in a reconciliation between being alone and being part of a community. Kerewin describes the home that will now take the place of her lonely tower: "I decided on a shell-shape, a regular spiral of rooms expanding around the decapitated Tower . . . privacy, apartness, but all connected and all part of the whole."

  Notice that in this example the writer also pulls loose ends together and briefly refers to the thesis.

- Without directly repeating your thesis, come full circle by relating the final paragraph to a point you made in your introduction.

  Preserving old-growth forests and finding substitutes for wood should concern everyone who cares about the environment. The days when Americans could view this country as an unlimited provider of resources are as gone as roaming herds of buffalo and pioneers in covered wagons.

- End with a story related to your thesis.

  On a recent trip to the airport, I stood at the ticket counter behind an angry woman. It seems she'd forgotten her photo ID and was being told by the attendant that she couldn't fly without it. After calling the clerk a storm trooper and threatening to sue the airline, she turned to me indignantly. "You tell me. Do I look like the kind of person who would blow up a plane?" I didn't answer, since the question seemed rhetorical. I wondered, though, how in the future this woman would react to a fifteen-minute interview about herself, or to a uniformed attendant patting her down.

Another way to conclude a paper is to summarize your points. But because summaries aren't particularly interesting conclusions, consider one only if your paper is fairly long and if one would be helpful to your reader. Keep summaries brief and avoid wishy-washy final sentences, such as *For all these reasons, the Internet should not be regulated.*

Revising and Editing

Since titles are important, choose one that is interesting and informative. Consider the formality of the writing assignment and the audience when selecting a title for your work. Try reading your draft aloud, and if possible, ask someone you trust to review your essay.

After the review is completed, edit and revise the essay. Editing, which can be done with most computers and word processors, involves looking at the grammatical and mechanical content of your work. Revising means not only looking at grammar, but also the overall effect of the essay. Editing and revising ensure that the final draft is appropriate for the assignment and audience, grammatically and mechanically correct, well organized and supported, and well crafted.

Titles

While you're writing an essay, if you have a good idea for a title, write it down. But often the best time to choose a title is when you've completed a first draft and read it over. You'll have a more complete picture of your essay. Be creative, but don't overdo it. For example, if you're writing a paper about deforestation, *"Knock on Wood"* might seem clever, but it doesn't accurately fit the topic.

Use good judgment when you choose a title. Consider the tone of your essay and your audience. *"No More Mr. Nice Guy"* might be a good title for a personal essay on the loss of your gullibility, but think twice before using it as the title of your analytical paper on Shakespeare's character *Macbeth*. (It's true, however, that one instructor who had received dozens of papers with unimaginative titles reacted well to the student who called hers *"Dial M for Murder: The Character of Macbeth."*)

The best advice is to take a middle road. Avoid both dullness and strained cleverness. Consider a good quotation from a work you are writing about, an effective phrase from your own essay, or an appropriate figure of speech:

"Sleep No More": The Role of Macbeth's Conscience
RATHER THAN Macbeth's Conscience

"I'm Nobody": Finding Emily Dickinson in her Poetry
RATHER THAN Emily Dickinson and her Poetry

Gaining Safety or Losing Freedom: The Debate over Airport Security Measures
RATHER THAN Airport Security Measures

Only Skin Deep?
RATHER THAN The Importance of Beauty to Today's Woman

Fit to be Tried: An Examination of the McNaughton Rule
RATHER THAN Judging Legal Sanity

Reviewing the First Draft

When you read your first draft, you will probably make your most extensive revisions. Here are a few suggestions that can help you in reviewing your first draft.

- If possible, leave some time between writing the first draft and reviewing it. Your objectivity will improve.
- Try reading your paper aloud to yourself; sometimes your ear catches problems your eye misses.
- Ask someone to read your draft and offer suggestions. Choose a reader you can trust to be honest and fair. And remember: You are looking for an objective opinion, not simply reassurance. Judge your reader's suggestions carefully, and decide for yourself their value, and whether or not to act on them.
- Remember that nothing is unchangeable. Until preparation of your final draft, you can change your thesis, your organization, your emphasis, your tone, and so on. A review of your first draft should *not* be limited to minor mechanical errors.
- Use a revision checklist to make sure you've reviewed your draft thoroughly.

Preparing the Final Draft

You may be able to move directly from your revised first draft to a final draft, but careful writers often prepare several drafts before they are ready to call a piece finished. Within your time constraints, follow their example. As you rewrite, you may continue to discover wordy constructions, poor connections, awkward sentences, and so on. Only when you're satisfied that you've done your best, should you prepare the final draft.

Writing and Editing a Draft

The computer allows you to produce a legible first draft that's easy to change by using a few basic functions, such as *delete, insert, merge, block,* and *move.* When you try making changes to a handwritten draft, on the other hand, you can end up with something so messy it's indecipherable. If you want to change a word-processed draft but aren't certain whether you'll want to keep the changes, save both your original and your revised drafts under different file names and decide later which you want to use or import parts of one into the other. You can also re-order the paragraphs in a paper with a few keystrokes.

You can do much of your editing directly on the screen. If you think of a better way to say what you've just said, make the change immediately and move on. For more global editing, however, many writers like to print out sections or complete drafts, mark them up by hand, and then go back to the computer to input the changes. This method has advantages. Working on the screen limits you to a small section of text; scrolling back and forth in the document can be confusing, and it's difficult to get a beginning-to-end picture of what you've written. Another advantage of printing out your document is that it forces you to slow down and read carefully. Sometimes, because you can write so quickly on a computer, your fingers may get ahead of your thoughts. Remember that good writing requires deliberation and judgment, and that you should always review a computer draft closely.

Spell-Checking, Grammar-Checking, and Search-and-Replace Functions

A spell-check function is useful for catching misspelled words, typos, and accidental repetitions *(the the)*. But be careful. The checker won't signal a word that is actually a word, even if it isn't the one you intended—for example, when you inadvertently type form for from. Spell-checking also doesn't distinguish between homonyms, so if you have trouble with its and it's, it won't help you. Consider the spell-checker as an aid, not a replacement for your own careful proofreading. Unfortunately, on the FSWE, the essay is handwritten, so you're left to your own spelling skills.

Grammar or style-checkers require even more caution because grammar and style are less clear-cut than spelling. Many writers don't use these functions at all, and unless you already have a good grasp of grammar, they can be confusing or misleading. For example, the checkers will catch pronoun agreement and reference errors but not dangling participles or faulty parallelism. Some checkers flag possible homonym confusions, usage problems (literal used incorrectly, for example), and passive constructions, but they also signal every sentence beginning with But, all contractions, and every sentence ending with a preposition—"errors" that current usage generally permits. If you use a checking function, do so critically. Don't automatically change a passive construction, or restructure a sentence ending with a preposition, for example, simply because the checker flags it.

A *search-and-replace* feature in word-processing programs lets you correct a particular error throughout your paper automatically. If you find you've misspelled a person's name, you can spell it correctly and ask the program to locate every instance of the name in your 25-page document and replace it with the correct version. Just be sure that the error is one that you want replaced in the same way every time.

Layout of the Final Draft

With word processing, you can produce a final draft that looks professional. Choose from different type fonts, use boldface type and italics, center titles with a stroke, create headings of different sizes, and use bullets or other symbols to highlight your points. You can create properly formatted and numbered footnotes, and place them correctly by selecting a footnote option and consistent page numbers by selecting automatic page numbering. If it's appropriate, you might want to present some materials in tables, charts, or graphs—which are easy to create with most programs. You can even import graphics. One note of warning: Don't confuse a good looking paper with a well-written one. Although your readers may be favorably disposed towards documents that are nice to look at, word-processing features can't compensate for meager content or poorly expressed ideas.

Checklist

Good writing often comes after revision and rewriting. If you can view your work critically, you will be able to improve it. Use the following checklist before you write a final draft.

Purpose, audience, and tone

These three elements deal with the overall effect of your essay and should guide you throughout your writing.

- If I am writing in response to an assignment, does my essay fulfill all parts of the assignment?

- Is my topic too broad?

- Do I state my thesis or main idea early in the paper? If I don't state a thesis or main idea, is it clearly implied so that there can be no mistake about my purpose?

- Is my thesis or main idea interesting? If this is an essay of argument, is my thesis statement fair? Do I take opposing viewpoints into account?

- Have I thought about my audience? Does my audience have any special requirements? Is my tone appropriate to my audience and purpose?

- Is my tone consistent throughout the essay?

Examples, evidence, and details

These are specific details in the writing process. When you read your essay, you can determine whether you have used these elements well.

- Have I adequately developed my thesis or main idea? Do I use specific details rather than generalities?

- Are my examples and evidence accurate, relevant, and convincing?

- Do I use quotations appropriately? Is too much of my paper quotation? Do I paraphrase carefully?

- Do I cite sources for the words and ideas of others?

Structure

Use an outline to determine the structure of your paper, but be aware that you may need to alter it as you write. Keep in mind the following:

- Do I have a principle of organization? Do I avoid repetition and digressions?

- Is my organization appropriate to my topic and thesis?

- Do I adequately introduce and conclude my paper?

- Are my paragraphs well developed, unified, and coherent?

- Does one paragraph grow out of another? Do I use transitions?

- Are my examples, evidence, and details in the best order? Do I save the strongest point for last?

Language and style

Rely on a dictionary and your word-processing tools to help you with language and style. Ask yourself some questions.

- Have I chosen my words carefully? Am I sure of meanings?

- Is my language appropriate to my purpose, tone, and audience?

- Have I avoided wordy expressions? euphemisms? clichés?

- Have I avoided pretentious language?

- Have I used idioms correctly?

- Have I followed the guidelines of current written usage?
- Have I avoided sexism in the use of nouns and pronouns?
- Have I preferred the active to the passive voice of the verb?

Sentence construction

Use your editing and revision skills to make sure your sentences are well constructed. Keep the following in mind:

- Are my sentences correct? Have I avoided both fragments and run-ons?
- Are my modifiers in the right place? Do I have any dangling modifiers?
- Do my subjects and predicates agree in number?
- Do I keep parallel constructions parallel?
- Have I avoided short, choppy sentences?
- Do I combine sentences effectively?
- Are my sentences varied in length and structure? Do I avoid monotony?

Grammar

Use this book to augment your grammar skills and keep in mind the following:

- Have I checked spelling (including correct plural forms and hyphenation) capitalization, correct use and consistency of verb tenses, agreement (nouns, verbs, pronouns), pronoun cases, pronoun antecedents, use of adjectives with linking verbs, and comparative degrees of adjectives and adverbs?
- Does my punctuation make my meaning clear? Have I followed punctuation rules?

    Commas with nonrestrictive elements; no commas with restrictive elements

    Commas with interrupting elements, with introductory phrases and clauses when necessary, between series items, between independent clauses

    Correct use of periods and question marks

    Correct use (and not overuse) of exclamation points

    Correct use of semicolons and colons

    Correct use (and not overuse) of dashes and parentheses

    Correct use (and not overuse) of quotation marks

    Correct use of other punctuation with quotation marks

While this section has dealt with most of the generalities of good writing, it's obvious that you can't bring all of these aspects into your Global History and Geography Examination. The questions are fairly specific on this exam, but the basic elements of writing are here and can be followed. You will probably not have time for "prewriting." You will not be able to do research on your topic on the Internet. But keep in mind that this exam, as well as many other Regents exams, will require you to write essays, and the skills you may learn in this section will accompany you as you continue your education, and take other types of exams that require strong writing skills.

Sample Thematic Essay Questions

Take the time to review the subjects of each of the following Thematic Essay questions, in order to have an idea of the broad range of topics that might be covered in the actual Global History and Geography Examination.

Although you may not want to write an entire essay here, it would be helpful to jot down some notes to yourself on how you would approach each of these essays. For example, in Essay I, who would be the two individuals you would choose? What were some of the changes made by these two people? Were the changes they effected positive or negative? A few words will suffice; just write enough to make sure you actually understand how to approach this essay and the others that follow.

Essay I

Directions: Write a well-organized essay that includes an introduction, several paragraphs addressing the task below, and a conclusion.

Theme: Change

> Individuals have brought about great changes in history. These individuals have had positive and/or negative effects on nations or regions.

Task:

> Choose *two* individuals from your study of global history and geography and for *each* individual chosen:
>
> - Discuss *two* specific changes made by the individual in a specific nation or region
> - Evaluate whether these changes have had a positive or a negative effect on that nation or region

You may use any individual from your study of global history and geography. Some suggestions you might wish to consider include Elizabeth I, Genghis Khan, Muhammed, Martin Luther, Napoleon Bonaparte, Toussaint L'Ouverture, Nelson Mandela, Fidel Castro, Boris Yeltsin, Deng Xiaoping, and Yasir Arafat.

Essay II

Directions: Write a well-organized essay that includes an introduction, several paragraphs addressing the task below, and a conclusion.

Theme: Geography and Society

> At various times in global history, human activity has altered or changed the land people live on and their surrounding environment. These changes in physical geography have affected society.

Task:

> Select *two* changes that a society or two different societies have made to their land or surrounding environment, and for *each* change:
>
> - Identify the society in which the change took place
> - Describe how the physical environment was changed by human activity
> - Discuss how the change in the physical environment affected society

You may use any *two* examples from your study of global history and geography. Some suggestions you might wish to consider include irrigation systems, terrace farming, road systems, canal systems, burning of fossil fuels, or the use of nuclear power.

Essay III

Directions: Write a well-organized essay that includes an introduction, several paragraphs addressing the task below, and a conclusion.

Theme: Geography

> Geographic factors have influenced historical developments and historical events of nations and regions.

Task:

> Choose *two* nations and/or regions and for each:
>
> - Identify and describe *two* geographic factors in each nation and/or region
> - Explain how *each* factor has influenced the historical development or a specific historical event in each nation and/or region

You may use any nation and/or region and any geographic factors from your study of global history and geography. **Do *not* use the United States in your answer.** Some factors you might wish to consider include deserts, river valleys, or oil in the Middle East; river valleys, monsoons, or the Himalaya Mountains in India; natural resources or the island location of Japan or Great Britain; the river valley or the desert in Egypt; the regular coastline or resources in South Africa; the Amazon rain forest or the Andes Mountains in South America.

Essay IV

Directions: Write a well-organized essay that includes an introduction, several paragraphs addressing the task below, and a conclusion.

Theme: Change—Turning Points

Political, economic, and social conditions have often led to turning points that have changed the course of history for nations and peoples.

Task:

Identify *two* turning points from your study of global history and for *each:*

- Describe the causes and key events that led to the turning point
- Explain how *each* turning point changed the course of history for nations and peoples

You may use any turning point from your study of global history. Do *not* use the United States in your answer. Some suggestions you might wish to consider include: Neolithic Revolution, the fall of the Roman Empire, Commercial Revolution, the year 1492, French Revolution, the year 1914, Chinese Communist Revolution, the collapse of European imperialism, the fall of the Berlin Wall/collapse of Soviet Union.

Essay V

Directions: Write a well-organized essay that includes an introduction, several paragraphs addressing the task below, and a conclusion.

Theme: Geography

> Geographic features can positively or negatively affect the development of a nation or a region.

Task:

- Select *one* geographic feature from your study of global history
- Explain how this geographic feature has had an effect on the historical development of *two* nations or regions

Be sure to include specific historical examples in your essay.

You may use any geographic feature from your study of global history. Some suggestions you might wish to consider include: river valley, mountain, desert, island, rain forest, and climate.

Do *not* use the United States in your answer.

Essay VI

Directions: Write a well-organized essay that includes an introduction, several paragraphs addressing the task below, and a conclusion.

Theme: Economic Change

> Since the ninteenth century, industrialization has had positive and negative effects on the lives of workers.

Task:

- Define the term "industrialization"
- Select *one* nation you have studied and discuss *two* specific examples of the ways in which industrialization changed the lives of workers in that nation
- Discuss the response of the workers, reformers, and/or government to these changes

You may use any nation from your study of global history *except the United States.* Some suggestions you might wish to consider include: Great Britain (ninteenth century), Japan (ninteenth or twentieth century), Russia (ninteenth or twentieth century), Korea (post–World War II), and Brazil (twentieth century).

Essay VII

Directions: Write a well-organized essay that includes an introduction, several paragraphs addressing the task below, and a conclusion.

Theme: Science and Technology

> Science and technology have played a critical role in altering the course of human history.

Task:

- Identify *two* scientific or technological advances that had a major impact on global history
- Explain the relationship between the scientific or technological advance and a specific historic event or period in history
- Analyze how these advances changed the course of history

You may use any scientific or technological advance from your study of global history. Some suggestions you might wish to consider include development of agriculture, irrigation systems, the astrolabe, the printing press, the telescope, nuclear power, steam power, and the microscope.

Essay VIII

Directions: Write a well-organized essay that includes an introduction, several paragraphs addressing the task below, and a conclusion.

Theme: Justice and Human Rights

> Throughout history, the human rights of certain groups of people have been violated. Efforts have been made to address these violations.

Task:

- Define the term "human rights"
- Identify *two* examples of human rights violations that have occurred in a specific time and place
- Describe the causes of these human rights violations
- For *one* of the violations identified, discuss *one* specific effort that was made or is being made to deal with the violation

You may use any example from your study of global history. **Do *not* use the United States in your answer.** Some suggestions you might wish to consider include: Christians in the early Roman Empire, native peoples in Spain's American colonies, untouchables in India, blacks in South Africa, Jews in Nazi Germany, Muslims in Bosnia, Kurds in Iraq or Turkey, or Tibetans in China.

Essay IX

Directions: Write a well-organized essay that includes an introduction, several paragraphs addressing the task below, and a conclusion.

Theme: Human and Physical Geography (Geographic Impact on Societies)

> Geographic factors such as land features, resources, location, and climate of nations and regions affect how people live.

Task:

- Select *one* geographic factor that influenced life in a nation or region *before* A.D. 1500, and using specific examples, discuss the influence of that geographic factor on the people of that nation or region

- Select a *different* geographic factor that influenced life in a nation or region *after* A.D. 1500, and using specific examples, discuss the influence of that geographic factor on the people of that nation or region

You may use any examples from your study of global history and geography. You must select a *different* geographic factor for each time period discussed. For example, you may not write about two rivers in different parts of the world. **Do *not* use geographic factors from the United States in your answer.** Some suggestions you might wish to consider include the Nile River in Egypt, the mineral wealth of Africa, the monsoons in South Asia, oil in the Middle East, Japan's location near China, the plains of Northern Europe, rain forests in Latin America, and mountains in eastern Europe.

Essay X

Directions: Write a well-organized essay that includes an introduction, several paragraphs addressing the task below, and a conclusion.

Theme: Conflict

> Differences among groups have often led to conflict.

Task:

> Identify *two* ethnic, religious, political, and/or cultural conflicts and for *each*:
> - Discuss the historical circumstances that led to the conflict
> - Analyze the effect of this conflict on *two* groups involved

You may use any examples from your study of global history and geography. Some suggestions you might wish to consider include the persecution of Christians during the Roman Empire, the Reign of Terror, the Armenian massacres, the forced famine in Ukraine, the Holocaust, Apartheid in South Africa, the Killing Fields of Cambodia, the conflict in Northern Ireland, the Sandinistas in Nicaragua, and the Tiananmen Square rebellion.

Essay XI

Directions: Write a well-organized essay that includes an introduction, several paragraphs addressing the task below, and a conclusion.

Theme: Change

> Throughout history, political revolutions had many causes. These revolutions affected society and led to many changes. The changes may or may not have resolved the problems that caused the revolutions.

Task:

> Choose *one* political revolution from your study of global history and geography, and:
>
> - Explain the *causes* of the revolution
> - Describe the *effects* this political revolution had on society
> - Evaluate whether the *changes* that resulted from the political revolution resolved the problems that caused it

You may use any example from your study of global history, but **do *not* use the American Revolution.** Some suggestions you might wish to consider include the French Revolution (1789), Mexican Revolution (1910), Russian Revolution (1917), Chinese Revolution (1949), Cuban Revolution (1959), or Iranian Revolution (1979).